The Otherness of Self

A Genealogy
of the Self in
Contemporary China

Xin Liu

ANN ARBOR

THE UNIVERSITY OF MICHIGAN PRESS

Copyright © by the University of Michigan 2002
All rights reserved
Published in the United States of America by
The University of Michigan Press
Manufactured in the United States of America
∞ Printed on acid-free paper

2005   2004   2003   2002   4   3   2   1

*A CIP catalog record for this book is available from the British
Library.*

Library of Congress Cataloging-in-Publication Data

Liu, Xin, 1957–
    The otherness of self : a genealogy of the self in
contemporary China / Xin Liu.
        p.   cm.
    Includes bibliographical references and index.
        ISBN 0-472-09809-8 (alk. paper) — ISBN 0-472-06809-1
(pbk. : alk. paper)
        1. Ethnology—China.   I. Title: Genealogy of the self
in contemporary China.   II. Title.
DS730 .L58   2002
305.8′00951—dc21   2001007709

Deng Xiaoping's socialist ideology: no matter whether it is a white or a black cat, as long as it catches mice, it is a good cat. Today's socialist practice: no matter whether it is a white or a black mouse, as long as it is capable of avoiding being caught, it is a good mouse.

AN ENTREPRENEUR IN BEIHAI

Contents

Preface and Acknowledgments

As an ethnography of a history of the present, this book compiles a genealogy of the self in contemporary China. A history of the present, as
Michel Foucault has shown, is an act of deconstruction and construction, projecting old elements of theory and story onto a new intellectual
horizon of the present, just as how a genealogy may be rewritten as a
new segmentation takes place in the southeastern Chinese lineage organization, where a focal point of worship can be established when a (usually wealthy) descendant sets up a new ancestral temple. In the sense that
I intend this phrase to convey, a genealogy of the self traces the effects
of dislocation within "a structure of conjuncture" of self-representation
in the context of contemporary China.[1] The representation of self—
understood in a broad sense as the search for an answer to the question
What is good (life)?—constitutes and yet is constituted by an ethical
space in which our condition of possibility of being as such dwells.

I argue that a moral earthquake is taking place in today's China.
Although we do not yet know how many buildings of existing goods or
evils will collapse and what will be the shape of a new moral outlook in
the near future, it is quite certain that the moral landscape of Chinese
society will not be the same in another couple of decades. This is an
attempt to capture the change of such an outlook while it is still changing, an adventure into the shifting ground of what good (life) is in the
history of the People's Republic, a glimpse into the question of what
they want to be. Specifically, I argue that a different conception of time
in the practice of everyday life seems to be emerging. Although tentative, this book sets to sketch the emergence of a new character, standing
on an ethical ground both familiar and strange, from the historical horizon of contemporary China.

This horizon is the home of a number of inventories of historical
forces. The notion of force is crucial here, for it is through these forces,

hierarchized and dispersed, that organizational and institutional power gain their life in everyday practice. A force is always related to another force, which is in turn related to yet another one, and so on. The relations between these forces are never equal; instead, each force is always subjected to another, or perhaps each is always in either a superior or an inferior relation to another force. Within the interior space of a force, a combination of social or cultural elements exists. These elements shape a particular force of which they are its constituent units. Whereas the combination of these forces makes up a particular social system at a given historical moment. The structure of the self is a historically situated (re)combination of the elements derived from all the possible forces at a given moment; a genealogy of the self is a system of several structural wholes. To capture this (re)combination of elements and forces in China at the present time is the ethnographic task of this book.

What underlies this book is a general theoretical orientation toward an anthropological understanding of the modern Chinese experience, and at the center of such an orientation lies my effort in trying to capture a particular mode of existence in and as *becoming*. From such a theoretical orientation, although the subject of my writing is different, this book can be seen as a continuation of my previous work, an ethnographic critique of everyday life in northern rural Shaanxi entitled *In One's Own Shadow* (2000). I believe that the modern Chinese experience has remained a riddle for the social scientist, and it is time to take up seriously the task of solving the riddle, to examine it not simply as "other modernities" but as an essential step toward a hermeneutics of the ontology of ourselves. Such an inquiry cannot be carried out unless a deep historical sensitivity is restored. This is therefore essentially a historical inquiry about "the structure of feelings," to borrow a term from Raymond Williams (1977, 128). This is not a study of political economy, a most popular mode of inquiry for the studies of postreform Chinese society; I am not dealing with material conditions of change. Instead, this book deals with the configuration of a discursive space affecting the way in which the stories about oneself and others are able to be told.

An empirical puzzle is that one often finds that Chinese society seems to possess a magic power that turns itself on and off quite unexpectedly, switching gears back and forth and revolving its wheels first in one direction and then in another. This possibility of switching gears—in both the domains of governance and of everyday life—was particularly true of the years of economic reforms in the 1980–90s. An ethnographer may find it surprising that a promising young scholar of physics has turned himself into a businessman within a year, working in a management position at a Kentucky Fried Chicken. What is striking is not that people have changed their jobs or professions; rather, they have changed characters as persons. This discontinuity in the personhood of a person is what I call the otherness of self: this book is an ethnographic account of the otherness of self in contemporary China.

Ethnographic materials for this book were collected from a very successful high-tech company, and this is an anthropology of the logic of business practice in Beihai, a southern Chinese coastal city. A city consists of an open space, quite different from a rural community—a long privileged site of field research in the tradition of anthropological studies of Chinese society.[2] A great deal of urban life in South China has been penetrated by transnational capital and capitalism, and the Chinese urban sphere is increasingly becoming an integral part of the global political economy. The subject of my writing can be located in space but is never local because it is a study of the conditions of possibility of social existence that cannot be experienced in one community. Methodologically speaking, this book is an ethnographic understanding rather than an ethnographic observation conventionally understood.

What underlies the urban question in and of China is a more general theoretical concern about the nature of anthropological knowledge.[3] Some prejudice and disciplinary habitus, such as that in favor of the exotic, may have been revealed to be an intellectual illusion, but the fundamental problem concerning the nature of anthropological knowledge is far from solved. This question was first brought to my attention when I was doing research in Japan in 1998: What is the significance of ethnographic experience in the anthropology of modern life? While traveling in Japan, a society where traditional forms of social ties, such as communal connections, are no longer central to the organization of cultural life, I began to wonder what a field approach would look like if the object of analysis was urban space. This book, if not always explicit, provides a critique of the classic mode of anthropological enterprise by shifting the focus of ethnographic description from the actual experience of a people to an account of the stories that they tell about themselves and others. Part of the reason for this shift in focus is because many aspects of business practices were not directly observable. For example, no businessman—insofar as China is concerned—would bring an ethnographer to the dining table where a deal would be sealed with the mayor, because personal favors might be offered that should not be witnessed by a third party. This example represents an extreme case, and a large number of business conducts in (South) China are not supposed to be seen in public. In such cases, ethnography can only mean hearing the stories told by those involved. If the term *experience* remains useful, I wish to give it a connotation as something embedded in commentary or memory or imaginary—already an interpretation of what happened or what would happen. Largely based on this kind of ethnographic materials, this book seeks not to describe what people actually do but what they want to be. Through the stories told, I hope to understand a history of the future. My understanding is that looking at the stories people told the ethnographer may enable an understanding of how they conceive of themselves and society at large. This shift in focus is linked to a larger theoretical concern that takes narrative as an essential feature of human experience. Following such a theoretical orientation in general, this book proposes to rebuild the grounding of anthropological analysis by a serious consideration of the significance of narrative in the constitution of reality and experience. In particular, to pose the question of narrative is not simply to state that social or cultural differences lie in the different ways of telling stories about oneself and others but also to raise the question about the relationships between narrative and experience to assert a theoretical stance that places a crucial significance on the narrative character of human existence: what we are and what we want to be are determined in the stories that we are able to tell about ourselves/Ourselves.

Truth is partial, and so is ethnography. If some readers, especially those not familiar with the history of twentieth-century China, wonder about the extent to which such an account of business life may represent the overall picture of (South) China, a response would be to invoke Ludwig Wittgenstein's idea of "family resemblance": this work is only an individuation of an overall process of change, a snapshot of the stream of a historical transition, a person in a segmented lineage of multiple generations. One can still tell that in some respects this person resembles his uncle descending from his father's line, although his mother's brother may see in this person's appearance another outline of features. Ethnography is like this person, sitting in front of a reader whose reading is not entirely constrained by what is written, though the ethnography as the instance of a family resemblance provides a best example for the anthropological imagination.

It is common for anthropologists to say that the object of their analysis is social (or cultural) system; however, the definition of the social itself is not always clear. Few would disagree with Clifford Geertz when he said that "human thought is consummately social: social in its origin, social in its functions, social in its forms, social in its applications" (1973, 360), but even fewer could explain what the social is supposed to mean in the contemporary world because in most cases the term is simply used as in opposition to the behaviorist or other reductionist approaches in social sciences, where individuals—particularly their physiology and psychology—are considered the genesis of everything else. Geertz continued, "At base, thinking is a public activity—its natural habitat is the houseyard, the marketplace, and the town square. The implications of this act for the anthropological analysis of culture, my concern here, are enormous, subtle, and insufficiently appreciated" (1973, 360). In such a statement, one may see a hint of Wittgenstein's later philosophy, in particular his celebrated critique of the idea of a private language.[4] If this is the case, the domain of the social here is defined as that of meaning.[5] Given the fact that it is increasingly difficult to locate the social in the house-yard, the marketplace, and the town center insofar as the case of urban development in (South) China is concerned, how can we define what is social and what is meaningful?[6] With reference to the work of Alasdair MacIntyre, Charles Taylor, David Carr, and others, I argue that the social must be defined as a relationship that allows a particular articulation of oneself to Ourselves in a historically specific cultural context. It is a meaningful relationship, but, more important, it is narrative in essence. I argue that what characterizes today's China is the difficulty in articulating the relationship of oneself to Ourselves in any coherent way.[7] The book addresses how such a difficulty emerged from the historical horizon of contemporary China.

The book is organized into two parts: the first tells a story of the success of a high-tech company in Beihai, Guangxi, South China, a region where economic development is rather slow. I chose this particular city as my field site to move away from Guangdong (including Hainan), Fujian, and Shanghai, where most attention has been given whenever the question of South China's development is raised.[8] It is important, in my view, to shift attention to a less studied, less developed region to balance our understanding of the effects of capitalist global penetration. By writing about the success of this high-tech company, the Beihai Star Group, I hope to capture the spirit of Chinese capitalism and to reveal the complex investment structure that involves social and political capital rather than technology and knowledge. The larger context of my writing is that since the mid-1990s, the government has claimed that the future of China lies in the development of high-tech industries, and all the provinces have set up special zones and policies for such industrial development. Chapter 1 introduces the city and the feeling of being there, from an outside insider's point of view, and provides an account of the economic and political background against which the Beihai story of urban (high-tech) development is told. Chapters 2 through 4 describe the main characters involved in the telling of the Beihai story, sketch the typical modes of plots that situate the characters in the story, and provide an analysis of the narrative structure according to which those stories about business and society are able to be told. It is an ethnography of the characters and schemes of plotting in the Beihai story of urban (high-tech) development. The second part of the book, although continuing to provide ethnographic details, will bring theoretical concerns implicitly addressed in the first part to the focus of attention. Chapter 5 defines and describes the structure of the self as a theoretical domain of analysis. The concept of self is carefully examined by reading a number of anthropological and philosophical texts and using them to lay a theoretical foundation for the book's ethnographic description. Chapter 6 analyzes everyday conception of time as a central element in the constitution of the self and argues that three historical moments of the modern Chinese experience may be understood as three different configurations of temporality in everyday life. Chapter 7 deals with the problem of subjectivity, clearing a theoretical space for further ethnographic investigation concerning the question of subject and subject position. In conclusion, I turn to the problem of memory and argue that a new character seems to be emerging, embodied in the practice of business life in (South) China; this character has lost his memory and could no longer utter any *We*. State agencies have encouraged and nurtured an increasing gap between the ideologies of the state and the social life of business practice. I am writing for these difficulties in speaking about Ourselves, for the discrepancies between the official world and the world of business life, and for the future already lived.

First, my gratitude goes to those who have helped me in the field. None of these people with whom I worked should be called informants because they were not simply telling me about their lives: they were telling me dreams or desires acted out in language. For this reason, I see a clear difference between informants in the conventional sense of anthropological understanding and peoples whose character can only be revealed in the stories told by themselves and others. In a sense, I am grateful not only for their revelation of their dreams and desires but also for the possibility of knowing them in such a way. It was certainly a transformative experience for me as a fieldworker, though not always confined to a geographic place.

For academic help and assistance, I am most grateful to Frederic Wakeman, who as a senior colleague in the China field at Berkeley has strongly influenced my thinking and scholarship. Since I joined the faulty in 1995, the Department of Anthropology at Berkeley has been intellectually stimulating, and I am grateful to my colleagues for their inspiration and for challenging and encouraging me in ways that I often do not fully appreciate until later. There is a long list of people, colleagues and friends, whose names must be registered here as a trace of my intellectual growth in the past few years. Some read chapters of this work and provided useful comments, some stimulated me in thinking about anthropology and China studies in general, some helped create for me a productive environment, and some are friends who have provided emotional support while I was working on this project. They include: Gerry Berreman, Stanley Brandes, Timothy Brook, Meg Conkey, Robert Culp, Prasenjit Duara, Alan Dundes, Dru Gladney, Tom Gold, Nelson Graburn, William Hanks, Steve Hershler, William R. Jankowiak, David Johnson, Rosemary Joyce, Patrick Kirch, Ryosei Kokubun, Hong-Yung Lee, Hy Van Luong, Laura Nader, Lili Nie, Aihwa Ong, Christian de Pee, William Schaffer, Nancy Scheper-Hughes, Gavin Smith, James Watson, Diana Wong, Chen Yang, Wenhsin Yeh, Shen Yuan, and Li Zhang.

Two anonymous reviewers for the University of Michigan Press have provided extremely useful and insightful comments that have helped me rethink some of the crucial intellectual questions of this project. This manuscript has benefited a great deal from their comments; and I believe that their comments will also leave a significant mark on my next project.

As time passes, I feel even more obliged to my supervisors, Mark Hobart and Elizabeth Croll of the University of London, where my initial training to become an anthropologist was provided. The Hellman Family Junior Faculty Research Grant, University of California at

Berkeley, assisted me for field research in South China in the summer of 1998. Supported by the Japan Foundation (Asia Center) and administered by the International House of Japan, Tokyo, the Asia Leadership Fellowship Program, which selected me as a fellow in 1998–99, provided a precious opportunity for me to work on some of the ideas conceived in the field.

Finally, my gratitude goes to the editors of the Press. Ingrid Erickson initiated the project and, after her leaving, Liz Suhay took over for a short period of time. I want to thank the Press for its excellent editorial assistance and, particularly, those working on this project.

Notes on the Text

Table for conversion of Chinese units of measurement

Length
1 *li* = 0.5 kilometer
1 *chi* = 0.333 meter

Area
1 *mu* = 0.077 hectare
1 *li* = 0.01 *mu* = 0.1 *fen*

Weight
1 *dan* = 50 kilograms
1 *jin* = 0.5 kilogram

Official Exchange Rates

1980	1 U.S. dollar = 1.5 yuan
1985	1 U.S. dollar = 2.7 yuan
1986	1 U.S. dollar = 3.5 yuan
1990	1 U.S. dollar = 4.8 yuan
1992	1 U.S. dollar = 5.5 yuan
1993	1 U.S. dollar = 5.8 yuan
1994	1 U.S. dollar = 8.6 yuan
1996	1 U.S. dollar = 8.4 yuan
1997	1 U.S. dollar = 8.3 yuan
1998	1 U.S. dollar = 8.3 yuan
1999	1 U.S. dollar = 8.2 yuan

Romanization

Unless otherwise specified, names and words are written in Mandarin, romanized according to the pinyin system.

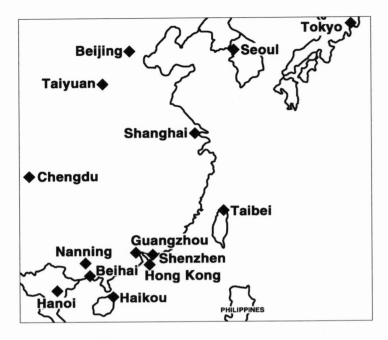

The network of cities

one ᴗ

The Dance of a Nissan

On a sweltering evening, a 1993 Nissan, relatively new and well kept but
with a noticeable dent on the left-side door, was moving, very slowly, as
if the driver were dancing with his car—perhaps not a tango but a
waltz—zigzagging across a very wide, brand-new avenue guarded by
two beautifully shaped lines of fine trees. The avenue was wide enough
to allow perhaps ten such cars to drive abreast of one another, but there
were very few moving objects on the road. The Nissan was right in the
middle of the avenue, completely ignoring the white lines marking the
lanes, as if the driver were the king of the road or perhaps as if the president of some country were visiting. The street was emptied for the Nissan as if it were the only vehicle allowed to be on the road. The Nissan
was too slow to keep up even with a couple of bicycles, the only other
vehicles, on which two young girls chatted with each other, their color-
ful skirts blown by a breeze. No one was in a hurry: everything seemed
to be on hold, a feeling of suspending or waiting. A very quiet—if not
too quiet—evening.

   If one were inside the car and looked out from the window, one
would probably be astonished by the newness of everything visible.
Even if one were driving in the night, one could perhaps still smell the
newness of the city; for example, the fragrance of newly planted pines
and other trees. These trees were still young, though some were huge,
and only through their shadows was it possible to see the new buildings
behind them on both sides of the road. It was then, if one were in the car,
that one would notice the darkness inside these buildings: some were
entirely without lights, while others had only very dim lights that
looked like reflections of candles or electric flashlights. Not every building was blacked out, but a large number of them stood in the motionless
darkness of their own shadows. Many of these buildings, beautifully
designed and modern, were not yet completed—not because they were

still in construction, with all the usual noises, but because they were on hold. Investments had been withdrawn and loans suspended. The buildings were abandoned, forgotten, left for nature to take over their fate. The most striking feature of these buildings, standing still and remaining silent in a space created by their own existence as the evidence to deny that very space, was the incomplete windows. The windows were like big, open mouths without any teeth, threatening to inhale immediately all flying insects. If one were to focus on any one of these windows, one would probably feel that behind each of these mouths was an abyss, not in the sense of not being able to find an end in it but in the sense of negligence, so obvious a darkness of human design that it would destroy any hope for their completion in the future. Most, if not all, of these buildings had no roofs due to the sudden halt in their construction, leaving steel bars and girders open and naked, as if bushes or jungles were growing out of the buildings' heads.

This scene was part of the Central Avenue of Beihai, a medium-sized coastal city located at the edge of Guangxi Autonomous District, a province known for both its beauty and its ethnic diversity.[1] Guangxi borders Guangdong in the east and Vietnam in the southwest. Although Beihai (literally, "Northern Sea"), which is probably most known for its tourist attractions, particularly its beaches, is not known in China as an important port city, it is possible to travel via sea routes to Vietnam or to Hainan Island, which used to be part of Guangdong and became an independent province in the early 1990s. The capital of Guangxi, Nanning, lies about 150 kilometers north of Beihai. Few people in China would remember that Beihai was in fact among the first fourteen cities initially granted the status of "coastal open cities" in 1984, an economic-reform experiment that allowed these cities to offer special economic policies to attract foreign investment.[2] Much public attention has been paid to cities such as Shenzhen in Guangdong, partly because of its strategic location in connection to Hong Kong. Few people in China would consider Beihai a member of the category of places that have achieved rapid economic growth. Beihai's economic performance can by no means be compared with that of Shenzhen, which developed very rapidly in the 1980s. A real moment of development in Beihai did not arrive until the early 1990s. During 1992 and 1993, in less than two years, there was an unbelievable flush of development—that is, a large amount of investment, primarily domestic loans and funds, poured into this small city and brought an unprecedented wave of construction of residential and office buildings, partly as a result of the provincial government's encouragement and partly as a result of the illusion generated by Deng Xiaoping's 1992 trip to South China.³ This heightened feverish moment of development quickly declined when Vice Premier Zhu Rongji took over the control of the central bank in 1994 and decided to freeze real estate investment across the country because the economy was believed to be overheated. All the investing companies withdrew their loans and funds, running away from the city; bank loans for real estate development were frozen; and the city's fever cooled, leaving all the skyscrapers half finished. Just a few years later, in 1998, the dead buildings remained a symptom of the city's terrible illness.

The Nissan was still right in the middle of the Central Avenue, dancing, not following any traffic rules—if there were any. The avenue was largely an open space, an avenue of quietness, which—at least in the minds of first-time visitors to the city—represented an unbelievable emptiness. Where were the people and traffic jams, the noise, so common to most Chinese cities? Inside the car were four people, including the driver, who was in his early forties, with a facial expression that said nothing about what he was thinking. Both hands were on the wheel, one rough and the other delicate, an interesting contrast, as if they belonged to two different persons. This was not an ordinary driver: this was the general manager of a famous Beihai company, the Beihai Star Group, a promising nationally known high-tech enterprise by the end of the twentieth century. His name was Haihun. Next to him sat a man in his early fifties, with a rustic complexion and a pair of quick eyes, as if he were constantly watching some moving object. It was difficult to make eye contact with him, because when an attempt was made, deliberate or not, his eyes would dart away. This pair of eyes did not focus on anyone or anything but rather were preoccupied with seeing some objects always beyond the focus of another person's sight. This was a man entitled, with considerable awe and respect, to be called Nee Chuzhang. Chuzhang is not part of his name but a title for an important position—section chief in the government hierarchy. Nee Chuzhang was in charge of the industrial division of the Guangxi Planning Committee, headquartered in Nanning, the provincial capital. His post was rather important, endowing him with responsibility for granting permissions for the export and import of industrial goods and technologies. Behind the driver's seat sat a slightly younger man, with a square face and a disproportionately large nose occupying the center of his face and making all of his expressions look as if he were smiling. This was Tu Chuzhang, Nee's vice chief and assistant. I sat next to Tu Chuzhang. An anthropologist from the University of California at Berkeley, I sought to understand the practice of business life in China at the turn of this century as a possible clue toward understanding what lies ahead for a society burdened with a revolutionary past. What was written on my face was not only excitement, brought about by the possibility of doing field research on a new project, but also a great deal of surprise at what I had observed during the past few days. I had traveled with Haihun to Nanning, eventually bringing two government officials back to Beihai for a "business trip" whose meaning I discovered only a few days later.

The Beihai Star Company, Ltd., which I shall refer to as the Beihai Star Group throughout this book, was run by a group of young people led by Haihun and his partner, Panton. It was categorized as a high-tech company. Between 1992 and 1998, the Beihai Star Group achieved remarkable progress in corporatization and became one of the most important enterprises in Guangxi. Two strategic achievements occurred during these decisive years. First, starting with almost nothing in its own stock, the Beihai Star Group successfully took control of two large state enterprises, both in Sichuan province, each of which had more than two thousand employees as well as a long history of producing basic electronic units for the Chinese space program. Both of these state-owned enterprises had been in debt, a severe problem for many such enterprises in the 1990s. With the idea of saving such enterprises from bankruptcy, the government agreed to let them come under private ownership, a reform strategy that was discontinued after a couple of years because, as the government soon realized, transferring public assets into private hands created problems in the form of economic and social disparities. During this short period of selling state enterprises, these two factories became subsidiaries of the Beihai Star Group, which owned a total of six companies in 1999. The second major achievement was that the company became listed on the Shenzhen stock market in April 1998. This listing almost guaranteed the company's success by giving it access to capital: the major problem troubling almost every enterprise in the 1990s was the shortage of capital for daily operation and management. The Chinese stock market was still in its cradle, and to make sure that it did not collapse, the state used strict procedures to select only the most promising companies to be listed (see Hertz 1998).

Only one or two Guangxi companies would have the opportunity to be listed on the stock market each year, and the Beihai Star Group managed to successfully go through this process, becoming one of the few privileged enterprises.

The Star Group was owned by its shareholders, both collective and individual. One of its main products was electronic chips, a very basic kind that could be used for a variety of purposes. The production line for this product was imported from Japan in 1996, when the company received special permission from the provincial government as a means of encouraging high-tech industrial development in Guangxi. Into the last few years of the twentieth century, official discourse increasingly emphasized the importance of developing high-tech industries. To accommodate this ideology, each province launched its own special policies. In Guangxi, if the Planning Committee identified a company as investing in the high-tech industries, this company would be exempt from import taxation. Of course, this policy was supposed to apply only to companies that were importing production materials for the development of high-tech products. However, if a company instead were able to get this tax exemption to import consumer goods, such as cars, it would be able to produce a huge profit over a very short period of time, because the taxes on some foreign products, such as cars, were extremely high.[4] The value of this permission was no less than the profit itself; and this permission could be granted only by the Planning Committee's industrial division, where Nee Chuzhang and Tu Chuzhang worked.

For fiscal year 1996–97, the Beihai Star Group was granted permission to import $280,000 worth of products, but the company did not use up all this quota, importing materials worth only $260,000. Although the original quota was supposed to be used for a single act of importation, Haihun decided to visit Nanning, hoping to convince officials that a small amount of production material still needed to be brought back to China to run the newly installed production line. I was not aware of what the company was trying to import this time, whether or not they were production materials. Before contacting the Planning Committee for another permission, the company had tried to import some materials into China but was stopped by the Customs Office and told that another permission had to be obtained. This was the reason for Haihun's trip, and I traveled in his car with him to Nanning. This was a couple of weeks after I arrived in Beihai in June 1998 for fieldwork, and by then I had become quite familiar with Haihun, partly because we both belonged to the class of 1978, an extremely significant group of Chinese college students. The class of 1978 connotes more a historical turning point than a group of classmates, because it was the first generation of students to enter college after the Cultural Revolution (1966–76), and group members went to universities through the system of the restored national exams.[5] Furthermore, I was pleased but somewhat astonished to discover that Haihun had received his doctorate in Marxism and demography in 1992 from the Southwestern University of Economics and Finance.[6] Largely as a result of his understanding and generous help, I came to know some hidden practices of (South) Chinese business life, such as how negotiations with government officials were carried out.

Late one afternoon, when we were driving close to Nanning, a much larger city than Beihai with a number of very impressive ultramodern skyscrapers, some entirely wrapped in glass, Haihun was once again on his cellular phone:

"Helloooooo, Old Nee, whaaaat? Nee Chuzhang, yes?"

. . . . . .

"What? No? You are not Nee Chuzhang, but I am talking to Nee Chuzhang. Am I talking to someone who is not whom I am supposed to be talking to? What?"

. . . . . .

"He is not there? You don't know, and you don't know who knows? Do you know who knows who knows?"

. . . . . .

"You don't know who knows, what? What? Oh, you are Nee Chuzhang. I thought I was talking to someone else. Whaaaaat?"

. . . . . .

"Who was on the phone? Whaaaaat? You were in the toilet, but you know I didn't know who was on the phone. You are funny, you know that?"

. . . . . .

"Hi, Nee Chuzhang, talk seriously, what are you doing tonight? I happen to be in town and want to see you."

. . . . . .

"You have a meeting until 7:00? What about after that? Fine, I will pick you up at your office at around 7:30."

Having settled the time, we drove to a hotel not far away from a huge sign, Ginza (*Yinzuo*) Nightclub, that was quite similar to billboards seen on U.S. freeways. I am not sure whether local people could imagine the kind of urban atmosphere associated with the Ginza, a famous avenue in central Tokyo, but it is quite clear that this borrowing suggested that searching for pleasures and good life understood in terms of material gains no longer bore any negative connotations. An ethnographer might be surprised to find that both Nanning and Beihai had a disproportionately large number of massage parlors and nightclubs, whose names were always most imaginative. After resting in the hotel for an hour or so, Haihun went out to pick up Nee Chuzhang for dinner and some sort of entertainment. I stayed in the hotel watching television. When Haihun returned later that night, I asked where they went. Haihun replied, "We went to a massage parlor. They like this sort of thing because they don't have money for it, and then they wait for us to invite them."

The following day, I went with Haihun to Nee's office in an old but well maintained building in the center of the city. Haihun told me that, after the previous day's entertainment, although business was not discussed at all, he sensed that there should be no problem in getting his favor granted. He came to talk to both Nee Chuzhang and Tu Chuzhang, whom Nee promised to bring to meet with Haihun. Although Nee was superior in rank, Tu was in charge of the everyday business of granting these permissions. When we came into Nee's room, he was lying on the bed, taking a break for tea and a cigarette and reading a newspaper. About twenty minutes later, Tu Chuzhang came in, apologizing for being late.

"I couldn't leave—in a meeting, you know."

"Have a cigarette, Tu Chuzhang. We just came anyway," Haihun said.

"You know, so many meetings. You are always in a meeting, you know, I bet you don't know, but I hope you know you don't know." Tu continued his apology while lighting a cigarette provided by Haihun.

"Tu Chuzhang, I think I need to ask for your help with a small matter," Haihun said a couple of minutes later.

"Oh, don't be so polite. Who are we? We have known each other more than a few days, haven't we?" Tu replied.

"We had this quota last year, and you allowed us to import something from abroad. We did not finish using that quota, and . . ." Haihun began to explain.

"You did, didn't you? Did you say you didn't?" Tu said.

"No, I didn't say we didn't."

"But you just said you didn't. Didn't you just say you didn't say you didn't?"

"I didn't say I said I didn't say we didn't." Haihun began to be confused by Tu's questioning.

"So you didn't say you didn't, but you didn't anyway." Tu was pressing.

"Yeeeees, we didn't finish the quota, but I didn't say we didn't use it. You are right. We used only part of it, and we still need to import more, and we want to use the leftover portion of the quota." Haihun took a breath and tried to follow up the conversation.

"Why didn't you finish it?"

"Because we didn't."

"So you did say you didn't. If you did say you didn't, why didn't you say you did say you didn't?" Tu brought the conversation back to a tongue twister.

"No—well, yes—anyway, we didn't. We still have some portion of that quota left." Haihun became a little irritated by Tu's questioning.

"If you didn't finish it, you can just go finish it. Why do you have to tell me you didn't?"

"Because we can't, Customs did not allow us to do that, because they said we did."

"But you just said you didn't, didn't you?" Tu smiled at Haihun, as if he caught Haihun in a logical confusion.

"Yes, I said we didn't, but they said we did."

"Who said you did?"

"Customs."

"If they said you did, why did you say you didn't?"

"Because we didn't."

"Then why did they say you did?" Tu was almost grinning.

"Because they said even though we didn't finish it, we still did, because the quota was given for one act of importation."

"So what is your problem?"

"We used only $260,000, and there was still $20,000 left in the quota."

"If there is some left over in the quota, why don't you use it?" Tu questioned.

"Because they said we didn't have anything left in the quota."

"If you don't have anything left in the quota, how could you use it?"

"That's why I come to you and Nee Chuzhang for another permission, because we need these materials to set up production."

"But if you haven't finished the quota, why do you want another one?" Tu Chuzhang began to appear a little cautious.

"Because they said we did, and instead of arguing with them, I would rather have another one, because we didn't." Haihun became obviously irritated.

"If you didn't, you should be able to use it; therefore, you don't need another permission, don't you? If you did, you should not be able to use it because you have nothing left, and therefore you have to apply for a new permission."

"What are you saying, Tu Chuzhang?"

"I am saying what you are saying."

"Which is?"

"If you didn't, you should be able to use it."

"But they said we did, and what shall we do?" Haihun was obviously trying to calm himself down, handing over another cigarette to Tu Chuzhang.

"You did say to them you didn't, didn't you? I think you have to talk to them because you didn't, didn't you?"

"Tu Chuzhang, let us do this another way. I am already here, and it's a small thing for you to get us another permission, as a special case for using the old quota. Otherwise, I would have to go back to tell them again we didn't." Haihun finally said.

Nee Chuzhang did not interrupt the conversation between Haihun and Tu, whose way of talking, representative of the official clarity in vagueness, was truly amazing. Sitting and sipping his tea while reading a women's magazine, Nee Chuzhang intervened at this point: "Perhaps we should help them this time. And then we should have a break in Beihai." Nee returned to his reading and tea drinking as if nothing concerned him. "A break in Beihai," as I understood a few days later, meant a weekend holiday in Beihai financed by Haihun. What was expected of such a weekend holiday was much more than simply rest and dining: this vacation would involve a series of entertainments, including singing in a karaoke bar and massages by the "invisible hands" of young girls. After Nee's interruption, Tu became a little more friendly and agreed to try the next morning to arrange something for Haihun. What followed that evening was entertainment for these two officials.

Everyone got into the car at around 6:00 and agreed that it would be better to find a karaoke bar where they could sing, dance, and eat. Karaoke bars have become a popular place for Chinese business gatherings and entertainment. The Nissan first headed to the northern part of the city, following Nee's suggestion that there was a good karaoke bar whose owner was a friend of his. After about a twenty-minute ride in the car, we arrived in front of the Guangxi Police Headquarters, with two soldiers saluting the Nissan with their guns. I was told that the police force had a huge building that had been used for militia training during the Maoist revolution. There were many rooms and dining halls that were no longer useful to the police and had been rented out to a private entrepreneur, who had begun to operate this karaoke bar a few years ago. The place did such good business because everyone believed that it was the safest place for a good evening—guarded by armed policemen and soldiers. Policemen in their uniforms walked around, and a number of patrol cars were parked nearby. It was indeed a very safe place. Karaoke bars might not be new to the Chinese people, even those who were not government officials, but singing inside a police headquarters was quite an experience for someone like me.

Unfortunately, we were told that every private karaoke room was taken, despite this being an ordinary Thursday evening. The popularity of this place was confirmed. There were only a few seats left in the big dance hall. We could take these seats, but there was no privacy, and we could not sing whenever we wanted. This was the major difference between having a private room and being part of a large audience in the hall. Nee's friend was not yet there when we arrived, and we decided to try another club. We went back to the car, heading to a restaurant suggested by Tu that was well known for its seafood dishes. Since the late 1980s, many restaurants began to provide karaoke facilities because many guests wanted to sing after a delicious meal. The second place disappointed us but in a different way. Because of the large number of guests, the restaurant could not immediately arrange for us to have *xiaojie*, literally "misses," meaning hostesses whose job was to serve and accompany the guests for singing, dancing, and eating. Lacking the patience to wait, the Nissan headed for another place, located in a tall building right in the center of the city. The elevator took us up to the twenty-seventh floor. Before the door opened, a breeze of fragrance greeted us. We were led into a private karaoke room with a huge television and a semicircle of sofas, and some girls appeared to help us eat and sing.[7] I noticed that Haihun was always addressed as *laoban* (the boss), a term for someone who would pay on such occasions. When we were in Nee's office, no one called Haihun *laoban,* but now everyone did so, including Nee and Tu. A large number of dishes were ordered, and the two Chuzhang were happy to enjoy themselves with food and singing.

The following day, we went to visit Tu Chuzhang in his office at the main building of the Planning Committee. Before we parked the car in front of the building, Haihun telephoned Tu, reminding him of the previous afternoon's agreement. After a few minutes, Tu came to the car, took some documents from Haihun, and went back to the office. About ten minutes later, Tu came back, asking, "Did you say you didn't finish the quota?"

"Yes?"

"It doesn't actually matter, does it? But there is this small problem, as I explained to you yesterday. If you did say you didn't, you didn't need to come to us."

"Tu Chuzhang, please. They said we did, and that is why we didn't go to them."

"Who is this 'they'?"

"Customs."

"That's right. If they said you did, why did you say you didn't? If you said you didn't, why did they say you did? Let me tell you straightaway: if you didn't, you didn't need to come to us; if you did, you didn't need to come to us either; you only need to come to us if you said you didn't but they said you did." Tu was very happy as a result of the previous night's entertainment, but Haihun was obviously irritated by returning to this kind of hopeless conversation.

"That is what I am saying."

"I see. That is what you are saying. Why didn't you say this earlier to me?"

"That is what I've been saying."

"Then why didn't you say this to me straightaway?"

"I thought I did."

"But you didn't. You see, this is your problem. Like all the businessmen of your rank, you always use an indirect language. Not like us. We, the officials, have to talk straight. That is the rule of our game. If we don't talk straight, nobody will understand us. If nobody understands us, there will be problems. You should have said everything to me at the very beginning, straightaway. Now I understand what you want, and I think I can help you fix it. But I have to make sure that Nee Chuzhang knows it, because he is my superior."

"Nee Chuzhang knows it."

"You know he knows it?"

"Yes."

"You mean he knows you know he knows?"

"I am sure he does."

"That is the only thing I want to know." Tu rushed back to his office to get a signature. From the dreary expression on Haihun's face, I understood his feelings. As an outsider to Beihai's business practices but an insider to Chinese society, I believe that Haihun's frustration came from the fact that a lot of things depended on the very last moment of negotiation. Even if an agreement has been reached, the success of a business deal cannot be guaranteed until it is finally sealed with the official stamp. The idea of trust is certainly not part of this kind of practice. The way that Tu Chuzhang talked to Haihun on the second day surprised me, because it seemed as if the conversation in Nee Chuzhang's office had never occurred. But especially when asking for a favor, one should not lose his patience. As a result, Haihun continued to show a great deal of respect throughout the dreadful conversations with Tu, although Haihun later complained to me that Tu was incapable of fulfilling his official position: "He is such a failure. He did not even know what he was talking about." The way that Tu Chuzhang spoke shows a couple of significant qualities of the official world. First, the officials do not simplify but complicate things. They create more work for themselves by making confusion for others. The confusion is introduced by repetition: everything must be said redundantly, as in the conversation between Tu and Haihun. In many such cases, what is said is not as important as continuing to talk. Entering the official world—that is, building a relationship for your business—means making officials speak to you. It is extremely important for businessmen to open this channel of noncommunication as communication, without which there is no way to succeed in business in today's China. In doing so, however, one must learn how to deal with this kind of conversation. All businessmen's efforts to entertain officials are meant to initiate or maintain this noncommunication as communication. Second, this way of speaking also indicates an asymmetrical relationship of power. It is—as far as my field experience is concerned—a way of showing who is in charge of a dialogue. In the case of Tu, his strategy was to employ a large number of pronouns, presuming that who they referred to was always clear to those present. He repeatedly used two simple Chinese verbs, *shuo* and *shi*, which I have translated as "said" and "did."[8] In doing so, Tu controlled the conversation as a master of what Erving Goffman would have called "the arts of impression management" (1959, 208–9).[9] To put it simply, conversation of this kind is not an equivalent to communication; rather, it is a means of authority and control.

Searching for an appropriate way to characterize this kind of activity, I settled on Geertz's famous essay on the Balinese cockfight, in which he talked about how the Balinese gambled: "The Balinese never do anything in a simple way that they can contrive to do in a complicated one" (1973, 425). If there are multiple ways of doing something, Chinese officials often choose a difficult one to enable them to demonstrate their official, superior position. In other words, things have to be done the official way not by their nature but rather by choice, by will, by preference. To be sure, complicating things does not increase efficiency in government management but instead increases the stock value of official capital in economic, cultural, social, and political investment. The full significance of obtaining official capital will be shown in the following chapters; here it is only necessary to make clear that such a category differs from, following Bourdieu's usage, either social or symbolic capital.[10] Official capital differs from social capital in that the official is at once narrower and broader than the social. It is narrower in the sense that it is constituted within the domain of the social; it is broader in the sense that it authors or authenticates the social. It is different from symbolic capital for a very plain reason: official capital has a real economic value that constitutes a necessary component of any investment for business opportunities.

That Friday, Haihun was on the phone from the moment he woke up. He needed to return to Beihai that night. After we checked out of the hotel, we stopped in front of a gray building, old but still in good shape, where Planning Committee officials had apartments. Haihun was not in a mood for conversation, and he did not tell me why we parked there. A few minutes later, Tu came out of the building, got into the car, and sat next to me, behind Haihun. Nee then walked out of the building, carrying nothing, and sat in the car next to Haihun. I then realized that they would be traveling to Beihai for a weekend break. I had previously sensed only that Haihun's trip to Beihai would be for business, but I remembered Nee Chuzhang's suggestion during Haihun and Tu's conversation the previous day. It was surprising that neither man carried even a small suitcase. Nee Chuzhang had not even changed his shirt, wearing the same garment that I had first seen him in. Was the lack of luggage a sign that everything needed would be prepared by Haihun in Beihai? Or was it simply a personal preference?

It took us about three hours to drive from Nanning back to Beihai on a new, high-quality freeway. I was for the first time properly introduced to the two officials. Our conversations were no longer about the Beihai Star Group, and they began to ask me what America was like. I was asked how much I earned, a common question for Chinese people to ask someone from abroad.[11] Neither Nee nor Tu was interested in my explanation of why my salary was not large or of the differences between the U.S. and Chinese economic systems. They began to complain about how little they received as officials, ignoring the fact that they had free housing and other benefits as well as the free trips to Beihai. "We officials are paid too little," Nee said, "fuck too little, in comparison to what you fuck make. You make $50,000 a fucking year, which is about 400,000 in our money. That is a fucking lot of money. Don't you fuck think? We have fucking nothing in comparison to that. I think the government has to increase our fucking salary to avoid corruption. With this little fucking money, there is no fucking way for people to be clean. We have to fuck survive, too." "True," Tu followed up, "we are paid too little, and we have to get something with whatever we have, don't you think? Particularly people like us, I mean, in the position of a Chuzhang. We run the office, but we are paid nothing. What else can we do? Of course, there will not be any corruption abroad, because they don't need to. They don't have to get more because their salary is good enough. Don't you think?" I did not think that corruption had much to do with one's salary, but telling them what I really thought would not be a wise choice. What interested me, as an ethnographer of urban China, was their deep assumption that an ethical or a moral decision depended on economic situation and their view that what a person was was entirely determined by the material condition of life outside himself.

Having talked a little about America, Nee turned to comment on his own recent experience in France: "The fucking fuck of France! We stayed in a fucking three-star hotel, but it was total shit. Nothing fucked.

It was like a small asshole. I mean they didn't have anything. I mean the fucking facilities were so fucking bad. If their hotel were three fucking stars, all our hotels in Beihai could be four or five fucking stars." The language was so animated that I could hardly follow what he was saying, but finally I realized what he meant was that the television in the room was too small. His comments were limited to the hotel facilities, and I did not get an opportunity to find out why Nee went to Paris, but it was quite clear that it was some kind of official visit. This was the first time that I heard Nee talk casually, and I realized that he was a good speaker but perhaps was a little too fond of one particular word.

Tu picked up the conversation: "A big place may not have good things. Last time, when we went to Shanghai—a big city, ah?—we wanted to have some girls. They said they didn't have any. We insisted, and then they got us some very old auntie. It wasn't a big trouble for me, but our director was really disappointed. A big place is not always good in offering good things."

"The best place is Beihai, isn't it?" Haihun joined in.

"Undoubtedly!" said both officials.

It was completely dark when we arrived in Beihai, and we went to the hotel close to the Beihai Star Group's headquarters. I had been staying somewhere else, but I decided to join the guests at this hotel. We got out of the car and crossed a very large, well-decorated hall on our way to the hotel's reception area. Tu and Nee suddenly jumped to look at a display of photographs of young girls in exotic costumes. This was an advertisement for the hotel's nightclub. The hotel also hosted a massage parlor and a karaoke bar. The girls in the photographs were not hotel employees but had permission to work for the nightclub, massage parlor, and karaoke bar. The nightclub's name was the Dream of Paris (*Men Bali*).

This was not a special hotel that catered to special guests. It was a very ordinary hotel, like many others in Beihai. Most, if not all, hotels depended for survival on the operation of such entertainment facilities. An attachment to the hotels' normal business, the facilities were often run on contract by people who were not formal employees. Without such entertainments, no one would come to the hotel. After checking into our rooms, we went down for a meal, where we were joined by Haihun's wife and nine-year-old daughter. The dinner was delicious but not so elaborate because of the presence of Haihun's family. After the dinner, we were shown to a karaoke room on the hotel's second floor. It was decorated in very high-quality materials, large and with a private dancing space. All the important people from the Star Group were already waiting in the karaoke room: it was a reception for Nee and Tu. What followed was pretty similar to what had happened in Nanning. Young girls were brought into the room, and a slightly older woman who knew everyone from the company introduced those girls to Nee and Tu. Each man chose a girl, and people began to sing or dance. The karaoke party lasted until about midnight, but I was later told that further arrangements had been made for the two officials from Nanning. They were brought to a massage parlor owned by the Star Group itself and were looked after by the "invisible hands."[12]

For those, ethnographers or otherwise, who wish to understand the configuration of business practice in Beihai in specific or South China in general, it is important to consider what was going on in terms of a social drama acted out by three main characters: *chuzhang* as an actualization of the official personhood; the entrepreneur, often addressed as *laoban*, who emerged in late-twentieth-century China; and finally the young women, unanimously called *xiaojie*, working in the nightclub, the massage parlor, the karaoke bar, and other entertainment facilities. To understand the plot of this drama, real or imagined, which I argue holds the key to understanding the logic of business practice in today's China, requires a close inspection of these characters, their ways of telling stories about their roles in the play, and their conditions of emergence in the context of a historical transition, to which I shall now turn.

part one

The Beihai Story

The key force that has led us to our victory is the Communist Party of China; the theoretical foundation of our thought is Marxism and Leninism.

MAO ZEDONG*

The key force that has led us to our victory is the Bank of China; the theoretical foundation of our thought is sex, money, and consumerism.

AN ENTREPRENEUR*

two

Characters of the Story

It is not unusual for an ethnographic account to open with a story about the ethnographer traveling to the field, and anthropologists with different theoretical orientations may employ a similar writing strategy of this kind.[1] In so doing, the anthropologist as an author creates, among other things, an ethnographic authority that rests on the fundamental assumption, implicit or explicit in writing, that these experiences are out there in reality. It is by now a commonplace to argue that ethnography is as much a particular genre of writing, with its own historical conditions of emergence, as it is based on the actual experience of the ethnographer; however, what is not as clear as some might have thought concerns the nature of experience itself. An examination of how ethnographic materials are obtained by personal experience, situated in the large context of relations of power, does not answer the question of what experience— both of the people under study and of the ethnographer—is supposed to be. That is, by focusing too much on the question of how ethnographic materials are obtained, one may have pushed aside another important domain of inquiry on what there is. Even if we know that there is a relation of power that sets up the context for some to become the object of knowledge, we still need to know what is actually out there, to be collected or experienced by the anthropologist in the field. A student of Malinowski might have said that there were three kinds of action and interaction out there in the field: what people do, what they say, and what they say about what they do. According to such a scheme of classification of what there is, two layers of reality are distinguished: what people do and say on the one hand and how people talk about what they do on the other.[2] What people say is taken here as part of what they do: for example, talking about the forthcoming election in a community is action. This is different from what they say about what they do in that it is meant to reason with one's own action or interaction, to give it an account in a culturally coherent way, to provide a discursive justification for action. If such a distinction is maintainable, I shall argue that there are in fact two possible modes of anthropological inquiry, with one focusing on the description of what people do and the other focusing on how they comment on their own practices. Any ethnography necessarily consists of, consciously or not, a combination of these two modes of inquiry: very few—if any—ethnographic works are purely descriptive of what people do, lacking some kind of account of how the people under study explain or interpret their institutions or systems of behavior. However, in terms of an ethnographic awareness of this possible difference in focus, anthropologists do not always prioritize how people comment on their own practices.[3] This experience, from the perspective of the ethnographer, is the experience of hearing or listening to—rather than watching or seeing—the way in which a cultural world is shaped. In other words, fieldwork can be either based on the mode of (participant) observation, a metaphor of empirical science that prioritizes the eyes of the observer, or based on (participant) understanding, scientific in another sense that gives a significant power to the ears of an anthropologist. The field project, on which this book is written, focuses on the commentaries of those under study—that is, on how the business world of everyday experience in Beihai or South China in general is talked about by those who are part of it.

These commentaries are not to be treated as gossip; instead, they will be considered constituent elements of lived experiences, moments of articulation of a story about oneself and others within a larger picture of society and history. It is true that how people comment on their own practices depends on the occasions for which these comments are produced. That is, there is always a "who question" whenever we wish to understand the effects of these comments. However, another question must also be raised: the question of the narrative structure by which a certain kind of speech is able to be produced. Instead of simply providing an ethnographic description of what was going on in Beihai, I focus my analysis on the form of these comments or stories. Two theoretical assumptions underlie my analysis, which I will elaborate in chapter 4: first, stories told on various daily occasions consist of characters, units of plots, and sites of plotting constituted in a particular structure of narrative, historically situated and culturally specific. A combination of characters, units of plots, and sites of plotting is essential for the narration of certain kinds of stories, but these elements are not necessarily actual in the sense that they were acted out in a specific time and place—although they might have been. They are real in that they constitute the conditions of possibility to be part of the reality envisioned, and this is the focus of my analysis. Second, my discussion is based on the assumption that, following David Carr and others, the actual experience itself is structured in and as a narrative; an analysis of the narrative structure as a historical form of social existence therefore provides a real possibility for understanding the mode of existence itself.

By orienting my analysis in such a theoretical direction, I do not mean to overlook the question of ethnographic coherence, which is indeed often the problem of some theoretically challenging ethnographies.[4] A coherent ethnographic description is a central concern for me; however, according to my understanding, ethnographic coherence means a full treatment of the functions of the characters that make possible the telling of the story of urban (high-tech) development in contemporary China. That is, ethnographic examples are governed by a theoretical thread that stitches the story of who one is and what one wants to be in a new discursive domain.

What Is a Character?

What is a character? In his influential book on the condition of our moral chaos since the Enlightenment, *After Virtue* (1984), Alasdair MacIntyre provides some interesting ideas for how a character can be defined and why it is necessary to consider such a definition for a sociology of culture. To be sure, *After Virtue* and his other works have little to do with any sociology of culture in a conventional sense; instead, they are concerned with rewriting the history of modernity by compiling a genealogy of Western morality and/or moral philosophy.[5] My reading of MacIntyre's work, though by no means constrained by his intention as an author, has helped me frame the central questions that I hope to raise in this ethnography, which ground my theoretical inquiry embedded in the ethnographic materials still unfolding. I will begin with a particular point about the character in *After Virtue*.

MacIntyre refers to Japanese Noh plays and English medieval morality plays as examples of what a character is supposed to be. To my mind, there is nothing more adequate than using the Beijing opera or perhaps other kinds of local operas in China as such examples of what a character is. Unlike those in modern movies, characters in these plays are immediately recognizable to the audience in the sense that the characters possess a stock of qualities that have defined them as certain characters, which in turn define possible developments of a plot. The interpretation of these plays depends on a culturally specified preunderstanding of these characters. MacIntyre particularly points out, "*Characters* specified thus must not be confused with social roles in general. For they are a very special type of social role which places a certain kind of moral constraint on the personality of those who inhabit them in a way in which many other social roles do not" (1984, 27). This difference is important. Social roles—for example, professional ones such as accountant or manager—are not characters; they lack the stock of moral qualities presupposed to be part of their possibilities of being such personalities defined as characters. In contrast, the official, as represented by Nee Chuzhang and Tu Chuzhang, is indeed a character because there is a stock of presupposed moral qualities—powerful and corrupt, among others. As MacIntyre continues to define the difference, "In the case of a *character* role and personality fuse in a more specific way than in general; in the case of a *character* the possibilities of action are defined in a more limited way than in general" (1984, 28). Social roles may thus possess some qualities that define what they are, but the definition in such cases is more general than in the case of characters. It is possible to say that characters are a very special kind of social role.

Why is it necessary to make this distinction? MacIntyre suggests that it is essential in outlining cultural differences: "One of the key differences between cultures is in the extent to which roles are characters, but what is specific to each culture is in large and central part what is specific to its stock of *characters*" (1984, 28). In applying this argument to contemporary China, the comparison is not between two different cultures but between two (or more) different historical forms of social experience. That is, one may follow MacIntyre in arguing that one of the key differences between the Maoist revolutionary period and the period of economic reforms after Mao's death in 1976 lies in the difference between the two historically distinguishable stocks of characters.

MacIntyre seeks to define characters as masks worn by different traditions of moral philosophy in the West—that is, he seeks to explain how these characters have embodied moral messages as relatively stable images in a given time or place. The embodiment of the moral message through a set of characters constitutes the moral language of everyday life, which is different from the explicit articulation of moral philosophy. Inspired by MacIntyre's discussion, I seek to develop an analysis of the characters as a particular mode of anthropological understanding of society and history. Despite the differences in our orientation, MacIntyre's discussion is very useful for an articulation of the character as a central category for my ethnographic description. In his discussion, two distinctions are drawn. One is between individual and social role, and the other is between social role and character. The first distinction possesses a clear difference: what an individual believes does not necessarily conform to his or her public role. That is, the relationship of individuals to their social roles is mediated by a number of internal elements, such as psychology or personal history. Conversely, in the case of a character, a different kind of relationship exists: precisely because characters are already socially determined from outside—that is, they cannot be mediated by an individual's experience—they serve as a means by which culturally (or historically) specific modes of understanding are possible. "A *character* is an object of regard by the members of the culture generally or by some significant segment of them. He furnishes them with a cultural and moral ideal. Hence the demand is that in this type of case role and personality be fused. Social type and psychological type are required to coincide. The *character* morally legitimates a mode of social existence" (MacIntyre 1984, 29). This is to say that characters are, as it were, appearances of certain cultural (or moral) qualities presupposed as such by the members of a society. There is a fundamental difference between MacIntyre's discussion of the notion of a character and an earlier trend in the anthropological studies on culture and personality that essentialized the fixed features of different cultures.[6] MacIntyre's point is that moral beliefs and ideas are of two kinds in a given culture. One lies in, for example, its philosophical articulation that is not directly accessible in everyday life, while the other type consists of images stored in a number of characters whose meaning is directly accessible in everyday situations.

The Maoist revolution offers an illustrative example. The landlord was a character through which peasants were to understand the suffering of their own lives, to understand what exploitation had been, to understand the direction of the future for the People's Republic. Especially during the land reform of the early 1950s, the character of the landlord not only was associated with greediness and cruelty but also always received an image, in both narrative and visual representations of the revolution, of a mean-looking appearance. The landlord as a character was indeed an ideological character, specifically designed by the Maoist government for its political purpose; however, how such a character functioned in society differed little from other kinds of characters. During the Maoist revolution, the image of the landlord invoked an emotional (moral) response from ordinary peasants whenever it was presented, either in mass meetings or in the revolutionary dramas. Such a response came from the ideological assumptions attributed to the character of the landlord, whose behavior and attitude, no matter how different in specific cases, could always be anticipated according to the structure of feelings. For example, the landlord as a character in a revolutionary drama would always represent the counterrevolutionary force. There was no possibility in representing the landlord as a character as favoring the revolution in making, although everyone knew that in reality many revolutionaries came from landlord family backgrounds and not every landlord was actively engaged in counterrevolutionary activities. The landlord as an embodiment of the counterrevolutionary force was presupposed by the members of the society as a whole. The character of the landlord is not an individual or a social role. It is an image essential to the making of the communist ideology. In everyday life, such a character acted as part of the language of the revolutionary ideology. The point is that there are two modes of moral (ideological) representation: an ideological discourse, often in writing or in speech, and a set of images made through the creation of the characters.

Having defined the character as such, I seek to provide an ethnographic sketch of the characters essential to the telling of the Beihai story of urban (high-tech) development as an example of the rapid change in today's China in contrast to the logic of practice during the Maoist revolution. In so doing, I assume that MacIntyre's notion of character can be applied in a more general way to an analysis of society in flux. I also take up *After Virtue*'s general theoretical stance in arguing that the moral or the ethical has to be understood in a broad rather than narrow sense to mean the very grounding by which we are able to be what we are.

Characters do not exist in isolation. There is always a set of characters whose full meaning can only be understood in relation to each other at a given historical moment. Characters may be considered the essential referential points according to which the stories about oneself and others may be told. This is the fundamental significance of my discussion of such a notion. An implicit assumption in my approach is that ethnographic accounts under the contemporary condition of life are only possible through an analysis of the stock of characters and the relations between them. The phrase "contemporary condition of life" means to indicate the shift taking place in our mode of existence, caused by globalization or capitalist global expansion, at the present moment. For example, one theme of David Harvey's influential *The Condition of Postmodernity* (1990) focuses on what he called "space-time compression" and the transcultural character of flexible accumulation of capital. Under such a condition, the conventional anthropological method— participant observation in a specific locale—is quite impossible, partly because it is increasingly difficult to assume the existence of what James Boon called "island-like cultures" (1982, 15), places or groups of people in isolation.[7] However, this problem cannot be solved by asking the ethnographer to travel with, for example, the floating population, a term describing the increasing volume of rural-urban migration in contemporary China; instead, what must be done is to make a conceptual reorganization that allows the anthropologist to focus on the stock of characters, where the boundaries between local and global, regional and national, and so forth, have little relevance. We should focus on the renovation of a particular society's stock characters rather than following around our subjects of research in a physical sense or simply increasing the scales of our analysis.

By this discussion of the notional importance of character, I have also meant to criticize, implicitly rather than explicitly, a popular theoretical tendency in the sociological studies of and in China that has always focused on the emergence of new social roles, such as peasant entrepreneurs and professional households. The weakness of such analysis lies in its blindness to the difference between character and social role, of which the latter is simply a matter of fact brought about by the changes in the sphere of economic and political life. Such analysis, if ironically called sociological, does no more than the official classification, recorded in government statistics, does or wishes to do. "The poverty of theory" in this case—to reverse the meaning of a term borrowed from E. P. Thompson (1978), who was arguing against the conceptual abstraction of Althusserism—is precisely the poverty of theoretical understanding.

Who Is in the Story?

We have given a considerable theoretical significance to the notion of character as a category of ethnographic analysis. A set of characters is relatively stable at a given historical moment; however, in the case of China, the question of regional and local diversity must also be taken into consideration. Some regional or local differences regarding the characters in the story of development do exist. There are two regional features in the Beihai story of urban (high-tech) development. First, Beihai is far away from the center of political power, Beijing, China's capital. As those in Beihai often said to me, "The emperor is not nearby," meaning that things that could not be done in Beijing might be done in Beihai. I heard so many complaints from managers at different levels in the Beihai Star Group that it was difficult to do anything in Beijing, from business negotiation to entertainment. Conversely, in Beihai, everything was said to be much easier. As the manager of the massage parlor owned by the Star Group once said to me, "Oh, don't believe it. Those people from Beijing—once we had some here—are so inhuman. They wanted something but they didn't have the guts to ask for it. In the karaoke bar, they spent hours wondering whether they could have girls singing with them. When I brought them to the massage parlor, no girl liked them because they didn't know how to take their pants off. Cash and fuck! This is what these girls want. They waited and waited, but in the end everyone did it. What is this? Why didn't you just go for it? A waste of time, theirs and mine. And those girls'. Unbelievable." This comment suggests that local officials, such as Nee Chuzhang or Tu Chuzhang, had little hesitation in going to places, such as massage parlors, where one might receive sexual services. In the case of an official from Beijing or other centers of political power, some degree of hesitation might have been the case.[8] This means that the official character in Beihai, in a sense, wore little clothes for his desires. By saying this, I mean that ethnographic descriptions of this book may be taken as an account of naked desires and practices. The nakedness here means that there is little need to hide what one wishes to do—for example, in the case of government officials accepting entertainment provided by businessmen. This was not always the case when dealing with the officials from Beijing. This is by no means to suggest local officials in Guangxi were worse than those in other places in terms of corruption but simply that these officials wore no masks.[9] A second regional feature is that the

Beihai area was far less developed than, for example, its neighboring province, Guangdong. A feeling existed among those in the less developed areas: to develop, every possible means should be allowed to be tried; moral values cannot exist without material sufficiency. This is indeed a reflection of a long tradition in Chinese moral philosophy linked to the doctrine of Confucianism, which said that virtue and morality came after the provision of food and clothing. This regional feature is representative of those in China who considered themselves as being left behind by the train of development (see Liu 2000, 1–16). The ethnographic description, therefore, is not cast from the perspective of an "already" but from the perspective of a "not-yet." Justification for action in Beihai was often articulated from this "not-yet-ness": a combination of desperation for quick material gains on the one hand and disregard for the regulations, official or customary, in controlling the modernizing process on the other.

The Beihai story will be colored by these two regional features, which will bring out some striking characteristics of urban development that outsiders to this region might not see as "normal." What concerns me is not the truth of urban development in terms of what actually happened but the conditions of possibility in telling a story about it, in which each character functions as a unit constituted in the whole of the Beihai story of urban (high-tech) development. One might also say that the focus is the truth condition of the narrative structure characteristic of today's China. Stories have different versions, told by different people or groups of people on different social occasions, but the structure of these stories, the way in which they are told, is historically stable. In this sense, the Beihai story is narrated, ethnographically and theoretically, in the singular. The plurality in terms of versions of this story is a given condition for us to search for a historically situated structure of social existence.

Under these two assumptions—the regional characteristics of Beihai and the focus on the narrative structure—three fundamental characters are identified as essential to the telling of the Beihai story of urban (high-tech) development: *chuzhang* (the section chief); *laoban* (the boss); and *xiaojie* (the miss). One must bear in mind that these are characters, not social roles defined primarily according to professional or occupational differences. For example, a *laoban* could be in charge of any kind of business, but as a character it is defined as the embodiment of the newly emerged personhood who is in charge of his fate by paying for others, a character different from any identifiable personhood in the stock of characters of the Maoist revolution. *Chuzhang*, in a narrow sense, indicates a particular official position but, as I will explain in the following section, as a character it signifies and resembles the official kingdom. A character is a function of understanding; social roles are not. Social roles are located in the real domain of experience; characters reside in the domain of understanding. The word *chuzhang* is a title: when it is used to mean a social role, it is made in contrast to other official titles. In contrast, when it is used here to signify the character of the official world as a whole in relation to *laoban* and *xiaojie*, it performs a crucial function of understanding in the telling of the Beihai story. Similarly, *xiaojie* can be used to name any young woman; as a character it occupies a specific location in the narrative structure of the Beihai story, referring particularly to those who worked in entertainment establishments.

Characters are defined in relation to each other as a functional whole constituting a structural necessity in telling the Beihai story of urban (high-tech) development. There are possibilities in further dividing them into subcategories or adding more secondary characters to this whole, but it will not change the fact that the elementary (narrative) structure of the Beihai story is determined by the wholeness of these three characters. They are not main characters in the ordinary sense of the term; rather, they are the main characters of a structural necessity. The structural necessity means that the relations within this functional whole are necessary and internal to the possibilities of telling any stories about urban development in Beihai (or in South China in general). In mathematical language, one would say that this whole of characters is a necessary condition for telling the Beihai story, but it may not be sufficient. In another sense, to say that it is a structural necessity means to emphasize that the relations between these characters, rather than the identification of each character in question, are essential in the constitution of this wholeness. Not the characters themselves but the relations between and among them define the narrative structure of the Beihai story. In specific versions of telling a story about business and society, an individual may refer to a social role as the representative of a character; in such cases, the social role is only the name of the character that functions to make the story able to be told. Social roles, in other words, designate an actual significance in its economic or political sense, whereas, in the case of characters, they function as the necessary means of understanding.

Someone in favor of the theoretical image of fluidity and multiplicity of reality might challenge my definition of characters and narratives as forcing a conceptual straitjacket on the body of real life. A dreadful conceptual error involved in this charge is that it is blind to the difference between things referred to by words and words referred to by words—that is, the difference between the actual and the conceptual. It is a truism to point out that concepts help us organize experiences but are not themselves the experiences. The expression of an experience, linguistically or not, may take a different form as a result of a different conceptual scheme employed in organizing it. This experience may vary according to the situation in and the perspective from which it is experienced by a person or a people; however, this is not the same as saying that there is no way to organize them in a coherent way to illustrate more effectively its characteristics. In arguing for the specificity of their particular brand of historical ethnography, Jean and John Comaroff have provoked us by using Edmund Leach as an example of the difference between the experiential and the conceptual, of which there are two different orders of things. In their comments on Leach's landmark work, *Political Systems of Highland Burma* (1954), Comaroff and Comaroff write,

> Leach would have scorned any postmodern suggestion that, because the world is experienced as ambiguous and incoherent, it must therefore lack all systematicity; and that, because social life seems episodic and inconsistent, it can have no regularity; that, because we do not see its invisible forms, society is formless; that nothing lies behind its broken, multifaceted surfaces. The very idea would probably have struck him as a lamentable failure of the analytic imagination. *Political Systems of Highland Burma*, remember, set out to disinter the dynamic structure underlying a diverse (dis?)array of social arrangements and representations, values and events; to show that, if our models are supple enough, they should make sense of even the most chaotic and shifting social environment. . . . We require good grounds for claiming the *non*existence of a system or a structure—the fact that we are unable to discern one at first blush is hardly proof that it is not there. Here,

then, is a preemptive counterchallenge to the deconstructive impulse of the 1990s: Absence and disconnection, incoherence and disorder, have actually to be demonstrated. They can neither be presumed nor posited by negative induction. (1992, 23–24)

I am not concerned here with a general response to what may be called postmodernism, which represents a very diverse field of inquiry that can by no means be considered as constituting a unified theoretical space.[10] Nor am I as comfortable as the Comaroffs were in using the term *deconstructive impulse* only in its negative sense. I am concerned with the coherence of conceptual tools that one must bring to the ethnographic analysis. What is important, as far as I can see, is not to confuse tool with material or concept with experience. This confusion arises when one cannot distinguish a model from what it represents, an old problem wearing a new suit in our own age.[11]

The (Holy) Trinity of Characters: Chuzhang, Laoban, *and* Xiaojie

The Character of Chuzhang (Chief)

Those whose object of inquiry concerns China cannot avoid the question of "the limits of state power" as Stuart R. Schram (1987) put it or "the reach of the state" as Vivienne Shue (1988) phrased it, no matter from what disciplinary perspective the inquiry is made.[12] Regarding the current transition under the name of economic reforms that has greatly affected the topological features of social and political landscape of that vast country, a political scientist might ask the question of the extent to which the individual was allowed more autonomy in deciding or taking responsibility for himself (see Davis 1995, 10). A sociologist might ask questions concerning certain newly emerged social problems, such as the increasing unemployment or the (re)emergence of prostitution, or questions about economic disparity or the formation of new social identities. As an anthropologist, however, I ask a different kind of question regarding the problem of the state: What are the characteristics of the character representing the image of the official world in everyday imaginations of state power? By asking the question in this way, I have presupposed that the effect of the state must also be understood in and as an image in everyday life—that is, as an embodiment of the ideology and morality of the state. Ordinary people in daily life might not be able to articulate the effect of the state, but they are always capable of portraying a character, consciously or not, as an image of the official world to tell a story about what is going on around them. This everyday understanding of the state through its image is a form of implicit knowledge that requires no definition from the point of view of those who are part of the social world under state control.[13] *Chuzhang* is a character that represents this official image through which everyday understanding of the state's effect is made possible.

Chuzhang consists of two Chinese characters and is best translated as "section chief" or "chief." The *chuzhang* occupies a strategic location in the bureaucratic machine of government administration. If the bureaucracy can be viewed as filled in by two layers of officials, those primarily making decisions and those primarily carrying them out, the *chuzhang* is situated at the conjuncture of the power to decide and the responsibility to carry out these decisions. Those below the rank of *chuzhang* have less responsibility in making decisions but more in carrying them out; those of higher rank have more responsibility in making decisions but less in carrying them out. The *chuzhang* is strategically located between these two layers of officials. This is a key characteristic of this particular official title. The bureaucratic machine under examination in this case is at the level of a city, the same level as a district in the countryside. At lower levels of government administration, such as a county (*xian*) or township (*xiang*), the title for those who stand between the two layers of officials may differ. But there is a stratum of officials strategically located between the two layers of officials in the Chinese bureaucratic machine, and as far as the Beihai story is concerned, this stratum is called *chuzhang*. The significance of this category of officials lies in the fact that it consists of a relatively large group, which means that, on the one hand, it is not impossible to become a *chuzhang,* and, on the other hand, the rank is a significant marker of one's place because of the power to decide.

Although a *chuzhang* is usually in charge of an office, as in the case of Nee and Tu, this title may also be given as a recognition of the rank to other officials. Even bureaucrats who cannot be promoted to be in charge of an office would still hope to receive the title of *chuzhang* at some stage of their careers. To be an official at the *chuzhang* level is a desirable but also achievable dream for many or most people working for the bureaucracy. I heard plenty of stories about officials who would refuse to retire unless they received the title of *chuzhang*. Anyone working for government bureaucracy would be shamed to fail to reach to that rank before retirement. Part of the reason for this shame was that important discussions or meetings regarding government policy making were often organized for officials of this rank and above. Those who lacked the rank of *chuzhang* would not attend those important meetings and would lack advance knowledge of new policies. Exclusion from these meetings means that one is not yet in the circle of real power. Without this title, even if one is part of the bureaucracy, one is not an agent of official power. *Chuzhang* can be divided into *zheng chuzhang* (chief) and *fu chuzhang* (vice chief). In the bureaucratic ladder of government administration, the difference between them is registered significantly as far as benefits are concerned—for example, use of a government car. Someone outside the bureaucratic system, however, will not always recognize such a difference. In the case of the industrial division of the Planning Committee of Guangxi, for example, Nee was *zheng chuzhang* and Tu was *fu chuzhang*, but managers from the Beihai Star Group addressed both men as *chuzhang*.

Practically speaking, if an entrepreneur needed to establish official connections, he would target the various kinds of *chuzhang* because, unlike lower-ranking officials who had little power to make decisions, the *chuzhang* was part of the power structure that made decisions and, unlike higher-ranking officials who did not oversee implementation of decisions, the *chuzhang* could help to move things around in the business world. It is not simply that reaching higher-ranking officials is more difficult but also that when a decision is made, the *chuzhang* is in charge of implementing it. The implementation of a decision requires both experience and practical knowledge, which higher-ranking officials no longer possess. In Haihun's dealings with the Guangxi Planning Committee, the key persons were the two *chuzhang* in the industrial division. As Haihun said to me, if they were willing to help, they could always convince their superiors that what they did was necessary, because their superiors would not know what was going on in the world of business operation. It was sometimes necessary to look after those working under the two *chuzhang* in the industrial division but, in general, subordinates could not refuse to carry out the *chuzhang*'s decisions. In other words, keeping good relations with those working under the *chuzhang* would be a friendly gesture but was not necessary.

The practical significance of the *chuzhang* lies in the fact that they have something to offer—that is, they control government resources. Despite the economic reforms intended by the government to create a market system under which the state would no longer directly control economic activities, the state's role and function have remained extremely powerful in the distribution of economic resources.[14] For example, when the state was trying to encourage the development of a private sector that would help transform the existing economic structure entirely based on the state enterprises, government officials decided how to redistribute these public assets. When the government tried to help develop certain areas of private industrial development, a number of favorable economic policies were established—for example, encouraging high-tech industrial development. In the case of Guangxi, the provincial government decided to encourage entrepreneurs to invest in high-tech industries by offering tax exemptions and low-interest bank loans. These favorable policies created in fact a game of social or political investment—that is, a game of securing a government loan with tax exemption, which would almost assure business success. Successful applicants would not receive loans and exemptions simply because they had investment opportunity and/or better technology; rather, being chosen by the government to develop enabled these entrepreneurs to obtain sufficient capital for success. Many individuals or small private companies hoped to get something from the state, but only a small proportion succeeded. The Beihai Star Group had great success in this game of inclusion.

How these policies were actually carried out was largely decided by those *chuzhang*, who decided which companies would receive state favors. This decision was never made in a vacuum; it was always made in a theater of desires (see chapter 3). The power of the *chuzhang* lies in their power to choose. The *chuzhang* as a character representing the image of the official world chooses to distribute state resources. Such power also enables the *chuzhang* to choose where and how he wishes to be pleased. As Tu Chuzhang once said, "A lot of times, things are not so different. Everyone is in a similar situation to begin with, without much capital or resource. It is we who decide which company is to be given these favorable policies. This is like a random choice. If we choose a company, it will certainly flourish. If we don't want someone to go ahead, we will always be able to think of something to stop him. To the government, punishment does not need an excuse." Even if this is only a partial truth, it is very clear that a good relationship with Tu Chuzhang is necessary to develop one's business. As a result, whenever possible, Haihun would always like to have Nee or Tu spend a weekend holiday in Beihai, for which the company would pay. Such exchanges were not unusual, as many others informed me during my fieldwork, because, compared to what the company received from the tax exemption and low-interest bank loans, the cost of such entertainment was insignificant. What surprised me, at least at the beginning of my fieldwork, was the fact that there was nothing secret about such exchanges.

It may not be unusual in China that, when a favor is asked of someone, the recipient will treat this person to a good meal. As I have argued elsewhere, food and its presentation constitute a system of signification that not only allows people involved to communicate their emotions and feelings but also makes them aware of the social norms of behavior on various occasions (Liu 2000, 83–106). However, the entertainment for *chuzhang* is never simply confined to eating but also often involves the provision of sexual services. In a general sense, one may argue that the everyday business world in today's China is sexualized in two senses. First, almost every conduct of human behavior—social, political, or economic—especially if it is concerned with the officials, can be talked about in sexual metaphors. Second, in the operation of the business world, *xiaojie*, the young women working in various entertainment establishments, have become a necessary condition for business operation. I will now return to the earlier example in which a Beijing official was reluctant to accept sexual services to show how sex could be a troubling yet exciting moment of business practice in the everyday world of experience:

> It is much better here [in Beihai]—I mean, in terms of doing business—because nothing is hidden. What they want, they let you know immediately. In Beijing, they want the same thing, but they don't say it. They wait for you to say it. But even if you offer something to them, they will not take it as it is; instead, they will wait for you to offer one more time. We had this experience with a Beijing official coming to us last year, when we were trying to get listed on the stock market. He was about fifty and perhaps never had been treated the way we treated him. Because of his importance to us, we had assigned two managers to accompany him wherever he wanted to go. We got him the best food we could find

in the world, and all different kinds of rare animals, protected by the state law, would be cooked for him if he wished to have them. In the evening, we brought him to the best nightclub in Beihai, and one of our directors had reserved a *xiaojie* for him, a beautiful young girl with a double master's degree in quantum physics and sociology. We even thought that he might like someone whom he could talk to. This was a *xiaojie* of the highest quality who could talk about theory of relativity or Max Weber when having sex with you, you know.[15] We also asked this girl to dress up in a uniform, pretending to be a college student. She did everything we told her to do. Nothing worked. He liked this girl but refused to take her to his room. While in the club, he sat there like a stick and went to the bathroom every other minute—yes, literally, every other minute. We thought that he had some sort of problem with his kidney or bladder. Anyway, it was too dark to see the expression on his face. Whenever the girl placed his hand on her leg, he stood up and went to the bathroom. No matter how much we said to him that this was Beihai, not Beijing, he still refused to take anyone to his hotel. At one time, we thought he didn't like this girl we had prepared for him, and we brought many different girls for him to choose from, but he still refused. He went to the bathroom even more frequently than before. Our director didn't know how to handle this guy. We even thought this must be a good guy who just didn't like it—a good government official, perhaps, but we couldn't figure out why he had to go to the bathroom so many times. He didn't drink very much. After he went back to his hotel room, we got this relativity-Weber girl to call his room, pretending to be someone else and asking him whether he wanted some kind of intimate service. You know what? He asked how much. What a strange guy! Why didn't he just take one from the club? If it were Nee Chuzhang or Tu Chuzhang, there would have been no problem of this kind. They would just tell us straightaway what they wanted. The Beijing officials are all bullshit but pretend to be flowers.

Such is a portrait of the character of *chuzhang* as an image of the official. Despite the other elements involved in this comment, it clearly shows that, from the perspective of those in business, entertaining relevant officials was a crucial part of business practice; and this entertainment went far beyond simply feeding the official rare animals. It is quite obvious that they believed that it was necessary to entertain the officials in charge to receive business opportunities or favors. Such entertainments would not simply help one's business but would hold the key to business success. It is through this conception of a particular kind of reciprocity—concerning not only the actual power of *chuzhang* but also the structure of economic transition—that the Beihai story is able to be told. However, this does not mean that every business conduct needs to be done this way or that each government department would have the same kind of attraction for those in the business world.

The *chuzhang* is a character in the Beihai story of urban (high-tech) development. It is not simply a layer of administration; it is the layer of administration that performs an extremely important function in connecting the official kingdom to the business world. To say that the *chuzhang* is a character means that it is neither an individual nor a social role; rather, it is an image of the official itself through which everyday imagination about how things are supposed to be operated is produced. As a character, the *chuzhang* is seen as someone of real power, able to decide on crucial matters, overseeing the implementation of government policies, knowing the rules of the business game and possessing a considerable amount of practical knowledge, directly controlling the process of distributing government resources, choosing which company will receive state favors, needing to be entertained—someone who pleases when pleased.

The Character of Laoban *(Boss)*

As a term of address for an employer, *laoban* had been part of the business vocabulary in traditional Chinese society but was abandoned during the Maoist revolution because of its exploitative connotation. Under the Maoist rule, everyone was supposed to be employed by the state or its agencies, and those who were in charge of a state work unit were supposed to be called *lingdao* (literally, "leaders").[16] *Laoban* returned to the inventory of everyday language after economic reforms were launched in the late 1970s and private enterprises began to emerge. The term was more likely to be used in privately owned companies or businesses. The political significance of this term does not lie in its function in designating an employer but rather lies in its representation of a character who owns a business or is in charge of the situation in which this term is called for. On daily occasions, a number of terms were used in the Bei-hai Star Group—*zong jingli* (general manager), *jingli* (manager), *dong-shizhang* (chairman or director)—but all of them differed from *laoban*, which maintained the essential meaning of being a boss. In particular, this term connotes a sense of being in charge of a situation, for example, being responsible for paying for others. When a group of people goes out for dinner or entertainment, one person usually pays the bill, and waiters and waitresses in particular would call this person *laoban*. As mentioned in chapter 1, when Haihun was entertaining Nee and Tu at the nightclub, they always followed others in calling Haihun *laoban*, although at other times they called him Lao Hai. (Lao means "old" or "older" and is commonly added to someone's surname as a way of showing respect.)

The person who pays is in charge; the person who is in charge owns; the person who owns takes responsibility for what happens; the person who takes responsibility for what happens is *laoban*. It does not mean that this term of address cannot be used, as a metaphor, by some-one who addresses a person in charge, such as an official calling his supe-rior, but in the story of development, particularly in South China, the word's connotations are determined by the emergence of an image of someone who is in charge by virtue of ownership. Who could be con-sidered *laoban*, for example, in the Beihai Star Group? In general, this question is implicitly asking who owns the company, who has the final say on payment and expenditure. To answer these questions, it is neces-sary to take a brief look at the company's structure. The Beihai Star Group is a corporation with six subsidiaries, mainly producing electron-ics but also with other business interests, such as real estate develop-ment. The idea was to build a modern shareholding company control-ling these subsidiaries via purely financial means. The daily management of, for example, the electronics factories was not part of the responsibilities of those working in the company headquarters in Beihai, although the managers or directors at the headquarters were more likely to be seen as *laoban* simply because they were significant shareholders. The company headquarters was in an eight-story building at the center of the city, with eighteen departments under seven divisions or offices: Office of the General Manager, Office of the Board Secretary, Division of Finance, Division of Sales and Marketing, Office of Development, Office of Management, and Office of Construction and Property Man-agement. The general managers were supposed to be in charge of the overall operation, and they worked with other members of the board of directors under the board of supervisors.

The head of each department or office may be considered a *laoban*, but in the headquarters the real *laoban* were the two general managers (*zong jingli*): Panton, in his late thirties, and Haihun, in his early forties. Both men owned a significant proportion of the company's shares. To call someone *zong jingli* is to acknowledge his title within the hierarchy of the management, but its connotation is different from that of *laoban*. *Laoban* is not simply someone in the highest management position; if it were, the term would lose its signifying function. *Laoban* is a character, whereas *zong jingli* is the name of a social role. The difference between these two is that the former signifies and is signified by the agency of private ownership, whereas the latter does not necessarily do so.

The managers in the Star Group can be divided into two further groups, those in charge of a whole department and those in charge of only a section of a department. Those in charge of whole departments were sometimes also addressed as *zong jingli* within their own departments. Once after a meeting of all the top managers, an employee called the manager of the Division of Finance *zong jingli*. Panton overheard and said, half jokingly, "If you are a *zong jingli*, he should also be a *zong jingli*," pointing to another manager, "and he should also be a *zong jingli*, and everyone here should be a *zong jingli*. If so, what am I to be?" One of them quickly responded, "You are our *laoban*, and that is how we should call you. Let me be the first: *Laoban*." Everyone agreed and began to call Panton and Haihun "*Laoban*" in an obvious flattering tone. "Wait a moment," Panton continued. "If you call me *laoban*, can you tell me what it means?" No one attempted to answer. Panton then said,

> I don't think that *laoban* is a bad term, but it has been so overused that it has become vulgar these days. Everyone is now called *laoban*, including those selling clothes or desserts in the streets. Don't you think it is funny? *Laoban* should be this specific character; he must possess a combination of three essential qualities. To be entitled to be called *laoban*, he must first be an owner of a substantial amount of property and capital; second, he must have some kind of taste in high culture—I mean, well educated—as well as know modern skills of management; and finally he must possess a group of talented followers working for him. One cannot be a *laoban* without his supporting managers just as an emperor cannot

be an emperor without his generals. You are all my generals. I rely on every one of you for daily management, and I pay you for doing so. Without any of these three qualifications, one cannot or should not be called *laoban*. Therefore, government officials should not be called *laoban* because they own nothing but their own positions. Those selling clothes or desserts on the streets may have some money in hand, but they have no taste in culture, and their education level is zero. It is a joke to call them *laoban*. Haihun and I deserve such a title. We have property, taste, and followers.

Everyone applauded this excellent definition of *laoban*.

Panton's casual response to the question of what *laoban* should mean later became accepted wisdom among the company's managers. Two very basic aspects of this conception of what *laoban* meant are that a *laoban* is a private owner of capital and that there must be people working for him. However, it is interesting to note that Panton stressed two further qualifications: first, a *laoban* should not be simply a rich man but must have a high taste in culture; second, he must possess modern management skills. Both of these qualities depend on receiving a good education. The emphasis on education as an essential quality for the managers of a private company, if not an entirely new phenomenon, is a striking feature of the Beihai Star Group, perhaps partly as a result of the nature of its business—electronic technology. In a more general sense, my field experience showed the emergence of a new kind of private entrepreneur who saw education as a significant predictor of business success.[17] In the administrative hierarchy of the Beihai Star Group, education functioned as a very important criterion in the selection of managers. One of the most significant characteristics of this company was that all the managers received some sort of degree from a university or a college. Among the five top managers, including Panton and Haihun, three had doctorates, one held a master's degree, and the other held a bachelor's. The average level of education of the managers in this company was much higher than in other enterprises. Both Panton and Haihun received their Ph.D.s in the early 1990s, and their authority in the company arose at least partly from their status among the best educated. An assistant manager once said to me, "I greatly respect our *laoban*, not only because they are good people, but because they know everything and have connections everywhere. I am happy to work for them, because they have knowledge that I don't. I got my M.A. in economics;

I will not work for a peasant entrepreneur who knows nothing about economics no matter how much I would be offered, because I will not learn anything from a peasant.[18] But I am learning every day from our *laoban*. When you go out with them, you will be respected because they are respected." Haihun himself truly believed that his doctoral degree increased his opportunity to succeed in business negotiations, and he said, "When I was in Beijing, talking to those officials, who tend to be arrogant, it was helpful to have a Ph.D. Every time I implied that I had a Ph.D. in economics, they became a bit modest, a little bit nicer, because they knew they could not babble nonsense as if no one understood what was going on. They could have done that to someone who was not well educated; they could not do that to me because I have my degree."

The general level of education in the Beihai area was quite poor; it was striking to know that the Star Group management was full of doctors and masters. If this case were representative, it would leave the impression that one's success depended on the level and quality of one's education. Indeed, people who were considered incompetent for their jobs often were said to have failed to receive enough or proper education. For example, the chief accountant was one of the core managers and had received a master's degree and worked extremely hard for the company for many years. However, after 1997, when the company was trying to be listed on the Shenzhen stock market, his performance was doubted because he knew very little about the stock market economy. When Panton or Haihun talked about him, they always said that he should have more training in a broader field of economics and finance or he would not be able to deal with the expansion of the company's business. I was indeed impressed by this orientation toward education as an essential quality of a manager. To me, this may be taken as a sign of a shift in the (mainland) Chinese business world, where education has begun to be considered a key element for success. Of course, one should be aware of the extent to which such a generalization can be made. When one looked into the situation of Beihai or Guangxi in general, one would find that it was quite unusual for a company to be managed by people with graduate degrees.

The word *education* may also have a different connotation for the employees of the Beihai Star Group. A higher degree may have real functions in making business connections. Many classmates of Panton or Haihun in different fields of economics and finance have become either university professors or government officials, positions in which they may help the development of Panton and Haihun's business. In this sense, the doctoral degree was not only a certificate of esteem but a passport into another world of necessary connections. One day when I was having lunch with Haihun in a Beihai hotel, a man joined us. Haihun introduced the man as a classmate at the Southwestern University of Economics and Finance, but he was in fact trained, as I later discovered, in a different field and was several years younger than Haihun. The men knew each other through a common friend who also graduated from the same university. This person, Mayuan, was now working in the Beihai local government's Office of Institutional Reform and had first come to Beihai to work through Haihun's connections. After becoming an important local government official, Mayuan helped Haihun in obtaining important business information and further connections.

Why did Panton and Haihun become businessmen after receiving so much education? Did many young people in those days not believe that education would help very little in their efforts to succeed in the business world? Panton's and Haihun's differing experiences provide good examples of the change in values among Chinese intellectuals. Panton was twenty-nine when he received his doctoral degree in economics from a provincial college. Everyone in the company believed that Panton was never interested in becoming a professor or an official of any kind, because he was, from the very beginning, constantly in search of pleasure and power in the business world. He was said to have studied for a doctoral degree because he thought that graduate school was a good place to begin his business practice. Indeed, he used those years in graduate school for traveling and looking for opportunities to establish his own business. Even before he graduated, he found himself a position in a promising young company in Hainan, a new province made independent of Guangdong by the central government as the largest economic free zone for further experimental reforms in the early 1990s. Immediately after his graduation, he went to Hainan, worked for that company for a couple of years, and then created his own business and moved to Beihai. Panton had no illusions about the usefulness of nonpractical knowledge. He never mentioned to anyone the subject of his doctoral thesis.

Haihun's experiences in becoming an entrepreneur were quite different because he had always prepared himself to be a scholar. When traveling, he often brought a book, reading sometimes Malthus and sometimes Confucius. In his hotel room, a book would often be lying open on his bed. In Nanning, when I was traveling with him, he was reading a Chinese classic on military strategies. Unlike Panton, his becoming an entrepreneur was unexpected, and a full account of his story will be provided in chapter 5. Briefly, Haihun received his bachelor's degree from a small provincial college of economics and finance, and after graduating he became a lecturer at the same college for a couple of years. He then went on to the Southwestern University of Economics and Finance for a doctoral degree in the field of Marxism and demography. He was supposed to return to the college to teach, and the college, even in his absence, promoted him to associate professor and increased his salary. But Haihun did not return; he paid the required compensation to leave the college and became a businessman. Haihun remembered a conversation with a college classmate that helped make the decision. This friend said,

> Let me tell you the truth, the only truth, nothing but the truth. Nothing exists in this world except things that can be bought by cash. What have you been doing all these years? Teaching? Talking to students? Reading Marx? But for what price are you doing this? What have you received by doing this? You have been reading Marx, but you have never understood him. What Marx has taught us? You actually do not know—although you have read *Capital,* and I haven't. The spirit of Marx is historical materialism. This is what we all know. "Historical" because we are still in an early stage of socialist or capitalist development, which means that we don't have enough things for everyone and that who gets what depends on how much one invests—in whatever means. "Materialism" means that there is no truth beyond what can be measured in cash. If you continue to do what you have been doing, you will be in the dustbin of history. Wake up! Marx told us that the material condition of life is the first order of existence; the spiritual development of our civilization is secondary. We are still in a primary stage of socialism, like the Party says. That is the lesson you should learn from Marx. The primary stage of development. I bought my parents a new house in Beijing, and I could get them anywhere for a visit any time I like—to let them enjoy the best hotel and food. Can you? You cannot. Every month, you sit in darkness, nervously counting your tiny salary and calculating how

much you may put in the bank as savings. If your father is ill, you will not be able to bring him to a good hospital; you will be in a hopeless situation, begging people here and there for help. These people will do whatever you ask if you pay them. I can pay a man to eat his own shit. This is what I learn from Marx and how I understand historical materialism. Look, I know you are a good son, but to be a good son these days means that you are able to bring your father on a trip without being worried about the cost of the airplane ticket or hotel bills.

This comment contains not only an ironic materialistic interpretation of history and society but also an emphasis on the stage of development. China is said to be at the primary stage of accumulation, and knowledge has little value in itself. Haihun became a businessman in 1992. His father was hospitalized in July 1998, and Haihun went back to Taiyuan, his home city, to look after his father, who was guaranteed the best possible treatment in the hospital because Haihun was able to offer several doctors cash and free holiday trips to Beihai. "Everyone in the hospital took my father," as Haihun said proudly, "as their own. I could not imagine this if I were still teaching in college." Similarly, many employees at the Beihai Star Group headquarters took their *laoban* as no less than a symbolic father. The appearance of the *laoban* would stir a feeling of nervousness if not fear. When waiting to get into the elevator, no one would go before Panton or Haihun if either or both of them were there. It was a common experience to see people holding doors for their *laoban: laoban* is first.

Once, at the dinner table, two managers were chatting with each other while I was present. One said to the other, "I don't particularly like this term of address, *laoban,* which does not sound good to my ears."

"Because you just came out of school, and you are not used to the real world," the other said.

"What is this? To call someone *laoban* sounds like he is the master and we are servants."

"You think you are not?! We are servants. What do you think you are? Your salary is paid by the *laoban*—not by anyone else. Don't be naive in thinking that you are not a servant. The sooner you realize this, the better for you."

Thus understood, *laoban* as a character in the Beihai story is a master who has servants whose fate is supposed to be decided by this master. The master owns the company; the master decides who is paid and how much; the master takes responsibility for the growth of wealth. If one had illusions, one would be left out of the stream of "historical materialism." This was the significance of the *laoban* as a character. This character is the agent of capital. What is an agent? R. G. Collingwood long ago distinguished instruments (what or who carries out action) from agents and patients. Agents command an action to be carried out and/or take responsibility for that action (1942, 8). Economic reforms gave birth to the character of the *laoban,* an agent of market and capital who is no longer entirely generated by the genetic codes of the state and the habitus of socialist practices. The moral image of this agent in everyday imagination is represented by someone who by virtue of paying and owning decides and cares for those working for him. In this sense, those who are paid by a *laoban* become his servants.

The Character of Xiaojie (Miss)

Xiaojie, consisting of two Chinese characters, is a term with two basic meanings in today's China. In a general sense, it means "miss" and can be used to address or refer to any young woman; in a specific sense, it means the young women involved in the various kinds of entertainment businesses—waitresses, hostesses, and so on. The distinction between these two senses of the term can only be established by context. For example, someone trying to catch a waitress's attention in a restaurant would probably say, "Xiaojie, please bring me another beer." However, if someone in a nightclub or a karaoke bar were asked whether he wanted a *xiaojie,* the term would refer to some kind of sexual service, though not necessarily genital sex. *Xiaojie* thus symbolizes a variety of roles that are all defined in terms of "the second sex" in the sense that it is always a means for achieving business success and never the end in itself.

The services that *xiaojie* provide include a very wide range of activities, many of them far beyond what would be considered prostitution in its usual sense. For example, a formal lunch or dinner for an important guest would often require an accompanying *xiaojie.* Later sexual service might be implied, but not necessarily: the presence of a *xiaojie* was considered necessary when entertaining socially or politically significant guests. Someone unaccustomed to being fed by a *xiao-jie* might feel embarrassed or even intimidated by the presence of several young females from which he could choose. If this were the case, one would most likely be laughed at by others as "uncivilized" (*bu kaihua*).[19] It is not important here whether sex or prostitution is involved; rather, it is important to understand that the function of *xiaojie* as a character is intrinsic to business practice, not because it helps but because it is an integral part of the practice itself. Why? This question cannot be answered without considering the importance of changes in the Chinese economy that have resulted in the emergence of a double structure, reflected in the ideology of "one country, two systems." In this structure, two economies coexist: the market economy and the state economy. To explain this phenomenon, it is necessary to understand how South China's businessmen conceive of official power.

During a summer 1999 trip to Haikou as part of my fieldwork in South China, I heard a story from a young man who went to search for opportunities in Hainan in 1992, just after it was declared an independent province for further reform experiments. The story reveals much about how businesspeople conceive of official power:

> When I first got down here, I knew nobody, because the person who brought me here left for prison because of some kind of fraud in his investment in his real estate business. The early 1990s were really something. A lot of people carried guns because there were so many desperate people trying to make something out of their adventures in Hainan. It was crazy. Well, I had to find a job because I gave up my work in Beijing. I was bored and then came down here. I forget how I got my first job, but I remember an important lesson given by my first boss. He taught me this very, very important lesson that has made me successful. When I went to his office for the first time, before he said anything to me, he threw on the table two notes, a hundred yuan note and a two yuan note, and asked me: "What is the difference between them, and how can one make money?" I was puzzled by his abrupt way of asking me this, although I did have a degree in economics. I did not want to say anything stupid, because I sensed that he was not looking for any book knowledge or political economics, so I kept silent for a second. Then I said to him frankly that I didn't know

what he meant but I was ready to learn from him. He stared at me
for a while and said to me that he was glad that I did not give him
any shit such as the principles of macroeconomics. "Listen, fuck
your college knowledge. This is Hainan, a real world. I have not
finished my elementary school, but I have made three million in
one year. If you ever wish to work for me, never fuck me with
your knowledge from college. Open your eyes and look at these
two notes." I looked at them again, carefully this time: on one side
of the two yuan note there is a print of two faces of ethnic women,
and on the other side of that note there is a scene from the Hainan
Island, tropical forest; on one side of the hundred yuan note there
is a print of the faces of four great men of China—Mao Zedong,
Liu Shaoqi, Zhu De, and Zhou Enlai—and on the other side of
that note there is a picture of a huge mountain of North China. I
still didn't know what I should say to him. He then said to me,
"Stupid guys who come to Hainan can only make small money—
this money," he picked up and flipped the two yuan note above my
nose, "and small money is here in Hainan, exactly as it is printed
on this note—two yuan." He then continued, "To make big
money, you need these, you understand? The big men, the official
men, the government. It is they that make the business world go
around! If one cannot make use of them, one will never be successful in business. But this does not mean that small money has no
use. You understand what it means by printing these two fucking
girls on this two yuan note? Do you understand? What moves the
great men around is women—*xiaojie*. This is the meaning of this
two yuan note: with it one can make an effective transaction. A lot
of men come to Hainan for money and women, but they do not
understand the secret relationship among money, women, and the
officials. If one has money, one may be able to get women, but one
may not be able to get *real* women, you understand? Real women
are the *xiaojie* that not only fuck but fuck in right places *and* at
right times to make you rich. If one gets *real* women, one will certainly get money, a lot of money. Therefore, the first thing for you
to do is to find real women and control them, and then you will find
where big money is, and then you will get big money by means of
xiaojie. Not the other way around, you understand? *Sex is the
weapon that destroys anything and everything it wishes.* Great men in
particular."[20]

Sex is the weapon that destroys anything and everything it wishes. This is the ideology of an era in the history of the People's Republic marked by the unique shape of development in Beihai or Hainan or South China in general. Two assumptions are apparent in this conception of business and society: first, the effect of the government, much more than simply its (govern)mentality, is real; second, there is a very fundamental assumption about the nature of men as captives of their sexual desires. Government officials were seen not only as men but also as special men who were particularly driven by the desire to consume women, precisely because the officials lacked the kind of freedom that businessmen had. Implicit in seeing the world this way is an assumption that the official world is a male world. It is an empirical truth that in places such as Beihai were there very few female officials in charge of significant offices for the local government. Therefore, for businessmen to assume that officials would be male is not groundless. The message of this teaching is explicit: one can only make big money by allying with government officials. By working hard or selling clothes on the streets, one could only expect to make small money.

There is a logic in this particular understanding of business and society. It is not the case that, as many people have assumed, businessmen have money first and then become interested in women. It is the other way around: those who have made a fortune for themselves know how to employ sex as a weapon for their success. For example, the Beihai Star Group operated a successful massage parlor that provided the company the most crucial part of its initial capital accumulation. "If one has real women, one will get big money" means that the *xiaojie* is not outside the process of wealth making but is inside this process as an integral part of money production.

Haihun once told me a story about a couple of government officials from Nanning who were for the first time entertained by the company. "They were good officials," as Haihun said, "because they had never been treated in the way they were treated in Beihai." They were invited to come to Beihai to inspect a factory owned by the Beihai Star Group. Both men were in their fifties and received massages after dinner. Haihun said,

> Can you imagine how they enjoyed it? In their fifties, to be massaged by young girls of eighteen! After a hot bath, to be treated with care and respect by a girl of their choice. What an experience

for them! That was their first time having sauna and massage. When they came out of the room, the two old men were almost in tears because they had never had such a relaxed experience. They told me that it was a world beyond language and expression. They are not bad men, and they did not wish to have sex with these girls. They enjoyed the massage to their hearts and bottoms. They never dreamed of such experiences like this. They had good job, good life, and good other things, but they never had this kind of experience. What is economy? This is economy. The function of "the invisible hands."

Haihun became friends with these men, who ultimately supported all of the Beihai Star Group's development plans for the small price of this massage experience. People outside China may not understand the significance of this example. For officials of this generation, who have been in the government office for many years, to visit a place like a massage parlor means a great adventure in their life. They could only have this experience in Beihai, because they had no money to go to this kind of place on their own and because they feared being caught if they went to a place not operated by their friends.

One should not consider the relationship of *xiaojie* to *laoban* as that of female to male, for what is essential to the female-male relationship is the gender difference, which is a relation of two terms, although often unequally constructed. In contrast, the *xiaojie-laoban* relationship contains a third element, the *chuzhang*. One typical plot involving this trinity of characters in the Beihai business story would be as follows: The *laoban* needed some kind of favor from officials and tried to build a good relationship with the *chuzhang*. The *chuzhang* was then invited for dinners and entertained by the *xiaojie*, who were of course paid by the *laoban*. After the *laoban* and the *chuzhang* became familiar with each other through singing and other entertainment, the *chuzhang* granted a business favor to the *laoban*. In such a plot, the *laoban* should be considered an agent, defined as someone who makes a decision and takes responsibility for it; the *chuzhang* should be considered a patient, on whom the *laoban* carries out action; and the *xiaojie* is an instrument in the sense that the action takes effect only by means of her involvement. Understood in this way, the *xiaojie* as a character in the Beihai story differs from the other two in that it is never considered an end in itself; rather, it is by definition a means of business success. To be acted on or to act on are both ends, not simply means, but no such ends can be conceived in the character of the *xiaojie,* even from the perspective of the *xiaojie* themselves. I often heard that a *xiaojie*'s purpose in being involved in such business was to make some quick money to open her own business. The relation between "to act on" and "to be acted on" is one of active versus passive, whereas the relation between the end and the means is one of agents/patients versus instruments. The character of the *xiaojie* as an instrument of business practice is a nonhuman being in the sense that it does not have to follow the moral codes of the human world, the world of agents and patients. It is like any other goods or commodities that may be purchased.

This is not to suggest that a *chuzhang* will never conceive of himself as an agent. What is suggested by this analysis is confined by the views of those who have been in business—that is, I hope to lay out the *laoban*'s view of the world of business and society, not only because the *laoban* were newly born of the economic reforms but also because the *laoban*'s vision of the world could serve as a significant indicator for the future direction in which China will travel.

three ·~

A Theater of Desires

Office of the General Manager

Each character in the Beihai story of urban (high-tech) development is associated—in both the real and the metaphorical sense—with a setting in which his or her practice of everyday business is supposed to be carried out. The real sense of a setting means the physical environment in which a character is situated—that is, an environment or a place to work. In contrast, the metaphorical sense of a setting indicates a site of desire and imagination essential to the functioning of a character being told in the story. In this latter sense, it is not simply an office or a massage parlor where one works; instead, it suggests the location of an image that partially defines the content of this image as a character. This metaphorical sense of a setting means a background, an immediate background, from which the character stands out. Two kinds of backgrounds may be distinguished here. The broad social and economic background is the setting of my writing. This immediate background constitutes a necessary part of the character, like a canvas to the portrait: without each, there will be no painting. This immediate background of the character is already part of the character. For example, when one talked about *xiaojie* in Beihai, one would inevitably think of the entertainment establishment as part of her character. This distinction between the two forms of backgrounds or between the two senses of setting is crucial for the understanding of plot in telling stories about urban development in South China. The most elementary form of plot—that is, articulating events and persons into a narrative whole—is placing a character in his or her immediate background and then situating this background in the larger picture of society. As an example, the office of *laoban* (the office of the general managers of the Beihai Star Group) is illustrative.

Observers of the changes taking place in the last two decades of twentieth-century China may still remember that when private enterprises began to emerge on the surface of economic life in the 1980s, a large number of "handbag companies" (*pibao gongsi*) came into existence. They were so named because they had no offices of any kind and moved from one place to another, doing business in locations such as private homes or restaurants, mainly because they did not start with a large amount of capital (most financial resources were still tightly controlled by the state). Most of these handbag companies were based on what may be called the mode of household production, a kind of family business through friends and acquaintances. These companies also operated in this manner because they did not wish to spend their money on offices. Few cared for where they worked: their sole purpose was to accumulate capital for further operation. However, this image of household entrepreneurs without offices stands in absolute opposition to the image of a successful *laoban* in today's Beihai business world. If one were in Beihai at the turn of this century, one would no doubt have the feeling that the *laoban* were competing with each other not only in economic or financial performance but also in decoration and ornamentation of their offices. Self-image, as they often said, had become quite important (cf. Bourdieu 1984). For example, the headquarters of a company came to mean a lot more than it had previously. It was a symbolic expression of power and wealth. The office of the general manager has therefore become the symbol of a symbol—the headquarters of a company.

The Beihai Star Group's headquarters was an eight-story building. Some floors were prepared to be rented out to others as office space, although they were not yet occupied in 1998 because business was slow as a result of the Southeast and East Asian economic crisis and as a result of overconstruction, which had produced many empty buildings. The headquarters building was completed only in 1996. More accurately, the completion was incomplete: the building had been planned as twenty-four stories, but Beihai's real estate development fever had cooled down in 1993–94, when Vice Premier Zhu Rongji ordered the sudden withdrawal of all loans and investments. Realizing the difficulty facing the company, the Beihai Star Group decided to seal the building at eight stories. The structure was beautifully designed—white, a bit flashy, decorated with artificial marbles. It shone under the daytime sun; at night, several huge neon signs singled out the building in the dark. The biggest neon sign atop of the building said, "Star Massage."

When I went to the Star Group headquarters for the first time, I was stopped at the door by a "policeman"—a doorman dressed in an exact replica of the city's new police uniform. He was quite polite and simply grabbed my shoulder and forcefully turned me around to see my face, since he did not know me. I was released after Haihun arrived and explained who I was. Then I noticed that this was a huge hall that looked more like a hotel entrance than the headquarters of a company. Several more "policemen" in uniforms stood around. I went with Haihun to the elevator, which impressed me even further with the luxurious intentions of the original plan for the building: the door of the elevator bore an engraved picture of two naked women—of the Western body in a posture of a ballet dancer. Haihun saw me staring at the picture and explained that the elevator had originally been obtained for the company's massage parlor. The massage parlor opened in 1993, soon after the Star Group was formed. The original plan would have moved the massage parlor up to the twenty-fourth floor to allow guests to enjoy Beihai's night scene, but when the plan was changed, the elevator was no longer needed for that purpose, and managers now used it to go up to their offices.

All the offices were located on the eighth floor. Outside the elevator was another huge reception area that looked very much like those in Hollywood movies: spacious, clean, and extremely well organized. A computer sat on a receptionist's desk, behind which sat two girls who looked like they were just out of high school and who had joined the company because someone had recommended them to Panton, as I later learned. To the left of the reception area were a number of small rooms used as offices by the managers or section chiefs; to the right were several conference rooms as well as the general managers' offices. Haihun's office was next to Panton's, which was in turn next to the board of directors' conference room. Everything was brand-new and compelled visitors to feel this brand-newness, which left no trace of anything preceding it. While standing in the middle of these offices, I could not sense anything that might help me trace a past of any sort indicating what the company would have been like before these arrangements were made. I also could not tell what sort of future this newness indicated. This feeling of being there, in the space of a business world, left a strong impression that nothing temporal existed except the presence of a present order of things.[1]

Except for a very refined wooden master desk and a pair of Italian leather sofas, everything touchable in Haihun's office was made of artificial marble. The master desk was huge enough to play table tennis on. The desk contained only a telephone and a color television. Behind the desk was what they called the *laoban* chair, a comfortable, movable chair, much higher than the chairs or sofas for guests. I was told that the *laoban* chair had been ordered from Hong Kong and the desk and sofas from Italy. When I was looking around, amazed by the high quality of the furniture, two local government officials came in to talk about whether Haihun would like to make a contribution to help some of the region's poor children return to school.

"Of course we do," Haihun said after offering the men cigarettes. "Beihai is our home. Whatever the government wants to do, we will go along with it, to support you, you know."

"We know that Haihun Laoban always understands our problem, and this is why we have always tried to do our best to promote your company's image," one official said.

"No problem. Why don't you just go to talk to Xiaohua, who is our special accountant in charge of this kind of matter?" Comfortably sitting in his chair and overlooking the officials, Haihun pushed a button somewhere underneath the desk. A secretary came in and asked, "Anything?" "Ask Xiaohua to come," ordered Haihun. I was sitting next to the window on a temporary chair, much lower than Haihun.

A few minutes later, Xiaohua came in. She was slender, not very tall, and wearing a long silk skirt and high heels, a very calm young woman, indeed. She spoke in a clear but soft voice: "Anything I can do, Laoban?"

"Oh, there is something that you need to help them with. Just do as we usually do." Haihun said to her.

What did they usually do with this kind of demand from the local government? Xiaohua seemed to know the answer very well, and she did not say anything more but brought the two officials to her office.

After they left, Haihun had a long telephone conversation, and I began to notice some construction problems with this splendid building. New air-conditioning equipment had been installed a few months earlier, but it seemed that when the building was designed, there had been no plan for having such equipment or at least not equipment of this kind.

The region's climate was close to tropical, and for seven or eight months of the year air-conditioning was required. The air-conditioning pipes and wires hung down from the ceiling; a window was broken to allow some pipes to exit the room, but the window looked as if it had been broken by a thief—the hole was too big for the pipe. I then noticed that my hands were wet, and I found that there was a leak somewhere close to the window. I thought the moisture came from the air-conditioning equipment, but I was later told that leaking was a severe problem for the entire building because the roof had not yet been properly completed. It had been only temporarily sealed because the company still hoped to complete the twenty-four-story building. Whenever it rained, damage to the Italian sofas became a serious possibility. Haihun spent more than an hour on the phone, and I continued looking around without knowing what to do. A carpenter who came to fix the lock on the door saved me from my dreariness. The lock had not been properly placed, and sometimes Haihun could not get in, although his secretaries often found the office door wide open. The carpenter was the person who made the door; the locksmith had already left the city. The man did something with the lock and a few minutes later told Haihun that everything was fixed—an easy job, he said. But it was fixed in the sense that we could not get out through the door, as we discovered an hour after the carpenter left. Another door connected to Haihun's personal secretary's office, but this door was locked and the secretary had gone home. Haihun had to call someone to come to open the door from his secretary's office so that we could get out.

It was about 5:00 in the afternoon, and people began to leave their offices. As we came out, we saw Xiaohua. She smiled at us and tried to close her office door with her right foot because the door was extremely difficult to close and had to be pushed very hard. Xiaohua kicked the door with her high heels as if it were the only way to shut it. She did not succeed at first. She then put her red handbag on the floor, moved back a little, like a soccer player preparing for a penalty shot, and then kicked and pushed the door closed. Xiaohua then locked it and smiled at us once more and left. Why were there so many problems with the doors and windows of this brand-new building? Was it simply a coincidence, or was it something more significant regarding the symbolic value of the *laoban*'s office? It is clear that as far as the *laoban*'s office is taken as a site of desire, what signifies the power of the *laoban* is not the perfection of details but the glamour and splendidness of his work space. It does not really matter whether there are leaks; what is most important as a symbol of power and wealth is the marble, the Italian leather, the master desk—the content of what he owns.

Banquet of Turtles

The significance of banqueting in Chinese society, past and present, need not be reiterated. Social and political relations are eaten (see, e.g., M. M.-H. Yang 1994); cultural events are marked by a calendar of food (see, e.g., Liu 2000, 88–89); ethnic and local groups are signified by their kitchen habits or table manners (see, e.g., Chang 1977). Food and table manners constitute a very crucial part of socialization that not only produces ties that link people together but also creates significance for the relations thus established. The practice of business life in Beihai is no exception to this general observation, but in addition to what has already been said on food and eating in Chinese society, I will emphasize: *power is eaten.* As a result, dining together is the first step toward or the minimum requirement for knowing one's location in the network of power relations, either real or symbolic. This sense of power, different from the Foucauldian notion of power as the essence of being in society and history, means at once the sweeping force, anywhere and everywhere, and the dynamic hierarchy, *here* and *now,* required for the specific moment of a configuration of Beihai business practice.[2] The banquet is a site of such configuration; it is a location where one's desire is being desired; it is a battlefield for symbolic struggles. It is important to remember that this is not simply lust or individual greed; it is the function of a character as told in the Beihai story. When thus told, they are considered characters, to be desired. This "toldness" is only possible from the perspective of a "telling." The plot of the story is already a desired description of what ought to be. In other words, the character in the story is always an embodiment of a desire that is in turn being desired by another character. As far as the function of the character is concerned, it is not a thing or an object but the desire of another that sets the story in motion. In this sense, one must say that the symbolic struggle involved is a struggle of power. This sense of power has little to do with political domination or exploitation but a great deal to do with symbolic control and subordination.[3]

The banquet is an essential part of the practice of business life in

Beihai. In a normal situation, the banquet represents the very beginning of what was called "a golden production line of entertainment" (*huangjin liushuixian*), designed for entertaining government officials or business partners and including three crucial steps. First, the guest would be invited to a banquet. What was provided or ordered for the guest would depend on his or her status. For people like Nee and Tu, I was told that some ordinary but good food would be enough because they did not care too much about what they ate. Their demands for Beihai centered less on food and more on singing, dancing, and other forms of enterntainment. Normally, when a government official was brought to Beihai, especially someone from Beijing or another big city, a proper banquet would be appropriate. The second step was to bring the guest to a karaoke bar or nightclub, where they could sing or dance while drinking with hostesses. It was surprising for me to find out that many officials, such as Nee and Tu, were great singers, perhaps partly as a result of their frequent practice in such places. Whenever they were singing, they often took on a very serious mien, entirely absorbed in the performance, as if they were becoming sober. The karaoke party would go on until midnight, and then the third and final step in the entertainment production would be to bring the guest to a massage (sauna) parlor for relaxation, potentially including sexual services. That local business people called this chain of entertainment "production" rather than "consumption" seems to suggest that the phenomenon was really part of business itself.

Those who came to Beihai for food were usually tired of the kind of food offered in ordinary restaurants. When an important guest was invited, it was necessary to find a restaurant that would cook and serve rare animals. In Guangxi, people prefer the taste of nonordinary meat. The first meal to which I was invited when I arrived in Beihai was at a very stylish restaurant inside a grand hotel. I was taken to dinner by Haihun's secretary, Hexiu, an elegant young woman in her late twenties. She ordered a very large plate of stir-fried chrysalides, blackish and oily, some looking as though they were still alive. Perhaps I was initially taken for someone with some sort of significance, or this may have been a common way of entertaining guests from North China, where people were not in the habit of eating fried insects of this sort. I hesitated but could not begin. Hexiu lifted her head and with a mouthful of chrysalides mixed with tofu and vegetables, said, "Gooood, ah?" She had been raised in this area and knew the best thing to order.

Because Beihai was a seaside city, shrimp and crab were not considered very special; however, turtle was significant in the hierarchy of food offerings. The best way to cook it was by steaming. As I was told by a manager, Beihai's local police chief was particularly fond of steamed turtle; every month or so, an excuse must be invented for him to be invited to have turtle. He also liked other kinds of rare animals and birds, which were supposed to be protected by law, but turtle was his favorite. Other officials might prefer monkey, snake, bear, tiger, or other animals. Although laws prohibited the consumption of many animals, they continued down the throats of businessmen and their guests. One young man who was always asked to accompany officials on their visits, said, "You see, people like rare animals because they are good for health. They eat these rare animals not because they simply taste good, you know, but because they are nutritious."

"Really? But a lot of things are nutritious, such as carrots," I said.

"Well, that is different. How long can you live? How long does a turtle live? See the difference? A turtle lives for a thousand years, but you cannot live more than a hundred. You see the difference? Then you understand why he likes turtles. You eat more turtles, you will be likely to live longer. This is what I mean when I say they are good for health. This is what everyone believes and why everyone enjoys turtles."

"If so, one should not eat chrysalides. They live only for a few hours, if I am right."

"You are wrong. They eat chrysalides not for that purpose. Young women in particular like them because they are supposed to be good for one's skin. You know, you don't want have skin like a turtle's, do you? Then you have to eat something like chrysalides for a change. Eating them helps keep your skin young precisely because they live only for a few hours. After you have enough turtles, you must have something else for different parts of your body." He was completely serious, and he continued, "Each animal, especially rare animals, has its own potential to increase your health. Snake, for example, is good for your kidney, and the kidney of the snake is good for your eyes. The only danger is that if you eat too much turtle, although you may live longer than others, you might also become more like a turtle in character or appearance. Don't you think that those officials look a bit like rare animals? I guess that part of the reason is that they have eaten too many such animals."

There are a number of metaphors or unconscious implications of this philosophy. As far as food was concerned, official guests favored rare animals. It has become a sensational topic: despite the central government's efforts through various laws forbidding the consumption of rare animals, eating them continued. Who was eating them? Officials, among others. Why were these rare animals favored? Because they were considered good for one's health? No. Because they were rare, expensive, difficult to find. This was the true reason for them to be favored. The guest came to taste the rareness of food. Having rare animals was power, as was offering them. The host and the guest were on two sides of the power relationship whose name is *rare:* rare in the sense of scarcity and in the sense of nobility. To swallow rare animals is a sign of being in control—or, rather, a sign of control of being.

Singing in the Karaoke Bar

The second step in the golden production line of entertainment was to bring the guest to a karaoke bar, usually located inside a nightclub. The term *yezonghui* (nightclub) usually referred to an establishment including a bar; a dance hall with a platform for some sort of professional or semiprofessional singing or dancing performance, often erotic; and a number of private karaoke rooms. However, small karaoke bars sometimes existed without other facilities. When locals said that they went to sing in a karaoke bar, they commonly meant that they went to a nightclub but sang in the karaoke rooms, which were rented out by the hour. Most people going to karaoke bars came in groups and would choose to have a private room. Each of these private karaoke rooms bore a name—for example, the House of Roses. These rooms differed in decoration and in size. Nee and Tu were invited to sing in the club's largest room, the Emperor's Suite. There were about thirty people altogether, including the *xiaojie*, but the room did not seem particularly crowded.[4]

As the guests entered the room, a woman—often slightly older—would come to talk to the person who was supposed to pay the bill later. In most cases, she knew the guests and would begin the conversation by complaining that they had not come to see her for a long time, even if it had only been a few days. While this conversation was going on, the headwaiter would come in and ask what kind of drink he could offer the guests. Imported wines and spirits were much more expensive than local products, and if someone had a taste for whiskey, for example, the cost of the entertainment might be much higher than the usual. Each room would have a fixed minimum price. For example, no matter how much was drunk, the Emperor's Suite would cost at least fifteen hundred yuan for the whole night. If only beer was drunk and no food was ordered, the cost probably would not exceed this amount. However, if more than the required minimum amount was consumed, payment would have to cover what was actually eaten and drunk. Payment was given to the management and did not include tips for the *xiaojie*. There was great regional variation in how much these hostesses earned. Although tips were supposed to indicate appreciation of the *xiaojie*'s service, the Beihai social norm was to pay each of them at least one hundred yuan for her presence. There was no upper limit, but few men would pay more than two hundred yuan if no other services were included.[5] The *laoban* was supposed to pay all such tips when an official had been invited. Therefore, the total cost for singing in the karaoke bar depended on a number of elements: (1) the room; (2) the number of guests and tips for the *xiaojie;* and (3) the amount and type of food and drink ordered.

After the drinks were ordered, the older woman would bring in a group of *xiaojie,* and first the guests would be asked to choose from among these girls. For example, when Nee and Tu were entertained in Beihai, the woman sat beside Nee and asked him in a whisper about what kind of girl he would like to have, at the same time placing his hands on her legs, which were uncovered. When all the girls had entered the dimly lit room, Nee was given first choice. He did not like any of them, and another group of *xiaojie* were brought in. All the accompanying managers from the Beihai Star Group were male, and they made their choices, partly because they did not wish to make further trouble for these girls, but Nee still did not. Then the older woman said, "I will find you someone you cannot refuse." She left the room and returned with another young girl. It was too dark to see what she looked like, but she was wearing something like a fishing net, as if she were a goldfish caught in it. Nee Chuzhang was happy to take her as his company. Subsequently, everyone began to take turns at singing. Nee was an excellent, enthusiastic singer, and never skipped a turn. He devoted himself to the music and concentrated passionately on his performance. Most of the popular songs were love songs, and many of them probably came from Taiwan or Hong Kong. The content of the various songs differed very little. Not only did Nee sing, but he was also very much into the story told by the song. As in any karaoke bar, there was a huge television set, usually showing some sort of love scene—a young woman rolling back and forth on a beach, a young boy chasing a girl on a rock, or something similar. It was interesting to note Nee's devotion to the television scenes as well as to the songs—he was almost yelling. The music was so loud that people could not hear each other well. In terms of displaying passion, Nee Chuzhang was much better than the actors on the screen. Although it was impossible to see clearly, it sounded like Nee was weeping for the hero in love when he was singing/yelling. As a matter of fact, Nee himself was the hero—that is, the focus of attention and the guest of honor. Whenever he finished a song, Haihun or another person from the company would applaud, with everyone else following suit. From time to time, Nee would sing a duet with his *xiaojie*, who was said to have previously been a professional singer. Haihun told me later that this girl was the queen of that nightclub and was always asked to look after the most difficult guest, although she had never been a singer. She was a nurse from Hubei, a province north of Guangxi, and she had become a *xiaojie* because her boyfriend, who had been working in a bank, stole some money from his office for gambling. He was caught and sentenced to five years in prison. The girl spent a considerable amount of money of her boyfriend's, felt guilty, and decided to move to another city to make some money to help him when he was released. She was indeed very good at singing and dancing, which made Nee happy. Having sung for about an hour, Nee took his *xiaojie* out to the dance hall. I was told that Nee was also a good, dedicated dancer. Of course, singing and dancing were not the only activities possible. Some men were playing a kind of dice game with their *xiaojie* while drinking and talking. But the managers from the Beihai Star Group focused their attention exclusively on the wishes of these two government officials, particularly Nee.

This environment was extremely alien to me and left me with an uneasy feeling. What struck me the most was the fact that everything seemed so natural, as if this were the only imaginable way of doing business and as if it had existed for the past five thousand years. Nee was very relaxed and familiar with everything in the bar, but why should he not be so? Only a few days later, when I reflected on this experience, did I begin to realize that what puzzled me was that my mental image of a government official differed very much from Nee. My image had somehow been shaped in the shadow of the Maoist communist cadre. From that sort of image, formed in a very different past, everyone would perhaps criticize the scene and claim that this represented corruption. I do not deny that there was a certain kind of exchange between the entrepreneur and the official in this case and that it might appear to others to be unfair. But it is more important to note that commercial exchange—for the first time in the history of People's Republic—has assumed a general function in the constitution of social relations. Because of the erosion of the ideological space of an older kind, social relations of very different forms were now generally considered commodities. This is what was happening in the karaoke bar in Beihai. That is, the relationship between the entrepreneur and the official has become a relation that is no different in function from any other kind of social relation. Being fed steamed turtles and accompanied by a *xiaojie,* there is no longer any assumed difference between the official and the commercial, the high and the low, the sacred and the profane. A sense of equality between these two characters is achieved by singing in the karaoke bar.

This is not to say that economic differentiation is not a fact of life in today's China. Some have gotten extremely rich while others remain on the verge of poverty. However, my point is that the difference between the rich and the poor is of quantity rather than of quality. The hierarchical space of social relations before and during the Maoist revolution was filled by qualitative differences. For example, a communist cadre could not be considered an equal to a landlord no matter how much they looked alike. However, the space of the social relations in today's China is constituted by the differences of quantity—how much one earns and how much one has in terms of material goods and commodities: there is no longer any substantial difference between one and another although they have dressed in opposite fashions. The difference is no longer a difference internal to the being of a person; it is simply a mask of an individual external to the nature of this person. This is why, when I was doing fieldwork in South China, I often heard officials say that they were human beings and that there was no reason why they should not enjoy themselves or have concubines. This is not, at least from the perspective of an anthropologist, corruption but a revolution in the constitution of social relations. In saying so, they have reduced their status, their sacredness, to the ordinary and the profane.

If one looks into the wider context of change taking place in today's China, one could argue that everything is being transformed under the regime of market as a transcendental agent into a system of exchange. Contrary to the popular argument presupposing the corruption thesis, I argue that what is happening is an erosion of any essentializing definitions of being or existence. There may be a great deal of similarities between the Chinese experience of becoming modern and that of others; however, given the complexity of China's recent history, a new story about its staggering footsteps toward modernity still needs to be told. To do so, one must not assume that what we have seen is no more than corruption due to the institutional arrangements of a society based on nondemocratic principles. Nee and Tu's behavior must be viewed not simply as corruption but as a sign of modernity where differences between one and another, between the sacred and the profane, can be nothing but appearance. By nature, everyone is now conceived of as made up by the "selfish gene," to adopt Richard Dawkins's phrase (1976). Equality takes a different shape in a karaoke bar. The difference is that among who pays, who does not, and who receives. The marker of difference is a double: men in relation to women *and* the commercial in relation to the official. Outsiders would quite often feel disturbed by this form of exchange because—ethnographers or not—they project their own moral visions onto the Beihai story of urban (high-tech) development. This book does not deal with morality itself but with a metamoral question in the sense that it draws a picture of the restructuring of the social space in transformation. It is too early to say what it will look like in a few decades, but it is almost certain that the boundaries that used to mark each social position began to disappear as singing in karaoke bars became an essential part of Beihai's everyday business practice. The kind of equality achieved in singing or yelling a love song in front of a huge television screen, by officials or not, does not indicate that everyone has had access to the same resources but does signal that no one is assumed to stand on a higher moral plane. As a result, no one was disturbed by the fact that these officials were entertained at the nightclub. Their identities were not a problem at all: they were simply customers.

"Invisible Hands" and the Massage Parlor

After midnight, everyone looked a little tired, and the manager of Star Massage came to tell Haihun that a car was ready outside the nightclub. Nee and Tu were taken in the car to the massage parlor for a sauna and massage, the last step of the golden production line of entertainment. Star Massage was a very important part of the company's businesses. It was not unusual for any Beihai company to operate a massage parlor—

the city had many such establishments. In some popular seaside restaurants, young women with much of their bodies exposed passed by and handed diners advertisements for sensual massage. The streets were crowded with signs advertising massage; Star Massage had one of the biggest and the brightest such signs.

How did Star Massage come into existence? Why did a high-tech company have anything to do with a massage parlor? How did the massage parlor become attached to the Beihai Star Group's headquarters?

Having met with Panton and decided to come to Beihai to work, Haihun tried a lot of different ways to accumulate the initial capital needed to run the business, but none of his efforts succeeded. Unlike Panton, who had planned to have a massage parlor from the very beginning, Haihun hoped to obtain his stake by other means. As he related,

> To run a business, you've got to get some money in your hands, to invite people to come over and even get an airplane ticket to go somewhere, and so on. But we had nothing to begin with. Oh, in those years, 1992 and 1993, when we had just begun, I tried so many different kinds of businesses. Nothing worked—I mean, nothing at all. I tried to operate a fashion factory, which is still there, but it has never produced enough profit for investment in other businesses. I tried real estate, which collapsed when everyone went away in the mid-1990s. I tried to operate a restaurant chain, but it did not work either because there were too many here already. The most painful experience I had was to try to sell fish and shrimp to the restaurants in Shenzhen, Shanghai, Beijing, and other major cities. You know, Beihai has fresh sea products, such as shrimp and crab, and people wanted them in Shenzhen or Shanghai or Beijing. In those days, I got up at 3:00 in the morning, rushing to the fishermen's market, which would open at about 4:00. I would have to take two drivers with me and some huge plastic bags. We waited there, bought some shrimp or crab or fish after bargaining with the fishermen, and placed the animals into plastic bags with water and air to keep the precious little things alive for a few days. I would send a truck to Shenzhen, about twelve or fourteen hours away by road, and then I would go with the other truck to the airport, ordering the fish to be delivered either to Beijing or Shanghai. Then I went home to change and

took the airplane with my fish to Beijing or Shanghai. After I arrived there, I would go from one restaurant to another, trying to sell to these places. Sometimes the bag was not fastened well, water leaked, and the fish died. Then nobody wanted them. You were in debt. Sometimes I could sell them to someone, but the trouble was that I would not be able to get my checks, because it was a strategy of the restaurants to hook you to them. They always said to me, "Well, next time. We will pay you when you bring more shrimp to us." They were customers, the king of the sea. If they said so, we'd better bring more shrimp to them. I was trapped in this circle of empty promises. Never got my money back. They just tried to pay as late as they could, but you needed the money to run your own business. Well, you dared not be angry at them because they were customers. What could you do in such cases? It was extremely exhausting. While I was trying all these business possibilities, Panton opened the massage parlor, which easily made three million yuan a year, enough to cover the everyday operating expenses of the office.

All of Haihun's attempts occurred within one or two years, which I did not think a long period. Then I asked Haihun, "You only tried for a short period of time. Might you have needed to wait longer to generate profits? Would you agree?" Haihun did not reply but opened his window and pointed to a flower shop across the street: "Do you see the sign for that shop?" he asked.

"Yes. It says 'Fresh Flowers,'" I said.

"When I moved into this office about a year ago, the sign said 'Fresh Fish.' Then a few weeks later, it became 'Fresh Meat.' Then it changed again last month to 'Fresh Beer.' Now it is 'Fresh Flowers.' It all took place within one year. The guy who owns the shop does not even remove the sign; he simply changes one character in the middle to make it another business.[6] Look at the sign yourself—the outline of the old characters is still there. They are simply covered by a new character. This is Beihai. If you cannot make money in two years, you are dead several times over."

Massage parlors seemed to have met this business requirement. Panton was a good businessman in the sense that he could smell investment opportunities. Panton had no doubt that a massage parlor would produce profits. Haihun and others were doubtful, simply because there were so many such places in Beihai. But Panton believed that he could make it work. He spent a month or so before opening Star Massage searching for good *xiaojie* by visiting every such parlor in the city. He sometimes went back to a massage parlor several times, requesting different *xiaojie*. Whenever he found someone good in character or experience, he would suggest that she come to work for the Star Massage, offering her a better salary. Not every *xiaojie* he recruited came to Star Massage, but a lot of them did because of the temptation to work in a better place and receive better treatment. In terms of its equipment, Star Massage was indeed one of Beihai's best. Panton recruited experienced and charming *xiaojie* into his business, and they brought with them their customers. It was said that other massage parlor owners would become extremely nervous whenever they saw Panton coming to visit their place, though it was too late for them to be cautious. When Star Massage opened in 1993, twenty-one *xiaojie* came to work for Panton.

The manager of the Star Massage told me in 1998 that the club had about fifteen regular *xiaojie*, each of whom averaged three or four guests per day, for a total of fifty to sixty customers. There were two kinds of sauna rooms, regular and luxury. Each customer would have to pay a base rate to use the facilities, about 150 yuan for a regular room. Each guest was charged 100 yuan per hour for the service received, and guests commonly stayed for two hours per visit. Hence, each patron would pay about 450 yuan to Star Massage. The *xiaojie* would receive a tip from the customer depending on the quality and the kind of service offered, but she would have to pay a portion of her earnings to Star Massage if the customer signed his bill instead of paying her in cash. Thus, the massage parlor would receive almost 25,000 yuan per day, from which it would not be difficult to produce a net profit of 10,000 yuan. In a year, there would be more than 3 million yuan, a little less than half a million dollars.

It was difficult to know how the massage parlor was actually operated, not because people refused to talk about it but because no one assumed that there was anything worthwhile mentioning. Sexual services were certainly part of its business but, as some locals insisted, people often went there simply for a relaxing sauna. Massage parlors were part of life for the people in Beihai. Here are the voices of some girls working in such establishments.

Case 1, *Xiaojie*

I graduated from a senior high school, but very few other girls here did. Many of them had no education at all and do not even know how to write their names properly. They came from the countryside, where there were too many people, and they had to find somewhere else to make some money. To be a woman is actually easy, because you can always survive by using your own body—in different ways, of course. But I am from Chengdu, the capital of Sichuan province. I had a reason to leave my home. My problem was that I was never given any attention by my parents, because they have my brother, three years younger than me, as their family treasure. In my family I am always the one who works but receives no respect. You know, what I needed, when I was at home, was a little respect and attention. When our relatives came to see us, they never really talked to me. It was as if I did not exist. That was the main reason I decided to leave my family to be on my own. My parents work in a factory in Chengdu, making very little money themselves. They tried to find me a job in a retail shop, but I did not like it: standing there all day, with your legs supporting your entire body—no way. I decided to come down to Beihai because there was a friend of mine who had been here. She told me it was easy to make money here. Then I came, and she brought me to this place. It was difficult in the beginning because I did not know anyone here. As a *xiaojie,* you have to cultivate your own customers. If you have some people regularly coming for your service, you will have no problem at all in this city. You can move to another parlor any time you like because you will bring your customers to the new parlor. Now I make more money than anyone in my family. I told them that I was working in a hotel as a receptionist. I do not know whether they know what I am really doing. I don't care. Nor do they. I don't think that they care about what I am doing. You know what happened when I went back for the New Year last year? I brought something for everyone, and all my aunts heard this and came to visit *me*, talking to me for the first time in a way that they had never done, because they wanted me to give them something. They were so nice to me. Why? Simply because I am rich now.

The feeling of being rich was not very difficult to achieve in this case because of her relatives' relatively low standards. The happy manner in which this woman told her story truly impressed me.

Case 2, *Xiaojie*

I came from a northern city in Shandong. I've never told anyone where I came from. I was happy growing up with my sister and my parents. The family was close—we would have felt uncomfortable if we didn't have dinner together every night. Our family was working for a state enterprise that produced some sort of agricultural machinery. I was trained in a professional school attached to this factory, as was my sister, who is two years younger than me. It was a good factory that had been operated by the state since 1955, but in the 1980s nobody looked after it, and the situation became worse and worse. All the state enterprises went bankrupt. My parents worked for it for their whole life; they still hoped that they could continue working for this factory. That was the reason that they got me and my sister into the professional school attached to this factory. It was the iron bowl of our family. We are good girls, not stupid, but not clever enough to get into universities. We were happy in the professional school because we knew everyone there and all the teachers were my parents' friends. The teacher I liked the most was my father's apprentice. He was so nice, an older brother to me. He liked soccer, and, therefore, I spent all my time watching soccer games with him, from the World Cup to the China Cup. I just wanted to be close to him, making him happy. When we departed from the school, we all got drunk. We did not call him Teacher Li any more; instead, all the girls called him Old Brother, with tears. What a wonderful time! In the 1980s, it was difficult but it was still fine, because the factory was still able to operate. I graduated in 1989 and began to work in the factory, earning about one hundred yuan a month. But in the late 1980s the factory was in serious debt. We were paid only half of our salaries. In the early 1990s, the financial situation further worsened because few peasants were buying our products anymore—we produced only some old-fashioned machines. The factory was in trouble, and the solution was to ask workers like my parents to retire, but without giving them any pension. For a few months in 1995, we were paid no salary. By this time, my sister had also joined the factory for a couple of years, having graduated from the same professional school and been taught by the same handsome teacher. Those who were in their late forties were asked to retire early; others, especially women, were simply asked to leave their posts [*xiagang*]. You know this term? *Xiagang* is a good way to say "being dismissed"—basically laid off. My mother retired at age forty-four; my sister and I were both dismissed from our posts; my father went home slightly later. But we were trained for this factory, and we only knew how to do the things we were taught. Three women and one man sat at home without any hope. We had no other means of survival. We had some savings, of course, but they would not last forever. My sister and I then both came to Beihai, searching for job opportunities. I think that we both made a good choice in coming here, not only because we could survive but also because we can support my parents. We send money home from time to time. At least we do not have to ask for money from our parents. How did I get this job? A friend brought me to work here. In the beginning I didn't know how to massage, but I learned quickly. I was very good at technical things; I was trained as someone like a locksmith. Well, most times, you don't need to know how to massage, because many of them come here for something else. It was fine with me, because I gave myself to the teacher, and I knew all these things between men and women. In the beginning, I was a bit shy because I didn't know the people whom I was serving, but I gradually began to like my work. My teacher always taught me that we should serve the people and make others happy. The most important is of course that I could support my parents in some way. I truly love them and talk to them on the phone every weekend. And I have also bought a lot of good clothes. I can see my sister every day, which is another pleasure of life.

It would be a serious error to take these two personal accounts as representative of all the experiences of *xiaojie* working for the golden production line of entertainment. These two ethnographic examples somehow stand out in my consciousness in trying to understand the condition of (urban) life in today's China, and each makes a good point about what I am arguing. First, as I have already suggested, a philosophy of money seems to be eradicating all social distinctions and replacing them with a different mode of moral configuration. What has become an underlying assumption for the practice of business life in Beihai is the emergence of this universal standard in the evaluation of all values. In today's China, everyone is equal not in front of law but in front of cash. This does not mean that there has not been a greater degree of social and economic differentiation in recent years. However, although the gap between the rich and the poor has been increasing, as is well recorded in governmental statistical yearbooks, it is more striking that there is very little difference in different social groups' visions of the future. As I have shown in the discussion of these three characters in the Beihai story of urban (high-tech) development, despite the sharp and almost oppositional differences in their locations in the social landscape, *laoban*, *chuzhang*, and *xiaojie* seem to share a very similar view of the nature of society.

Second, the first *xiaojie*'s relatives became friendly to her after she had made some money by working in Beihai. Every relative might not have been as friendly as she wished even after she became relatively well-off, but the point is that the conditions of possibility for telling the story were set up by some larger forces in society. This way of telling one's story is a condition of life for all three characters—that is, despite their different subject positions, the narrative structure by which they are able to tell their stories about business and society is the same.

Third, the second *xiaojie* brought up the idea of *xiagang*, which was central to the experiences of a large number of people working in the state enterprises. In the late 1990s the state's strategy was to carry out reform by trying to get rid of those state enterprises in debt, with the result that a large number of workers were laid off—that is, *xiagang*. *Xiagang* is a nice way of telling someone to leave, to be unemployed; however, the problem is that the employees of the state enterprises usually had been trained in specific skills. They knew very little about anything else and had no financial means to open their own businesses, a nearly hopeless situation for people in their early fifties or older. If one were young and female, one could probably try to work for Star Massage or other such places. But how long could one continue working in these establishments? Everyone working there openly admitted that it was a business of youth. If someone asks what a *xiaojie* will do in the future, the answer is usually, "Who knows? Who cares! Perhaps settle down with a good man if I am lucky. At least I can make money now with my youth."

When I finally got an opportunity to ask Panton why he thought the massage business had succeeded, he said, without any hesitation, "The market. You know the power of the invisible hands." Adam Smith was used in the plural.

four

A Grammatology of Pleasure

The Narrative Nature of Human Experience

The question of narrative—or, rather, the recent revival of intellectual interest in this question—can be traced to three main streams of thought. First, it has always been part of the discussion among literary scholars, for whom the question of narrative essentially concerns the form of literature—how a certain literary content is or is able to be represented. Therefore, it is essentially an inquiry into the nature of representation.[1] Second, the question of form, in the hands of some historians or philosophers of history, turned into a serious debate about what the historical fact and its representation are supposed to mean. This debate goes back at least to the 1960s[2] and reached its intellectual height with the 1973 publication of Hayden White's *Metahistory*.[3] To social scientists, what was interesting was the interrogation of the factual, either historical or ethnographic, in the history and literature debate. The literary and historiographical streams of thought converged on the question of the form in the representation of reality, and this convergence was linked in an important way to the structuralist innovative approach to the problem of narrative, which will be discussed in some detail in the next section of this chapter.

The third stream of thought on narrative, with which I am concerned here, is philosophical. A philosophical reading of the problem of narrative constitutes the background of the ethnographic description in this book, although such a theoretical concern does not always appear on the surface of the text. The world of a text is a landscape of sign and signification, where its topographic features are undermined by an underlying geological structure of meaning. What needs to be made clear here is a difference between the philosophical discussion of narrative and the other two streams of thought. For example, in David Carr's argument, derived from a discussion of the Husserlian idea of "internal time consciousness," the question of narrative is no longer concerned with the representation of reality; rather, it has become a question about the nature of reality itself. The notion of reality is meant to be the human reality that consists of experience, individual or collective. Therefore, Carr's argument essentially asserts the narrative nature of human experience. This is a different inquiry from the other two streams of thought on the subject because it no longer simply takes narrative as a form— that is, as something added onto human experience for the experience to be represented. Instead, it focuses on what is out there, in the world of social (or business) life, on the question of what there is. This difference between the philosophical discourse on narrative and the other two streams of thought lies in that, in terms of its mode of inquiry, the former is ontological and the latter epistemological.

The theoretical lineage out of which Carr's argument grows is particularly marked by Husserl's (1964) treatment of time consciousness. If memory is used as an example, Husserl has made a crucial distinction between two forms of memory: retention and recollection.[4] Recollection is the usual sense used to describe what happened in the past, that which can be retrieved from the storage of memory and brought to present consciousness. This is *re*-collection. Retention is not the kind of past that lies in the storage of our mind; instead, if it were the past, it would be the just-past, that which serves as the background for the present to be recognized as the present. That is, it is the past without which there is no way to identify the present as the present. For example, in the case of listening to a speech, each word uttered by the speaker must be placed in a series of just-pastness; otherwise, there will be no possibility for understanding any sentence. This sense of pastness is different from remembering what, for example, Mao Zedong said fifty years ago, which is recollection. Husserl singles out this just-pastness to show the presence of the past. It is essentially different from the normal sense of the past: recollection differs from retention in that the latter is not the past of the past but the past of the present. As Carr explains,

> The best way to understand retention is to turn, as Husserl does, to the comparison between the experience of space and the experience of time. Present and past function together in the perception of time somewhat as do foreground and background or focus and horizon in spatial perception. To see a thing is to see it against a

spatial background which extends behind it and away from it and from which it stands out. Seeing always "takes in" this background as well as the particular object seen; that is, corresponding to the horizon is a horizon-consciousness that belongs to every perception. Just as there is no object without background (and no background without object; the two notions are correlative), so there is no perceptual consciousness of space which does not include horizon-consciousness. Now Husserl says that the temporal is experienced by us as a kind of "field" like the visual field: the present is its focus and the just-past forms the background against which it stands out. Consciousness of the present always involves retention as the horizon-consciousness of this background. (1986, 21–22)

To use a spatial metaphor for the discussion of the internal time consciousness is crucial. The present cannot be present unless it is set in the background of just-pastness. This immediate or primary pastness is not the past as it is usually understood—something behind us in time—but part of the structure of the present by which perception is made possible. The same can be said of the future: expectation in the normal sense, which means to call to mind some sort of future event—a birthday party, for example—differs from the primary expectation or anticipation, which, to parallel retention, may be called *protention*. The difference and function of this distinction between expectation and protention are the same as those between recollection and retention. "Taking past and future horizons together, then, one may speak of the temporal as a 'field of occurrence,' in which the present stands out from its surroundings, and of our consciousness as a kind of gaze which 'takes in' or spans the field in which the focal object stands out" (Carr 1986, 23).

When Husserl talks about "field" or "horizon," dealing with time consciousness via the employment of spatial images and metaphors, he does not take space as the objective space of geometry; instead, he takes it as lived experience—that is, as it is well known in the phenomenological tradition, the latitude of intentionality, which is the structure of experience that is not reducible to the experience itself.[5] The spatial image of a field or a horizon is employed to show that there is an orientation toward the future, not simply that the future is presented as a chain of events that one anticipates; instead, Husserl stresses the openness and interconnectedness of the now-ness with its immediate past and future, as a field of lived experience or a horizon of past-present-future from which the now stands out as the focus. The fundamental point, with reference to the metaphor of space, is that "the temporality of an experience of a temporal object is not itself an object but a structural feature of that experience" (Carr 1986, 26).

Carr radicalizes Husserl's discussion of internal time consciousness, extending it to the field of human action in everyday life and therefore arguing that experienced time is a structured and configured time: "Our experience is directed towards, and itself assumes, temporally extended forms in which future, present, and past mutually determine one another as parts of a whole" (Carr 1986, 31). This is a very different theoretical stance from the conventional understanding of human action, in which we either take experience or action as preconfigured pieces of a whole and analyze it from an outsider's perspective, as in the case of Parsons and Shils (1951), or take experience or action as the experienced, because, as Alfred Schutz said, "only the already experienced is meaningful, not that which is being experienced. For meaning is merely an operation of intentionality, which, however, only becomes visible to the reflective glance" (1967, 52).[6] Carr argues against two theories of action. The first is perhaps best represented by the structural-functional approach to action in Parsons and is essentially an understanding of human action from outside—for example, from a functional point of view to see how each action may be understood as part of a whole, as in Radcliffe-Brown's definition of social structure.[7] This is not denying the importance of such analysis; it is meant to suggest that such an approach has omitted an examination of the internal qualities of human action—that is, of the structure of experience *as being experienced*. Of course, the structural-functional model contains an implicit or explicit focus on the causation of an act—its functional relation to another act, and so on. Such a model of action, as Carr argues, presupposes that action is passive, though not in the sense that action does not cause other actions but in the sense that it is not viewed from the effectiveness of the agent in action. Recalling Weber's argument on meaningful action, one may argue that such a model cannot explain meaning in action because the significance of action is subjective.

Schutz's account of action, which is a critical reaction to Weber's theory, is an attempt to render action meaningful by taking into account its subjectivity and experience in the social world of everyday life. In his account, the problem of meaning in action is given a systematic treatment, and the question of the activeness of action is partially answered.

The problem of Schutz's model, as Carr argues, is that it takes seriously some aspects of the Husserlian innovation but misses others, and it focuses too exclusively on the already as the locus of meaningful action. "Schutz seems to me to overlook here what is genuinely valuable in Husserl's analysis and adopt its least appropriate features. The merit of Husserl's concept of retention-protention is precisely that it recognizes the structured and organized character of pre-reflective experience. . . . [T]he Husserlian notion of meaning-bestowing as an objectivating act is geared to contemplative or theoretical understanding and seems least appropriate to the sphere of action, at least as performed by the agent" (Carr 1986, 37–38). Schutz's overintellectualization of action has resulted in the overlooking of the structural features of action in its pre-configured mode of existence.[8]

As Carr argues, a solution to the problem of experience is provided by the Husserlian idea of retention-protention as a horizon from which the experience of being experienced at the present moment stands out. Against this horizon, the possibility of now is possible; and a temporal whole is assumed within this now-ness. Action not only is meaningful when it is completed but is already meaningful when it is being acted out because there is an immediate retention and protention involved in the now-ness of an experience. Carr's point is that even in the preconfigured human experience, in the very basic mode of simple everyday action, there is already a temporal structure, a certain sense of past-present-future. This argument challenges the usual conceptualization of human experience as devoid of any structure, let alone narrative structure.

Even if we accept the argument that preconfigured experience is already a temporal whole, it does not necessarily mean that the configuration of preconfigured experience must be configured as narrative is. Narrative is simply one of several possibilities of configuration. This is one of the main tasks that Carr sets for himself to explain in chapter 2. To do so, Carr draws attention to the basic structure, the temporal closure, of event, experience, and action, which are supposed to be considered in contrast to sequence, series, and process. The latter does not necessarily have a beginning or an end, whereas the former does. Carr basically argues that taking the very basic element of human experience, as being lived, there is always a temporal structure in it and it can only be understood as having a beginning, a middle and an end, which is also the most sketchy and common understanding of a narrative structure. For example, what are the structural features of someone's experience of a dog barking across the street? Suppose that this person is sitting in front of his door and reading a book, and his attention is caught by the bark as the now-ness of his consciousness. Therefore, he raises his head—the beginning of an action. Looking instead of reading his book is what he is intending at the moment of now, which is only meaningful to him as it is a standing out from the just-now as a precedent moment of intention. He is not stopping in the middle, looking at the dog, unless something else occurs on the other side of the street. His anticipation of a future event will come to an end when there is nothing that happens except for a boy kicking the dog. This event as lived experience will come to a close with the man's return to his book. Although there are different possibilities for further action, there is always this one of returning his orientation toward an immediate future—that is, the protention.

The point is that the unity of an action or the wholeness of experiencing an event, when observing from within, "is grasped in protention-retention by the person who experiences it" (Carr 1986, 47). This is the nature of human experience. So far, Carr's argument is built on examples of basic events or actions as lived experience. The argument can and should be extended to the complex temporal structures of social situations in larger contexts. Carr's point is that, if we look into the way in which basic events or actions are made into complex forms, "they combine according to the very same principle by which their elements combine to make them up. That is to say, events combine to make up large-scale events of which they become structural, not merely sequential, elements" (1986, 52). This is the essential argument of the first part of Carr's book: the nature of human experience is narrative in character. When Carr uses the word *structure*, he means the structure of intentionality in the phenomenological tradition, which is a structure of experience as being lived.

My ethnographic account of the Beihai story of urban (high-tech) development is based on such a theoretical position: recognizing the nature of human experience as structured in narrative forms. The human experience, even in its preconfigured form, as raw material of everyday life as well as of the object of ethnographic description, is already structured in time. Contrary to some recent anthropological writings on Chinese society in transition, which emphasize the significance of narrative only as a form of representation imposed from outside on the social world by the forces of the state,[9] I emphasize that narrative is essential to the configuration of experience: it is the way in which we are able to be. This theoretical reorientation primarily brings our attention to focus on the question of existence and time. If the pre-configured experience, simple or complex, is already structured in certain narrative forms, it is possible, as well as necessary in my view, to study these forms to understand the experience itself. In the second part of his book (chapter 5 in particular), Carr indeed deals with the question of *We* as a collective subject of experience; however, his discussion begins with the "I" as the agent of intention. From an anthropological perspective, I strongly argue that, given the narrative nature of human experience, what needs to be described or discussed is precisely the specific form of a particular cultural structuring of human experiences at a specific historical moment. The starting point of our investigation is already plural. As I will argue in chapter 6, as a collective experience of the temporal, there seems to be a new structure of past-present-future emerging from the historical horizon of contemporary China.

Such a theoretical reorientation presupposes the internal correlation of being to time, which is the central argument of the second part of Carr's book, reflecting more a Heideggerian influence on the condition of human existence: narrative structure is "the organizing principle not only of experiences and actions *but of the self who experiences and acts*" (Carr 1986, 73; emphasis added). Thus, the lived experience has truly become being lived, for the self as the configuration of an ethical or moral space, defined in a broad term, raises in essence a question about our being as such—that is, the conditions of possibility of being what we are. The question of the *We* must be raised from such a theoretical perspective because what happens to us in history or society is conditioned by Ourselves as the wholes of ethical or moral configurations. The question of the *We* is a question about the condition of possibility of being in history or society, and it lays out a domain of inquiry for the second part of this book.

I will now clarify a couple of points. As I stated earlier, it is important to note that anthropologists have always been interested in the question of how people comment on their own practices. This emphasis on the importance of commentary is conventionally meant to draw a distinction between saying and doing as two distinguishable planes of social action. One may argue that speaking is action (Austin 1962); however, commentaries on one's own practices must be taken as a particular kind of action, because they not only produce an effect, as an action does, but also lay out the intention(ality) of an action constituting part of a discursive formation. Nevertheless, we often presuppose the centrality of action as a model for discourse rather than the other way around. This has been, consciously or unconsciously, explicitly or implicitly, an epistemological position that supports conventional anthropological practices. A discussion of narrative such as I have provided is meant to reverse such an epistemological prejudice. Insofar as my own experience is concerned, this theoretical awakening comes from my field approach to the understanding of modern life, which is what I deal with in the rest of this chapter.

What needs to be emphasized one more time is that my discussion is not about whether ethnography is a form of storytelling, a question raised in the heated debates on fieldwork and writing in the 1980s. Even those who have defended the scientific nature of anthropology often share with others—those who are less convinced about this nature—the view that ethnographic representations commonly take the form of a narrative. In other words, ethnographies are often written, consciously or not, as if the ethnographer was telling a story. I am not concerned with that matter here. Rather, I am interested in the temporal whole within which our being as such is constituted. Therefore, this discussion of David Carr should not be seen as a continuation of anthropology's ongoing epistemological dilemma. Instead, I seek to make a new room for a different kind of discussion.

Furthermore, anthropological readings of—particularly—the literary message on narrative is not always positive. As Maurice Bloch (1993) argues, the extension of the narrativist argument into a general theory of culture is very problematic.[10] According to Bloch, such a theory is based on two elementary assumptions: first, people with different cultural heritages or traditions tell stories in different ways; second, these different ways of telling stories about themselves and others help in understanding the differences between these different groups of people. Therefore, for narrative theorists of culture, to understand cultural differences means to look into the ways in which stories are told differently. Underlying such a thesis is the rather old assumption, as Bloch points out, that culture as a schema organizes the experiences of a social group. It is true that experiences are always organized by a schema of some sort, but where to draw the boundaries between different groups of people is a highly problematic question. Bloch's reaction to this thesis is that people in the same tradition do not always tell stories in the same way. In other words, there is a richness of everyday experience that cannot be reduced to one or two schemes of narration because people change both their stories and their ways of telling them according to the situations in which these stories are told.

In my view, Bloch's criticism may be justified only insofar as it denies the sort of cultural relativism in such an argument. However, Bloch's criticism of the narrative approach to culture should not be read as if he were arguing against the philosophical message that is the subject here: that is, being ourselves is embedded in a temporal structure. The essence of narrative is Time/time. By bringing the temporal into the analysis, I examine the shifts in the organization of everyday experience in the social world of contemporary China. I assume that by analyzing the conception of Time/time in structuring the stories about oneself and others, it is possible to understand the condition of existence in that vast society in radical transformation.[11]

I will now turn to the other side of the problem of experience to look at how such assumptions about real experience are no longer adequate for the study of contemporary life in many situations, such as in Beihai or, in a perhaps even more striking case, in Japan. During the autumn of 1998, after doing fieldwork in China, I spent five months in Japan, joining a fellowship program sponsored by the Japan Foundation and the International House of Japan, primarily working with a group of Southeast Asian scholars on the idea of development and culture and traveling extensively. It was a sort of fieldwork. I had no intention of seriously including Japan in this ethnographic study. I was a traveler in the usual sense of the term, wandering from one train station to another, sometimes without a plan for my next stop. What arose from an idler's experience was a reflection on the nature of experience in contemporary society that has become part of my project on the anthropology of modern life.

No other society can compare with Japan in terms of its fascination with the various kinds of electronic games. So popular that they have become a sign of the ultraurbanity of social life, gamelands usually contain many different kinds of machines for a variety of entertainments.[12] Although all the games depend on a limited number of technological inventions, the games' cultural or symbolic contents, by which the player gets access to a different universe of things, vary greatly. One probably could not really understand the term *virtual reality* without entering a gameland and joining a Saharan car race, gunning down some bad guys in Manhattan, surfing off the coast of Perth, or trying to beat the Brazilian soccer team in a World Cup match in Peru.[13] Taking the term simply according to some journalistic understanding, one may consider virtual reality the equivalent of a certain kind of imagination, the kind of imagination that feeds back into reality. However, such an understanding is wrong in assuming that virtual reality is something added onto reality rather than reality itself. The gameland lacks boundaries between the real and the virtual. It is a good place to see how reality is no longer real in its conventional sense—meaning actual and truthful at once. Virtual reality creates a new domain of the real that is not necessarily actual or truthful in any sense.

Nothing better illustrates this than the epistemological stance of classical anthropology. Classical anthropology contains two fundamental presuppositions. First, anthropological knowledge is derived from the experience that the ethnographer is supposed to have in the encounter with his subjects of study. In other words, anthropological knowledge is a form of knowledge dependent on experience and obtained by the ethnographer's personal experience. Second, the anthropologist studies other people or cultures as and in their wholes. This assumption is closely linked to the functionalist proposition that the whole is greater than the sum of its parts. In other words, certain qualities belong to the whole itself rather than to the individual parts that comprise the whole. Because of these two presuppositions, classical anthropologists find convenient sites for fieldwork—the community, a tribe or a village or a neighborhood. Only in the community can the wholeness of social life be studied by experience. When anthropologists move to study modern society, where the traditional mode of communal life no longer dominates, can they still carry out ethnographic fieldwork assumed by the epistemology of classical anthropology? The question of methodology is crucial for anthropology, not only because anthropology is a discipline that depends on one single method but also because this method—participate observation—is intrinsic to the justification of anthropology as a scientific discipline.

What is experience? Let us continue to examine the problem of the real from the perspective of ethnographic method. Ethnographic experience is personal, the experience through which ethnographers reach their knowledge and the experience in which the people as the object of ethnographic knowledge are made to be themselves. This doubleness of the ethnographer's experience and the experience of the people under study is presupposed as the very heart of anthropology. What underlies this is a further assumption that people are made by their real experiences. Therefore, only by experiencing the experience of the study's subjects will ethnographers be able to understand the meaning of the subjects' lives. If so, the question of the real is inevitable. Anthropologists who are ready to leave for fieldwork often have two senses of the real in their minds. The first is that the real means something that actually happened. Events—that is, actual happenings—receive priority in the conceptualization of the real. This sense of the real also suggests that the nature of these happenings is objective rather than subjective. What actually happened must happen in a specific place. The specificity of a place in which events take place is therefore presupposed in this sense of the real. Following this logic, ethnographers cannot know what happened unless they go to that specific place to witness by their own experience. The second sense of the real is that of truthfulness, which concerns the way in which agents render experiences into meanings. What actually happened is experienced by a certain group of people in a specific place, and these experiences will be processed into meanings by those who have experienced them. This second sense of the real implies that there is a truthful rendering of these experiences into the correct meanings. This is not an objective process because it is concerned with how people make sense of their own lives; this sense of the real assumes that there is a—and perhaps only one—truthful rendering of these experiences. And ethnographers further assume that their task is to reach that truthful process. That is, in terms of how "what actually happened" makes sense for the agents, what is truthful is real. This means not only that the production of meaning needs to be truthful for the agents but also that the ethnographer's truthful experience sets up the foundation for anthropological knowledge.

A whole set of assumptions and presuppositions lies behind the belief in real experience. These assumptions and presuppositions have brought serious consequences on those who believe in them. One of these serious consequences concerns the conception of events in time. Because what is real is considered to be what actually happened, and what actually happened could only happen in the past, those who hold such a sense of the real tend to view the chain of events in terms of a single direction from the past to the present and then to the future. In addition, because the truthfulness of an experience can only be the experience of what has been experienced, an order of things tends to be arranged in a way that gives what has been experienced priority over what will be experienced. That is, in the authority of real experience, the happened determines the happening. In other words, in such a way of making sense of the lived experience, there is a tendency in associating cause with past actions or events.

The modern experience of the Japanese gameland, in some interesting yet complicated way, defies this conception and its associated convention of ordinary language. The convention of language allows us to distinguish between "what happened," "what is happening," and "what will happen." And the sense of the real, as it is usually understood, is embedded in this possibility of differentiation in everyday language. In the case of playing an electronic game, however, with the image provided by being part of it, "what happened" or "what will happen" is always what is happening. The condition of possibility for designating what is real, in everyday language, is the tense system, for it is always possible to confirm actuality or truthfulness by employing the past tense. This is not to say that a large part of everyday life is no longer registered by such a system of difference in designating what is real and what is not. The point is that another mode of reality, actual and truthful in an entirely different sense and symbolized by the gameland, has emerged on the horizon of the contemporary world. For example, "what actually happened," taken as a designation of the real, means either the completion of an act or the taken place of an event. The establishment of this sense of the real lies in the actualization of this act or event. In contrast, in the experience of playing a game in the gameland, "what actually happened" is constantly on hold, able to be erased at any time, as if it were in the body of the happening itself. There is no completion in this happening; it goes on and on. Its actuality is repetition. Nor is there any sense of anticipation in the normal sense, because anticipation or expectation is presupposed in a temporal development of action or event. Virtual reality, carrying within itself another sense of the real, is essentially a spatial organization of the actual.

This is the nature of a gameland: it inhabits a real world of action but without the ticktock of a clock as the internal measurement of the temporal flow of events. Everything is reversible; the chain of past-present-future has merged into a space of spontaneity. "What actually happened" has lost its power to determine "what is happening" or "what will happen." Everything falls into itself as an endless game of play and playing. The person who plays the game may not know or like what happened. Seio, a college student, was playing a soccer match in a noisy gameland in Osaka. He was a friendly young man and did not hesitate to talk to me. I was interested in talking to him because I had read in a California newspaper that the 1998 World Cup Final, between Brazil and France, had been virtually played out by a Japanese game expert, with the result that France lost to Brazil, two goals to one. I was in Osaka during the first week of October 1998, and the real World Cup had ended with France beating Brazil, three to zero. I could not understand what the newspaper had meant when it said that the game was virtually played out, though the result was wrong, until I watched this young man playing a soccer match. Seio controlled one team, which meant that he was in charge of the speed and direction in which his players ran and when they passed and shot the ball. The machine controlled the opponent. One could make a number of choices regarding the kind of games to be played as well as the level of difficulty. I asked Seio why he had chosen to play England against Argentina, both among the world's best soccer teams. To my surprise, Seio said that he had never watched either of these teams on television and knew nothing about their performance. His interest in playing soccer games resulted from a high school friend's influence. It did not really matter to him which team he chose to play, and he later admitted to having no particular interest in sports. He was only interested in the games, and the soccer game was one of the most popular. He had chosen England because he wanted to go there to improve his English; he had selected Argentina because his father had recently traveled there on business. "I am fond of both these countries," he added.

I am not even slightly tempted to argue that Seio is representative of all the other gameland players. Most of those who play the soccer game machine probably know something about the teams with which they choose to play. The ethnographic example that I have detailed here is meant to show how the question of real experience came to my attention. It is by no means a new question for anthropology. For example, with reference to Dewey and Dilthey, Victor W. Turner (1986) argued for the social character of experience as constituting an intersubjective field of expression, best exemplified in drama. Given Turner's usual theoretical emphasis on the symbolic forms of everyday experiences, it is understandable that he would argue for the importance of drama as a crucial form of everyday social experience. However, as I argued earlier in this chapter, I deal with the problem of experience for a different reason: with the technological and structural changes taking place around us, the contemporary world has begun to be filled with a different kind of real experience that has presented a different outlook of the world in the mirror of ourselves.

To what extent, one may ask, does this kind of game playing represent a different mode of experience by which the very question of being, being what we are, must be raised? This is a significant question brought about in the debates on postmodernity (see, e.g., Habermas 1987; Lyotard 1984; Harvey 1989; Jameson 1991; Anderson 1998). If drawing a sharp line between modern and postmodern is unwise, it is at least useful to make the effort as a conceptual exercise. In my view, there is indeed an empirical ground to be considered—for example, the difference between rural China and Japan or, perhaps, between northern rural Shaanxi and Beihai.[14] There appear to be two quite different modes of experience that entail two different senses of self. What is real in the playing of games in the gameland differs from the conventional understanding of the real—for example, in the case of living in a rural Chinese lineage village—because Seio's experience projects onto itself a different display of temporality. Time for Seio is a display rather than a flow, and this difference is crucial in the constitution of experience.

The question I have posed here concerns the changes that might have taken place in the shaping of ourselves/Ourselves. By this analysis, I do not mean that there is only one version of experience in Japan and that everyone plays in gamelands. Rather, such a reflection on the question of experience in the contemporary world, constituting a different conceptual formation, is derived from my ethnographic experience. In the actual world, I am sure that, as always, there is a multiple space of social life layered with different kinds of experiences combined and recombined at any moment of individual or collective action. But we must develop a new concept of the real partly because of the changes symbolized by the gameland. If such is the case, if such reconceptualization of the real is necessary, there will be direct implications for anthropological practice. Continuing to use the term *experience,* which used to anchor the disciplinary epistemology, might have a different significance in the contemporary world—the one with which we struggle.[15]

From the conceptual stance I have attempted to portray, the idea of studying from within a community is quite problematic. Those whose experience of reality is modeled on game playing do not contextualize their experiences in real space. I do not mean that no form of community still exists in Japan, nor do I mean that the existing communities do not provide a social context in which those who live in them can act. But the general mode of experience in the gameland—if taken as a mirror of that society—is best placed in contrast to the conventional understanding of communal life. It seems to me that the gameland is a better image for modern life, and the real experience is no longer rooted in a community defined in terms of geographic location. So how can anthropologists understand those whose experience exists in virtual reality? This book is devoted to this question, and I hope to build new conceptual ground by turning to the problem of narrative.

I have so far argued for the notional significance of narrative in my theoretical and ethnographic approach to the complex (social and political) investment structure in the Beihai story of urban (high-tech) development. On the significance of narrative, my argument is cast from two opposite poles. On the one hand, following David Carr in specific and the phenomenological school in general, I have argued that the human experience itself is structured as and in narrative. On the other hand, I have also argued that there is a need to reconceptualize what experience is supposed to be in the contemporary world, suggesting that a shift in the understanding of what is real may be taking place. These two arguments are not contradictory in any sense: to argue that what constitutes real experience needs to be reconceptualized does not defy Carr's argument, which is that the human experience carries within itself a temporal dimension, as does narrative. This being so, however, the question of what constitutes "real experience" is different. In the contemporary world, the question of what is real has also directed our attention to the problem of time, which is the central theme of the second half of this book.

Morphology of the Beihai Folktale

"The word 'morphology' means the study of forms," wrote Vladimir Propp in the foreword to his masterpiece, *Morphology of the Folktale* (1968, xxv), a key step in the journey of a great literary adventure—

Russian formalism—at the beginning of the twentieth century.[16] Summed up in one word, formalism is a mode of critique that later triggered a transcultural intellectual movement across Europe, (post)structuralism, whose repercussions continue to be felt today.[17] "Our method," as one of the grandfathers of the formalist movement, Boris Ejxenbaum (Eichenbaum), clarified it, "is usually referred to as 'Formalist.' I would prefer to call it morphological, to differentiate it from other approaches such as psychological, sociological and the like, *where the object of inquiry is not the work itself,* but that which, in the scholar's opinion, is reflected in the work" (quoted in Erlich 1955, 171; emphasis added). Anyone, whose life was imprinted by the Chinese Cultural Revolution, as an example of the general socialist experience of art and literature, would have difficulty in resisting the temptation of the formalist calling because during these years the only form of art or literature was the sociology of it. Art or literature was supposed to speak for a class interest; its meaning was supposed to lie outside the work itself—that is, in the context of social or political struggles of the time to which the author belonged. Thus, Balzac was said to be as good as Jack London because both tore off the mask of capitalism and revealed capitalists' naked desire; Tolstoy was not too bad because he was a mirror of the old Russian society, as Lenin said; Hugo's humanistic novels should be read with caution because they failed to show the true nature of misery, which concerned not human evils but the capitalist mode of production; and so on. In such a context, formalism was a serious attempt to emerge above the ideological water.[18] Formalism's intellectual energy lies in its insistence on the priority of internal (formal) factors in the explanation of art or literature, whereas the socialist ideology tried to explain anything and everything through factors external to the work itself.

Economic development in South China is often understood, as far as recent scholarly work is concerned, as the effect of global capitalist expansion, which—implicitly or explicitly, consciously or unconsciously, intentionally or unintentionally—presupposes external factors as the fundamental source of explanation. The question of global capitalism is extremely important because it is a dominant force, penetrating all layers of social and political life of our globe. I invoke an old school of thought, Russian formalism, because we must consider how we are able to reach a better understanding of the global effects of (transnational) capital. I argue that there is a need to return to some internal factors, to focus on the work itself, in searching for an understanding of the reincarnation of capitalism in Beihai or South China. This is not an innovation; rather, it is a reorientation.

One theoretical thread that has stitched together my ethnographic materials is the concern with narrative, and this concern assumes that an analysis of a historically situated mode of narrative structure holds the key for understanding the experience of contemporary China. How can such an analysis be carried out? Some of Propp's assumptions and analytical strategies may be useful here. "The study of forms"—that is, the morphological analysis—is a study of the structural qualities of all the tales taken as a whole, which differs from historical analysis of folktales by tracing their origins and transformations over time.[19] Morphological analysis aims at "a description of the tale according to its component parts and the relationship of these components to each other and to the whole [tale]" (Propp 1968, 19). At the time, this idea represented an innovation in the study of folktales.[20] The point is that, despite an extremely wide range of variations in the characters of fairy tales or folktales, there is a morphological stability in the functions that these characters serve in the stories, and these functions are stable, identifiable, and—I might add—structural.[21] As Paul Ricoeur commented,

> Propp's morphology is essentially characterized by the primacy it gives to functions over characters. By a "function," he means segments of action, or more exactly, abstract forms of action such as abstention, interdiction, violation, reconnaissance, delivery, trickery, and complicity, to name the first seven of them. These same functions occur in all the fairy tales, in innumerable concrete guises, and they can be defined independently of the characters who accomplish these actions. (1984, 2:33)

A fairy tale may appear to create very different characters. For example, the tale about the princess and the peasant may differ greatly from that about the king and the hero; however, what is essentially stable in these tales is the functions that these characters serve in telling these tales— that is, "a tale often attributes identical actions to various personages. This makes possible the study of the tale *according to the functions of its dramatis personae*" (Propp 1968, 20). Propp defines function as an act of a character from the point of view of the act's significance to the tale as a whole. As for the nature of the function, Propp makes four points:

1. Functions of characters serve as stable, constant elements in a tale, independent of how and by whom they are fulfilled.
2. The number of functions known to the fairy tale is limited.
3. The sequence of functions is always identical.
4. All fairy tales are of one type in regard to their structure.
    (1968, 21–23)

The key point is that "the number of functions is extremely small, whereas the number of personages is extremely large. This explains the two-fold quality of a tale: its amazing multiformity, picturesqueness, and color, and on the other hand, its no less striking uniformity, its repetition" (Propp 1968, 20–21). Thus, as it is well known, Propp discovered thirty-one functions in Russian fairy tales as a group. All of the tales share the same structure and offer a variation of the functions taken from their storage whole.

For Propp, although the fairy tale has a stable structure, the tale is still a tale in the sense that those functions are supposed to appear in a sequence: "if we read through all of the functions, one after another, we observe that one function develops out of another with logical and artistic necessity. We see that not a single function excludes another. They all belong to a single axis and not, as has already been mentioned, to a number of axes" (Propp 1968, 64). For Propp, the importance is to note that there is a "logical and artistic necessity" in the development of the actions in a tale: the order of a narrative sequence, a sense of time, is internal to the inventory of the functions as a whole.

There is a difference between Propp's approach and the approach later developed by structuralists such as A.-J. Greimas.[22] "French Structuralism," as Fredric Jameson said, "is related to Russian Formalism, less as nephew to uncle, in Shklovsky's phrase, than as crossed cousins within an endogamous kinship system" (1972, 101). But the crossed cousins indeed have an essential difference insofar as the analysis of the fairy tale is concerned. This essential difference, as shown in Lévi-Strauss's structural analysis of myth, is whether the sequence of functions can, or should, be further reduced to a structural whole without any reference to time. For example, in attempting a method of structural semantics, Greimas tried first to further reduce the number of functions and second to turn the "logical and artistic necessity" of the functions into a matrix of possible permutations. The first step is prepared for the second, and the essence of the second operation is to turn the narrative of a tale into a structure without any reference to time. Drawing on Propp's idea of function as action in the tale, Greimas aimed at "a description of the relationships between functions which, although organized into narratives, could, at least, in theory: (a) appear in a sufficiently reduced number to be grasped as simple structures because of the redundancy which characterizes any discursive manifestation, (b) offer at the same time, because of their sequence in the narrative, appreciable elements allowing us to explain the existence of models of transformation of the structure of signification" (Greimas 1983, 223). The result of Greimas's analysis, what is known as the actantial model, closely resembles what Lévi-Strauss called "the elementary structure," which appears to be a matrix of four elements in a number of possibilities of permutation and transformation (see, e.g., Lévi-Strauss, 1967, 1969).[23]

What, then, is the significance of this discussion of Propp and Greimas? What is the relevance of invoking such sounds from an old instrument that anthropologists have never particularly favored? My analysis in this section relies on a formalist-structuralist doctrine: despite the great variations in the actual experiences of a people whose stories are the subject of my study, there is a deep structural stability that conditions the possibilities of experiencing and narrating. Just as Propp has argued with regard to the Russian fairy tale, I will argue that everyday life as the object of ethnographic description is of a double quality: its amazing multiplicity in concrete situations—its picturesqueness, color, and difference on the one hand and its no less striking uniformity, repetition, and sameness in the organization of these experiences into cultural forms on the other.

I will now use some examples of ethnographic description from previous chapters, repeated here only in skeleton form, to show how the uniformity in form is born from a very diverge range of empirical experiences.

1. Haihun went to Nanning, the provincial capital, in search of a business favor. He ended up in inviting two government officials back to Beihai for an entertainment trip, "a golden production line of entertainment" that began with a banquet of turtles, included singing in a karaoke bar, and ended with a sensual massage by "the invisible hands."

2. A young woman went to Beihai in search of a better life and

ended up working for the entertainment establishment, potentially including prostitution. She did so either because she could not find any other way to make a living—for example, because her parents had been laid off by the state enterprise for which they used to work—or because she was tempted by material commodities.

   3. Managers of the Star Group, or at least many of them, had not prepared themselves to be businessmen when they were in graduate school. Some, like Haihun, had intended to pursue academe, but changed their paths and went to the tip of South China, searching for opportunities to—in an official 1980s political catchphrase—"get rich first."

Actual experiences vary tremendously in such elements as a person's age or sex, the time and space in which a particular individual experience was enacted, and the personal point of view impressed on the story; however, a number of stable features, in a structural sense, are also apparent. The stories told and retold in today's China always included a traveler, transgressing both physical and social space, in search of material gain, in the form either of capital or of consumer goods and for which there is always a direct or indirect transaction or exchange. My analysis focuses precisely on this uniformity in the narrative structure of the stories told—that is, the morphology of the Beihai folktale.

   However, in contrast to Propp's emphasis on the importance of function over character in the fairy tale, I stress that each function in the Beihai story of urban (high-tech) development is always clothed in the moral image of a character. For this reason, I have referred to MacIntyre's discussion of the significance of the character in the formation of an ethical configuration in society. Characters constitute, as I argue in chapter 2, the moral language of everyday life.[24] Ordinary life does not speak in and for itself a philosophical language; instead, it speaks only in the image of these characters. Therefore, the function, as Propp and Greimas defined it, is in my use equivalent to the character under discussion. In the everyday life of business practice in Beihai, there is a small number of functions/characters: essentially the trinity of *chuzhang/laoban/xiaojie*. Without each of them, the Beihai story of urban (high-tech) development cannot be told.

   In a sense, my treatment of the narrative structure of the Beihai story is somewhat close to Greimas's because I have reduced the manifolds of actual experiences to a trinity of characters, and I have set aside the question of sequence in telling a specific story about oneself and others. If such is acceptable, then the elementary structure of the Beihai story (see diagram) has two fundamental dimensions of coordination for contemporary Chinese society. The horizontal one, which is the coordinate of social space, is named here "the gender of sex," by which I mean to emphasize that, as recent feminist scholars have forcefully argued, gender means not simply the differences between the two sexes. A woman may and can play the role of a *laoban;* however, the image of the *laoban* presently is male in a historically specific way. The masculine and the feminine under this heading are the attributes of the image of *laoban* and *xiaojie*. These images are not the actual features of the person being discussed; rather, they are the sexual images of these two characters. According to such a division of social space—that is, the sexualization of society—the *chuzhang*, the incarnation of the official power, is neither masculine nor feminine, neither man nor woman. It has no gender. Again, when the character of *chuzhang* is discussed, we are dealing with its discursive location in the constitution of this social space, not an official's individual sex.

Further, as the diagram shows, my use of "the public sphere" as the vertical coordinate of the hierarchical space emphasizes that, contrary to the conventional understanding of the state versus (civil) society in Western social theory, there is no clear boundary between public and private in Chinese society. Social space in China is vertical: social

The elementary structure of the Beihai story

The Gender of Sex

the masculine ——————————— the feminine

the official   *Chuzhang*

the stream of needs
(outer circle)

The Public
Sphere

the flow of "gift"
(inner circle)

the unofficial   *Laoban* ⇄ *Xiaojie*

relations of any and every kind embed a hierarchy that can be finally traced to state power. A distinction should be drawn between the terms *official world* and *world of officials*. The former is the discursive totality of the official world, encompassing all the provincial and the local worlds of officials, whereas the latter is a part of the official world, such as the Guangxi world of officials at the provincial level. An official always occupies a place in a world of officials on the one hand and, on the other, represents the official world in opposition to those who are outside it. The public sphere is here defined as the intersection of the official world acted out in the world of officials and the nonofficial world of *laoban* and *xiaojie*, representing an emerging space of exchange and market. I have already discussed in chapter 2 the *chuzhang*'s function as a strategic link between the official world and the nonofficial world.

Finally, the diagram also shows two circles of flows. The inner circle is the circulation of "gift" and the outer circle is the circulation of needs. The outer circle of flow is characteristic of the Beihai story of urban (high-tech) development, where the *xiaojie* is dependent on the *laoban* for material income; the *laoban* is in turn relying on the *chuzhang* to provide business favors; and finally the *chuzhang* needs the *xiaojie* to fulfill physical desires. Let me reemphasize that *xiaojie* does not refer to women in general; instead, it is a particular *gender* of women, as an image of the character that represents a subject position in the social space. Each of these characters is only a link in the chain of (material) needs that characterizes the modernizing process in (South) China. The inner circle of flows is essentially a gift economy par excellence. It is not an economy in the normal sense because there is such a strong symbolic content in the exchange taking place that, following Marcel Mauss, there is an almost spiritual obligation to repay and return favors with some kind of gift.

I will now offer some detailed comments on the relations among the three functions / characters in the triangle. First, the *chuzhang-laoban / laoban-chuzhang* relation. It is clear that this relation is not a gender relation; instead, it is a relation of the official world to the nonofficial world and vice versa. Such a relation is characterized by the confrontation of the hierarchy of the official world with the market world of the entrepreneurs. This relation, in other words, is of a conjunction of two different worlds, two different structures. This is what may be called a structure of conjuncture. From the perspective of the *laoban*, what needs to be done is to lift one's own grounding to become closer to the center of power of the official world. In contrast, from the *chuẓhang*'s perspective, it is an opportunity for exchange, because the *chuẓhang* controls policies as an economic resource. Although some officials indeed receive cash from the *laoban*, most *chuẓhang* feel that it is much safer to enjoy turtle soup, to sing in karaoke bars, and to have massages by "the invisible hands." There is no trace of bribery if they receive such a form of gift. From the point of view of the *laoban*, it is also more convenient to bring the *chuẓhang* for a banquet of rare animals than to hand over cash for exchange of favors. Such a relation is an exchange of the collective resources signatured by the official world with the personal pleasures of the world of officials in the emerging market space. This exchange, seen from the world of officials, is humane and natural; seen from the official world, however, it is bad and immoral. Nevertheless, as long as this structure of conjuncture continues to exist, as long as there are two senses of the identity of being an official, this form of exchange will go on, perhaps even after the realization of the four modernizations.

More specifically, the relation of the *chuẓhang* to the *laoban* is a relation of "looking after," which means that public resources are in the hands of the *chuẓhang*, who has the right to choose to whom such favors shall be given. If one is to be looked after by the world of officials, one will have to return something for the favors received. This logic is that of the Chinese gift, or *guanxi*, though the difference here is that the gift enters another sphere of social life. The "looking after" as an official act also implies, as it were, a responsibility. Conversely, the relation of the *laoban* to the *chuẓhang*, the opposite direction of the same relation, is a relation of "looking for," a searching. In the specific case of business practices in Beihai or South China, this searching is for a path into the world of officials. "Looking for" is looking to be "looked after" in this case. This is the reciprocity of the relation between *chuẓhang* and *laoban*.

Next, I will turn to the *laoban-xiaojie/xiaojie-laoban* relation. *Xiaojie* may be classified into several categories. This discussion is confined to the upper stratum of this social group, whose services are beyond the possible reach of ordinary salarymen. In other words, this stratum of *xiaojie* exists for the business world. The *xiaojie*'s existence, both in a symbolic and a material sense, depends on the existence of *laoban* and on their entertainment needs. What is the nature of the transaction between the *laoban* and the *xiaojie?* On the surface, there is a commodification of sex: *xiaojie* live off their bodies. Deep down, there has emerged a rule of business, the iron rule of market economy that is ironically called in today's China "the law of the invisible hand." If one sees only sexual meanings in this transaction, one has been misled: it is important to note that the *xiaojie* functions as a medium for a dialogue between the world of officials and the world of entrepreneurs. The *xiaojie*'s value is primarily in transaction: any sort of sexual use is secondary to the function of facilitating the exchange between the two worlds. As Lévi-Strauss once said in a similar context, irritating many feminists, women—from the perspective of the *laoban*—can be used as a means of transaction and exchange. To say that Chinese society is sexualized tells only part of the truth: the *xiaojie* is a sign of the emergence of a third space, located between the official world and market as a growing force. The conjuncture of these two forces has brought the *xiaojie* to the foreground of the Beihai story of urban (high-tech) development.

The relation of the *laoban* to the *xiaojie* is a relation of want—that is, to buy, like a customer buying goods at the market. The want is a command, though it can be refused or too expansive to be fulfilled. The relation of the *xiaojie* to the *laoban* is a relation of needs—that is, desire for material gain. One cannot desire, in any actual or practical sense, to be in command in a world of officials, but one can desire to be rich through the means of *laoban*. Due to the growth of market forces late-twentieth-century China has bred a large number of different types of wants and needs. However, one must note that this is a different relation from that of *chuzhang-laoban/laoban-chuzhang*, where the relation, even if already established, remains asymmetrical: on the one side it is dominated by exchange and transaction, and on the other it is shaped by hierarchy and order. The "looking after" and "looking for" are not symmetrical relations. They are manifestations of the differences between the two structures of the social. The relation of *laoban* to *xiaojie* and vice versa is symmetrical in the sense that it is an exchange of something one has for something one does not have. What an official has is not exactly what he has. The official is simply a goalkeeper for resources authorized by the official world. Both the *laoban* and the *xiaojie* own what they have: money and body belong to them. In this sense, it is possible to say that this is a symmetrical relation of exchange.

Third, the *chuzhang-xiaojie/xiaojie-chuzhang* relation is without trace. No name, no face, is shown in this relation. What is involved is the exchange of "use value." The *xiaojie* is paid by the *laoban* rather than by the *chuzhang*, which makes the relation anonymous. There is exchange but no business involved between the *chuzhang* and the *xiaojie*. The only business in this relation is the business of the sensual. The sensual is the use of what has been exchanged—the use of the body, which is for pleasure, but nothing else. There are thus three kinds of exchange involved in the Beihai story of urban (high-tech) development. First, in the *chuzhang-laoban/laoban-chuzhang* relation, the transaction exists almost purely for its exchange value—that is, pleasure for favor. It is obtaining capital by getting access to the official world through a particular world of officials. Second, in the *laoban-xiaojie/xiaojie-laoban* relation, there is a form of exchange in its normal sense, an exchange of what one has for what one wants or needs. However, what one wants or needs is already structured by the structural change taking place in today's China. Third, the *xiaojie-chuzhang/chuzhang-xiaojie* relation contains a form of exchange only for its use value, a naked form of exchange with a long history. The operating force lies outside the persons involved in this exchange; they lay their hands on each other's bodies without knowing how much it costs.

This is the elementary structure of the Beihai story of urban (high-tech) development. The actual experience of telling a story about business and society is conditioned by such a structure, though it may not always be conscious to the storyteller.

This analysis, though referring specifically to Beihai, has some important general implications for the present transformation taking place in China as a whole. In terms of the logic of business practice in Beihai, these three characters are sharply focused through an ethnographic lens into a system of relations. In other situations, the group of characters may differ, but the relations between them may be analyzed in the same way as I have done here. One likely criticism of such a model is that it is too neat and too systematic. The debate on the function and relevance of models in anthropology is an old one and needs not be reiterated here (see, e.g., Lévi-Strauss 1976); it suffices to say I am interested not in the immediate experiences of individuals but in the structure of feelings and motivations that characterizes the ongoing transformation.

In understanding the reincarnation of capitalism in Beihai, one should not forget—as I have argued earlier—its regional (or local, if one prefers) features. Although the experience was more or less universal during the years of economic reforms, Beihai still stood out as an extreme case in its suffering from the central government's sudden withdrawal of bank loans and investments. The incomplete buildings in Beihai signify this developmental sickness, a silence among the noise of modernizing discourse. This may be a reason that the Beihai entrepreneurs worked harder on the world of officials, but it is a truth that every inch of the skin of a vast body of development has been tattooed by "the myth of the state" (see Cassirer 1946). Second, as stated earlier, Beihai is unusual because it is not a capital city, it is relatively small, and it is far from the center of political gravity. Thus, it is possible that what I observed in Beihai is not the norm and does not represent typical situations in other parts of the country. Even if so, the Beihai story remains significant in revealing the sickness of a normal body of modernization.[25] What was often the current beneath the water of development in other places could be dead fish floating on the surface in Beihai.

As I described in chapter 1, if visitors from abroad or other parts of China who had never before been to Beihai visited the city in the late 1990s, they would have felt the city's incomplete newness. Riding in a car along the city's central avenue, it would be impossible not to notice the silence of the incomplete buildings standing in the darkness of their own shadows. This deadly silence is evidence of what may be called structural ruptures—a series of sudden brakes on the developmental process, often as a result of direct state intervention. By calling it structural rupture, I mean that the disruption, imposed from outside the local economy, is not predictable; it is the effect of the double structure of the economic system in today's China. It is not something that is unexpected but still lies within a predictable routine of development; rather, the irregular itself has become a routine of business practice. Forging ahead of someone else depends on avoiding being crushed by such structural ruptures in the everyday world of business life. The Beihai Star headquarters was a sign of the structural disruption. "We had planned to build twenty four floors," said the director of this company, "but suddenly everyone was running away with their money. Although we could go on to finish it, what is the point? Most people will no longer be here. They have gone. They may come back sometime in the future, but for the moment there is no reason for building higher than what we have now. What we thought we would do was to build a huge building and rent it out or sell it for business purposes. Since everything was cooling down when our project was in construction, we stopped, as many other people did, in the middle of our construction. We did not build it higher. We have eight floors now, which is good enough." What is called routine in the everyday world of business in Beihai is precisely this unpredictable effect of disruption. Therefore, being good in business in Beihai meant being lucky enough to avoid the effects of the structural rupture.

This kind of irregularity is not the normal kind that may appear in any economic environment. The normal irregularity that appears, for example, in the stock market is unpredictable only in result, which is supposed to be handled by the invisible hand. In other words, what cannot be predicted is the result of a game, but the game itself is very clearly defined beforehand. However, the kind of irregularity in Beihai is entirely different: the rules of the game are unpredictable and may change any time. If one may say that the irregularity in the stock market in the capitalist society is internal to the rules set up for the game, in the case of Beihai or (South) China in general, it is an irregularity external to the game—beyond the control of the entrepreneurs involved. It is a fact of life that this external factor has become a routine part of Beihai's business rationalization. The half-finished skyscrapers serve as a manifestation of this structure of ruptures, which is an irregular regularity. In addition to affecting how business is done, this structure of rupture has also affected how people tell stories about business and society.

First, the idea of luck is central to the plot of any success story because this idea disconnects achievement from effect or capability and refers only to chance when an explanation of success is required.[26] This is obviously linked to the reality of business practice in Beihai: the routinization of irregularity. Official discourse may portray economic reform as a heroic departure from the Maoist revolution; however, in the world of everyday life, luck and chance were the most common ways of plotting a story about business success. For example, when other people talked about the success of the Beihai Star Group, they would always say, "Oh they were lucky, because they got the money from the government just before the loans and investments in real estate development were frozen. Otherwise, how could they build up their business so quickly? Anyone could do it if one got this amount of money." This kind of statement, true in some sense, was not at all the whole story of the success of the Beihai Star Group; however, it was the most common way of telling a story about it. Indeed, the Beihai Star Group managed to secure a bank loan to participate in the feverish real estate development; the group purchased some land from the government at a low price, sold it quickly, and profited out of it. But it is also true that the company did many other things in trying to succeed. Their success cannot be simply explained by luck: both calculation and the chance made the Star Group succeed.

I heard in Beihai a most interesting story that has become very popular in the late 1990s in China. It appeared in both newspapers and fiction writing, though often in different forms. This particular story concerned the success of a millionaire peasant who could not read or write. He was said to have grown in northern China, never having left the village of his birth until relatives drew him to Hainan, the largest special economic zone, to search for work in the early 1990s. (At that time, Hainan was the typical setting for the imagination of wealth.) "Stock fever" (Hertz 1998, 71–73) had infected the ordinary people of Hainan. He could not find a proper job for a few days and had no place to stay, but he happened to lie down in front of an unimpressive door. When he awoke some time later, he realized that a long line had formed behind him. He became even more puzzled when a policeman gave him a piece of blue paper with a number on it. He was about to leave and throw away the number, but a fat man in a red tie came over to him and said, "Would you like to give me that number in exchange for ten thousand yuan?"[27] The peasant did not even have a chance to react; the fat man took away the paper and left an envelope. In the envelope was more money than he had ever dreamed of having or even seeing.

Why did people want this number so much? What was it for? Why were people lining up in front of this small door? In the first few years of the operation of Chinese stock markets in Shenzhen and Shanghai, public and individual buyers created an incredible demand for shares. Since the number of shares and of companies chosen by the state to be listed was limited—far less than the demand on the streets—local authorities instituted a lottery system for share purchase applications (*rengouzheng zhidu*). Prospective buyers had to go through the lottery system to obtain a certificate before purchasing the stock.[28] These certificates were supposed to be randomly assigned to lottery participants. The certificates themselves became valuable and could be sold to others, and standing in line on behalf of other people became a profession. The peasant from North China happened to be sleeping in front of the door where the lottery was supposed to be executed. His number secured his place in the line—even though he didn't know what the number was for.

Wang Qinghui tells a similar story in *The Key* (1997), a novel about development in Hainan, which in some aspects resembles the Beihai story of urban (high-tech) development. In the novel, the peasant left with the money, planning to return to his home village to show off to his relatives. He first went to have a haircut and took a bath, and he could not resist the temptation to stop and buy some clothes for himself. He had a good dinner and decided to try a hotel in town. With a new self-image, he walked into a huge building for some sort of fun. No sooner had he entered than a young woman grabbed his arms. She was a salesgirl, selling office space in the building, which was an exhibition hall used for a real estate festival featuring many companies buying and selling new buildings in Hainan. The hero was brought to a table and asked whether he wanted to buy some office space in a new building that looked extremely beautiful in a picture. The salesgirl was very friendly and said that he did not need to pay anything immediately but could transfer the payment to their bank account in three days. He did not understand what she was saying and simply nodded his head, unable to speak, shattered by the entirely different vocabulary used in the bright exhibition hall. The salesgirl looked at his smile and helped him sign a contract to buy two entire floors of this new building at a cost of millions of dollars. Near the end of the process, the peasant began to realize what was going on, but placed his thumbprint on the contract, making it official, since the salesgirl said that he did not have to reveal his personal bank account for this transaction.[29] He did not have a bank account. He planned to leave Hainan the next day and return to his own world. He already had enough money to marry three times locally. But in the morning, the salesgirl came to his hotel with a middle-aged man, an official who had gotten some government funds to play the real estate game. Because everyone believed that the price for the building would rise tremendously, the two had come to see whether the peasant would like to sell the space he had purchased. The salesgirl had arranged everything: using government money, each of the three would reap a considerable profit. The biggest beneficiary of this transaction was the peasant, who made a couple of million yuan from this deal.

I heard several versions of this story from different people in Beihai.[30] However, the key component of this story is its reliance on the idea of luck: the person involved did not know what was going on, and it did not even matter that he did not know. He would get rich if he was simply lucky enough to be in the right place at the right time. This story's message is also the Beihai story's message, and, to some extent, it is the message of the story of the Chinese modernizing process. The frequent retelling of this story simply shows that people did not believe that the increasing economic disparity could be a result solely of effort. A place must be prepared for chance.

Because of the importance ascribed to luck, very little effort was spent in making long-term plans for a company's future development. Everything seems to have been carried out, ironically or not, according to what Deng Xiaoping said about the economic reform: "We are crossing the river by probing the stones in it." We did not know the next step, only the present location of our feet. Few Beihai entrepreneurs could explain what was going on in terms of what had happened; few could foresee their future development from the perspective of the present. It is interesting to note that even when talking about recent happenings— for example, events in the early 1990s—the managers of the Star Group could not provide a clear account of the sequence in which one decision led to another. This is not to say that they did not remember what happened in the past few years; instead, I am suggesting that they could not organize these events in a meaningful temporal sequence.

The second part of this book will argue that there was a lack of narrative coherence in the stories told by Beihai's entrepreneurs. By the term *narrative coherence* I mean the kind of temporal organization of events required for a normal understanding of what is supposed to be a story, which consists of a logical order of temporal flows of events— with a proper beginning, middle, and end. However, this was not the way in which the stories of business life and success were told in Beihai. The temporal in a story's plot should build up a chain of causes and effects between events in time. That is, it is through the logical connections between the events that the temporal unfolding of a story becomes meaningful. Because these events become meaningful in a time sequence, the logical connections between these events will therefore obtain a temporal character. In the case of Beihai, however, logical connections do not exist between events in time. The dependence on the idea of luck was an indication of such a lack of coherence. And I believe that this phenomenon is related to the structural rupture imposed on the regional economy from outside.

Another effect of this structural rupture is the emergence of a discourse about supernatural power. Because success is conceived as dependent on luck, it is necessary to believe in something beyond one's own control. Supernatural power was often used to provide an explanation for how to avoid being unlucky or counter evil forces. On one occasion, I was having breakfast with one of the Star Group managers when a young man joined us. This man was the vice chief of the Beihai Economic Reform Office, a very important and powerful government office, and he was in charge of making government policies for further reforms in this area. After greetings and some casual talk, he began to talk about the reason for the erection of a pair of stone lions in front of city hall, where his office was located:

> You have seen the new building across the street, haven't you? That is the new building for our finance department. They have money, and therefore they have built this amazing building, huge and modern. It is perhaps good for them, but not for us. Their location has blocked our good fortune. It was a good *feng shui* [geomancy] spot. They have built it too high. As soon as they finished the building—in fact, on the day after the building was completed, one of our chiefs, the guy in charge of the fishing and agriculture section, died. All of a sudden. He had been a very healthy man, but at the age of fifty, he suddenly died of a stroke. He had been eating all these good foods for his health. Anyway, he was in charge of the fishing and agriculture section, and he got all these fresh shrimps for free. Can you believe it? He ran every morning, did Falun Gong and many other things. We used to joke about him, saying that he would live longer than Jiang Zemin. He went away without a blink. A week later, another chief of our industrial section died, exactly in the same way that the other chief did—a stroke for no reason. Both of them were still young. What happened? The building across the street has brought us this misfortune. Every one of us was in a bit of panic after we realized this. We talked about it, thinking about what we should do. The mayor, Lao Wang, he really understood what was going on. He suggested that we should have a pair of stone lions in front of our gate to protect us from losing more people. We ordered the lions from Guangzhou and placed them right in front of our gate. And then no more deaths. The lions have suppressed the evil spirits and brought us back good fortune. It was kind of scary. At one time, we were talking about who would be the next to die. Whatever one does, one just cannot afford not to believe in this kind of thing. The stone lions can do a lot more than you think. The whole building is safe now. It is the truth of life. There is something that we cannot control. We can order to change the city, but we cannot

change our own fate. Without this pair of lions, I don't know how many chiefs would disappear. There is something more powerful than the government, the good and evil spirits.

He was completely serious in telling this story. Perhaps not everyone in the city would believe that the pair of stone lions fenced off the evil forces from the building across the street, but the message is that the universe of business and everyday life was believed to be sheltered by supernatural forces outside human control. This certainly does not mean that people did not try hard to find a better or a more secure business environment—for example, by means of building stronger or more effective networks of social relations. Instead, people were unable to understand why some people could not avoid misfortune or failure in business or life and others could. Once again, though from a different perspective, this ethnographic example shows that explanation of one's luck must be made with reference to the external factors.

I will now turn to other salient characteristics of the Beihai story, the strategic subversion of official discourse by sexual metaphors. There is no better example than the Beihai case to show that whatever the state said was always ironically subverted into a sexual metaphor. It is incorrect to think that official discourse is spoken only in the world of officials. As a matter of fact, official discourse, understood as an authorized ideological representation of the actual, can be employed by anyone, official or not, on an occasion for which the employment of it may generate certain effects. It is not unusual for Western ethnographers to be surprised to hear ordinary Chinese people speaking the language of the state.[31] The misunderstanding, especially in the case of some feminist writings on Chinese society (see, e.g., M. Wolf 1985; Judd 1994), is to overestimate the state's ideological power. This confusion arises partly from the fact that ethnographers are misguided by their own theoretical prejudices. I am not saying that people could not be ideologized by the state; rather, more often than not, the situation into which a discourse is adopted holds the key for understanding what it means. In other words, much like Wittgenstein's emphasis on the use of language, the effects of a discourse impregnate the meaning of an utterance.

Official discourse has a life of its own, independent of the situations in which it may be adopted. When I say that official discourse is subverted by sexual metaphors, I mean that the discursive foundation of the official discourse is shaken or threatened by the image of sex or sexual behavior, often very explicit. What made this strategy of subversion effective and interesting was its eroticism or, perhaps better, linguistic pornography—cast entirely from the perspective of the male. The following is an excellent example that became very popular in the business world in 1999:

> There is a city in Shandong province called Rizhao, a word that consists of two Chinese characters: *ri* primarily means "the sun" but is also slang for "to fuck"; *zhao* in this case means "spreading out." The meaning of the city's name is therefore "sun (shine) spreading out." One day officials came from a special office in Beijing, the Socialist Spiritual Civilization Office (*Shehuizhuyi Jingshenwenming Bangongshi*), to inspect the program of socialist spiritual civilization. As usual, the people of Rizhao prepared several huge posters to welcome the guests: the main one was supposed to read, "We Sincerely Welcome the Socialist Spiritual Civilization Office to Rizhao for Inspection of Our Work!" (*Relie Huanying Shehuizhuyi Jinshenwenming Bangongshi Lai Rizhao Jiancha Gongzuo!*) The city's party secretary thought that this sentence was too long to fit on the poster and suggested, "Let us shorten it to 'Sincerely Welcome the SCO to Ri." But the abbreviation for the Spiritual Civilization Office, SCO sounds exactly the same in Chinese as "Sucking-Cock Office."[32] With the shortened city name, therefore, the poster supposedly read, "We Sincerely Welcome the Sucking-Cock Office to Fuck Us!"[33]

The setting of Rizhao was not important; this joke was primarily a subversive strategy targeting the idea of socialist spiritual civilization. Such an idea represented an ideological move by the present government, which has failed to develop any powerful discourses on morality and ethics for the modernizing process. This is a good example of how the state's present ideological discourse easily becomes a joke, a sex joke. The Socialist Spiritual Civilization Office has been set up at every level of government, but the meaning of it, in the language of everyday business, was turned into an erotic pan: it sucks until it ejaculates. I want to stress that this is not an isolated case: a large number of similar sexual metaphors were employed in subverting official discourse. This is only one of the many instances that the ideology of the state was turned upside-down. It is important to pay attention to this kind of coloring of the Beihai story: the business strategy of dealing with the state was not to resist its discourse but to subvert it, to turn it into something else, into a different landscape of meaning full of images of sex or eroticism.[34] The Beihai story is colored both by the idea of luck as a significant means of creating plot and by a pornographic rendering of the official discourse. Both suggest that the world of business life differs from the life of the official world.

What are the theoretical questions implicated in my ethnographic description of the practice of business life in Beihai as an example of the ongoing modernizing process in (South) China? I will now turn to this question.

part two

The Question of the We

A beggar pretended to be a mute and received quite a lot of money from sympathizers. With the money he went to have a drink in a bar. After he finished his first glass of beer, he said to the waiter, "Get me another one." The waiter was surprised and asked, "Aren't you a mute?" He replied, "Without any money, who could actually speak?"

JOKE TOLD BY AN ENTREPRENEUR

five ·~

The Structure of the Self

P*lacing the ethnographic impression* of the logic of business practice in Beihai into the background, I will now turn to an analysis of the structure of the self, defined as a system of relations internal to a historically situated mode of existence, by which I mean to distinguish the notion of individual or individual agency from the structure of normal personhood as the conditions of possibility for what is supposed to be a self in a given social context. The word *normal* is here employed both in the sense of what people want to be and in the sense of what they think they should be, both within and outside the official discourse and ideology. The departure of my analysis is transindividualistic: I wish to grasp not the agency of an individual or a collectivity in the Durkheimian sense or the significance of a particular subject position; instead, my analysis should be seen as an attempt in trying to capture the historical character of an entire generation at the present moment.

There is a theoretical interest in drawing a distinction between the concepts of self and of identity, although in the anthropological or historical literature such a distinction is not always maintained. I hope to focus on the form rather than the content of an identity by stressing that the form of an identity concerns the question of how it is made rather than what it is made of. For example, when discussing Shanghai sojourners in the 1920s and 1930s, Frederic Wakeman and Wen-Hsin Yeh have used the term *identity* to mean what these people were made of, such as their backgrounds and modes of belonging (Wakeman and Yeh 1992, 11–12). In such cases, this term often means the identification of a group of people with their historical heritage or cultural background, which is not what I am concerned with. When I use the term *identity,* with or without coupling it with the word *politics,* I am referring more to the actual experiences of belonging. In contrast, by using "the structure of the self," I hope to focus on the conditions of possibility of belonging, which may not even be conscious to the agents involved.

"Sources of the Self"

The following consists of a reading of four texts, two by anthropologists and two by philosophers, and it provides a frame of theoretical reference for my inquiry into the structure of self in contemporary China. To say that this section is a reading of these texts brings two points into view. First, what is read is read by readers with their own intentions and considerations. In reading these four texts, I intend to search for a theoretical language that will enable me to speak about the structure of self as an object of analysis. This is not a systematic treatment of each individual author's work on such a subject, nor is it an evaluation of their contribution to their fields. Second, what is read is the text, not just the author's intention. This is a doctrine of hermeneutics, at least according to Paul Ricoeur's interpretation (1991, 105–24). To put it crudely, the birth of a text is the death of its author.

Geertz

With his understanding of anthropology as an interpretive science, Geertz has provided a classic example of analysis of the different senses of self in Java, Bali, and Morocco. His analysis views these three senses of self in terms of different cultural configurations of the person. As he argues, in each case, there is a different conception of what is supposed to be a human being.[1] The sense of self in Java, as Geertz argues, is based on the making of a double conceptual contrast: one between "inside" and "outside" and the other between "refined" and "vulgar." "The 'inside'/'outside' words, *batin* and *lair* (terms borrowed, as a matter of fact, from the Sufi tradition of Muslim mysticism, but locally reworked) refer on the one hand to the felt realm of human experience and on the other to the observed realm of human behavior" (Geertz 1983, 60). He has specifically pointed out that this contrast should not be confused with the Western dualist conception of soul versus body, because the contrast between inside and outside in Java has little to do with spiritual or material quality of human beings; instead, the terms refer to two domains, internal and external, of human life. *Inside* denotes more an emotional world, while *outside* points to the world of interaction in everyday life. "These two sets of phenomena—inward feelings and outward actions—are then regarded not as functions of one another but as independent realms of being to be put in proper order independently" (Geertz 1983, 61). The proper order is supposed to be achieved by refining oneself in both internal and external life. This notion of refinement is central to the second pair of terms, *alus* versus *kasar*—that is, "refined" or "civilized" in contrast to "vulgar" or "uncivilized." The goal of refinement is to achieve *alus,* or purity. "The goal is to be *alus* in both the separated realms of the self. In the inner realm this is to be achieved through religious discipline, much but not all of it mystical. In the outer realm, it is to be achieved through etiquette, the rules of which here are not only extraordinarily elaborate but have something of the force of law" (Geertz 1983, 61). The result of such a conception in Java is that all individuals would engage in constant redefinition of themselves to achieve the ideal of *alus,* which is not defined from outside as a set of definite qualities but is instead a goal defined in the process of becoming purified or civilized.

In contrast, the Balinese sense of self is quite different. The conception of a person in Bali is defined from outside by a series of characters, a notion that I discussed in some detail in chapter 1. A character is a public representation of a certain type of person or an image of a certain kind of person idealized or typified, as in drama. "It is dramatis personae, not actors, that endure, indeed, it is dramatis personae, not actors, that in the proper sense really exist" (Geertz 1983, 62). Geertz's well-known analysis of the Balinese system of names and addresses may be taken as a good example of how a person is supposed to be fixed as an image according to a hierarchy of titles and status by which such a person is identified or made identifiable (1973, 360–89). As he says, "In both their structure and their mode of operation, the terminological systems conduce to a view of the human person as an appropriate representative of generic type, not a unique creature with a private fate" (1983, 63).

The conception of self in Morocco, however, differs from that of both Java and Bali. The Moroccan conception neither relies on the internalization of a process of refining oneself nor depends on the externalization of viewing a person by the image of a character dramatized on stage. The Moroccan sense of self, a mode of understanding of what a person is, is defined according to situations that vary and change. Therefore, a contextual understanding of the combination of a set of immanent characteristics embodied in a person holds the key for understanding what a person is supposed to be. In other words, a person or a self in Morocco is considered as an embodiment of certain immanent characteristics; a person is supposed to be understood as a combination of these characteristics according to each situation in life. That is, "persons can be identified in terms of supposedly immanent characteristics (speech, blood, faith, provenance, and the rest)—and yet to minimize the impact of those characteristics in determining the practical relations among such persons in markets, shops, bureaus, fields, cafés, baths, and roadways that makes it so central to the Moroccan idea of the self" (Geertz 1983, 68).

The significance of Geertz, insofar as my analysis is concerned, is that he has shown how to raise the question of how a sense of self is supposed to be brought to light. The three understandings of what a person is are only distinguishable if they are taken as different cultural forms. They are not about how an individual may understand what his neighbor means to him; rather, they represent three discursive formations of self-understanding by which people in these cultural universes make sense of what a human agent is supposed to mean. To say that they are cultural forms is to stress that they are not reducible to the agency of any individuals. The long tradition behind such analysis can be traced back at least as far as Marcel Mauss, particularly to the argument presented in his last essay, "A Category of the Human Mind: The Notion of Person; the Notion of Self" (1938) (see Carrithers, Collins, and Lukes 1985, 1–25, for an English translation). Mauss belonged to, of course, a brilliant sociological tradition, the Année Sociologique school, but in the field of cultural analysis, a potential danger, if one exaggerates Geertz, lies in the possible return to the trap of a once powerful paradigm in American anthropology, the school of culture and personality (see Harris 1968, 393–463; Wallace 1961). The potential danger is to essentialize others in terms of what Ruth Benedict called "patterns of culture" without being able to see that cultural forms are historically contingent in nature. Cultural forms are historical constructs, and this is a presupposition for the other three texts to which I will now turn.

Comaroff and Comaroff

"History is culturally ordered, differently so in different societies, according to meaningful schemes of things. The converse is also true:

cultural schemes are historically ordered, since to a greater or lesser extent the meanings are revalued as they are practically enacted" (Sahlins 1985, vii). Comaroff and Comaroff (1991–, vol. 1)[2] provides a good example for such a point of view.[3] Their book concerns the historical process in which a particular group of Nonconformist Christian missionaries, of British origin, sought to change the hearts and minds, signs and practices of an African people. It is a historical ethnography of the experience of colonial encounter that covers approximately a century between 1820 and 1920.[4] By telling this story of a specific Christian mission to southern Tswana, they mean to reveal a more general post-Enlightenment process of colonization in which Europe set out to grasp and subdue the forces of savagery, otherness, and unreason. It is a huge text, a "thick description" if one likes; my interest here is limited to the part of the book in which the authors trace the sense of self, newly emerged in Europe as a result of the complex historical transformation in the capitalist world.

Why is it relevant to discuss the sense of post-Enlightenment self, represented by a specific missionary group of Christians in London? "This is a study of the colonization of consciousness and the consciousness of colonization in South Africa" (Comaroff and Comaroff 1991–, 1:xi).[5] By raising the question of colonization of consciousness, the authors argue that to know what was brought to South Africa, one must understand not merely the general condition of European society at the time but its specific shape in England. One must first understand who these Nonconformist missionaries were, their social and political backgrounds, their dilemmas and their ambitions—in short, their mode of personhood or their sense of self.[6] Three significant historical factors were central to the formation of this particular sense of self: the ideology of industrial capitalism and its relationship to Christianity; the structural change, such as rapid urbanization, in Britain that affected the mentality of Christian missionaries; and finally a reinterpretation of God.

The purpose of their analysis is to situate the development of a particular mode of self in the larger picture of a historical transformation that brought "the rise of utilitarian individualism, in particular the celebration of the virtue of the disciplined, self-made man; of private property and status as signs of personal success, poverty as a fitting sanction for human failure; of enlightened self interest and free market, with its 'invisible hand' as the mechanism for arriving at the greatest public good; of reason and method, science and technology, as the proper means for achieving an ever more educated, civilized and cultivated humankind" (Comaroff and Comaroff 1991–, 1:60). The key feature of this transformation is reflected in the voice of classic liberalism that "posited a world consisting of self-contained, right-bearing individuals, who, in seeking to maximize their own well-being, created society by the sum of their actions and interactions" (1991–, 1:61). As Bertrand Russell once observed, "Philosophical individualism and the cult of the hero went easily together. In its popular form, this philosophy saw the person less a product of a social environment than as an autonomous being with the innate capacity to construct himself—at least to the extent he put his energies and powers of reason to the task. Note here, too, the gendering of the imagery: in the stereotypic representation of the age, the universal person was always Man" (quoted in Comaroff and Comaroff 1991–, 1:61).

Two crucial characteristics of this modern personhood are, first, that he is capable of turning himself into an object of self-scrutiny. The *I* is a center from which one looks out and works on the world as well as an object that can be worked on by oneself. Through this newly reconstructed mode of self, social values of the bourgeois ideology could have become internalized as the necessary human qualities. "Hence, discipline, generosity, respect, loyalty, and ownership, to name but a few, became virtues of individual personality embodied in self-control, self-denial, self-esteem, and self-possession" (Comaroff and Comaroff 1991–, 1:62). For this modern personhood, the essential doctrine is self-improvement. To better oneself became a sign of salvation. In everyday life, the self as a subject was made to watch itself as an object: to keep him clean, smell good, dress well, maintain health, and so forth. The practice of everyday discipline is a sign of worthy heart and an alert mind (cf. Foucault 1977; Elias [1939] 1994).[7] Another significant aspect of the development of this sense of personhood is the partibility of the self: soul and body were firmly divided. That is, the self-object was made into bits and pieces, as it were, to be able to be sold piece by piece in the emerging capitalist market. The point is that, with the assistance of Christianity, bourgeois ideologies were not only spread, reaching a much wider society, but also secured as natural and given. For example, divisions existed not only between the poor and the rich and the worker and the capitalist but also, and most importantly, between man and woman. "Inequality of male and female was also taken to be a fact of life, a natural feature of the social world, . . . so they reinforced the gendered image of self and society that lay at the core of bourgeois ideology. These images were cogently contained in the idealized domestic group, a household based on the nuclear family with its sexual division of labor." This sexual division of labor might not be entirely new but "it was during the eighteenth century that this family-household took on the status of a 'natural atom,' the God-given foundation, of civil society. Its enshrinement in the social canon of Protestantism was to assure that it would become a vital part of the civilizing mission to 'undomesticated' savages abroad" (Comaroff and Comaroff 1991–, 1:68).

By this partial reading of the Comaroffs' text, I mean to bring two points to light. First, what lies at the core of their writing is an effort to cross existing conceptual or theoretical boundaries, to travel from one historical domain to another, from one cultural field to another, from one theoretical formation to another. They do not wish to stop at any fixed concepts or to draw any lines between ethnography and history, between theory and practice, between writing and imagination. This effort to draw a picture of how things are historically as well as culturally, materially as well as symbolically, connected, linked, related is the true spirit of their project. Second, it is also important to note that these connections, conceptual or real, are historically specific. Comaroff and Comaroff are working on the particular formation of a specific articulation of self in the general historical transformation of post-Enlightenment modern Europe. The historical specificity of any cultural experience is presupposed in such an effort, which, reflected in a long anthropological tradition, remains valuable.

Taylor

Taylor (1989) should be seen as part of a serious effort by a number of major contemporary thinkers—including MacIntyre, Foucault, and Habermas—to reassess the history of modernity and to reevaluate the consequences of the Enlightenment. What underlies such an effort is an increasing awareness essential to the intellectual horizon of our time: the possibility of being what we are is still implicated in the history of modernity yet to be (re)written. Taylor attempts to rewrite such a history in an encyclopedic manner, dwelling on two fundamental assumptions. First, in contrast to Foucault, Taylor views this history in an image of topographic changes: even though a number of drastic earthquakes may have taken place to change the topography of ourselves, he insists on a geological continuity in terms of the long-term configurations within which the shape of modernity was formed.[8] The sense of continuity in Taylor is achieved by assuming the coexistence of a variety of discursive possibilities—though only some of them are visible to the present generation. His second assumption is that, in the configuration of the topography of ourselves, a large number of ideas and practices were formed to represent a diverse field of conflicting ideologies. By no means can such a history be read, as the reader is frequently reminded when Taylor moves around in the conceptual space of this huge text, as a system of unilineal descent, to use a kinship metaphor, in which responsibility and membership are traceable along one line of descent.[9]

Taylor's account of such a history consists of a triplex that traces three intertwined but different genealogical connections of a discursive field. To again use a kinship metaphor, with a particular reference to the lineage organization in southeastern China, a triplex may be considered as the family tree of a lineage with three main segments, each of which contains a number of extended families, linking in specific ways to the genesis of an ancestry. As Taylor writes,

> I focus on three major facets of this identity; first, modern inwardness, the sense of ourselves as beings with inner depths, and the connected notion that we are "selves"; second, the affirmation of ordinary life which develops from the early modern period; third, the expressivist notion of nature as an inner moral source. The first I try to trace through Augustine to Descartes and Montaigne, and on to our own day; the second I take from the Reformation through the Enlightenment to its contemporary forms; and the third I describe from its origin in the late eighteenth century through the transformations of the nineteenth century, and on to its manifestations in twentieth-century literature. (1989, x)

Each segment in this triplex, just as in southeastern Chinese lineage organization, is a partial whole with the potential of regenerating the whole of a lineage; each element derived from these genealogies is an individuation of a family resemblance. Taylor treats such a history of family resemblance by tracing what he calls "modern inwardness" to Plato, in whose vision the "mastery of self through reason brings with it these three fruits: unity with oneself, calm, and collected self-possession" (1989, 116). Augustine stands on the way from Plato to Descartes in the sense that Augustine, as an authoritative representative of a whole tradition of the theological Middle Ages, radicalizes the existence of an inner space within oneself, which is what Taylor calls "radical reflexivity."

> In our normal dealings with things, we disregard this dimension of experience and focus on the things experienced. But we can turn and make this our object of attention, become aware of our awareness, try to experience our experiencing, focus on the way the world is *for* us. This is what I call taking a stance of radical reflexivity or adopting the first-person standpoint. . . .
>
> Augustine's turn to the self was a turn to radical reflexivity, and that is what made the language of inwardness irresistible. The inner light is the one which shines in our presence to ourselves; it is the one inseparable from our being creatures with a first-person standpoint. What differentiates it from the outer light is just what makes the image of inwardness so compelling, that it illuminates that space I am present to myself. (Taylor 1989, 130, 131)

This kind of conceptual opposition—inner-outer or inside-outside—is not unfamiliar to anthropologists; indeed, earlier in his book, Taylor referred to Geertz's discussion of *batin/lair* in his interpretation of the Javanese sense of self, discussed earlier in this chapter. What is interesting to note is Taylor's emphasis on the historical character of this inner space, defined as a deepening of the awareness of one's own awareness. This inwardness is not simply an attitude or a mode of feeling; rather, it is a structure of self dependent on reason.[10]

To move on, it is necessary to return to the beginning of Taylor's text, to explore his framework of analysis to discover what lies in the background of his discussion. What Taylor calls "Inescapable Frameworks," the title of chapter 1, indicates a general theoretical proposition: to understand our idea of what is supposed to be a human agent, a person, a self, one must have an understanding of the evolution of notions of good. "Selfhood and the good, or in another way selfhood and morality, turn out to be inextricably intertwined themes" (1989, 3). The question of the good concerns—to put it simply—what makes life worth living. This concern with the moral configurations of ourselves differs from that of traditional moral philosophy, which is often narrow in scope and limited in theoretical ambition.[11] As Taylor writes,

> Much contemporary moral philosophy, particularly but not only in the English-speaking world, has given such a narrow focus to morality that some of the crucial connections I want to draw here are incomprehensible in its terms. The moral philosophy has tended to focus on what it is right to do rather than on what it is good to be, on defining the content of obligation rather than the nature of the good life; and it has no conceptual place left for a notion of the good as the object of our love or allegiance or, as Iris Murdock portrayed it in her work, as the privileged focus of attention or will. (1989, 3)

The question of the good must be presupposed as the background for an inquiry of the self. This is not only an important theoretical assumption that underlies the search for the making of the modern (Western) self but also an instance of a theoretical tendency marking a significant shift in a historicalized philosophy of history, of which the best example is MacIntyre (1984). The question of the *We* that I have posed is also grounded in the question of what is good (life)? Here I hope to emphasize the significance of this mode of questioning both for Taylor's discussion of the constitution of modern (Western) self and for my later treatment of contemporary Chinese society. To raise a question about something or to question something indicates a presupposed subject that enables this question to be raised. If one wishes to question the presupposed subject position from which a question is raised, one cannot simply work on the question itself. That is, one must ask a new question, seeking a relationship of the questioning to the questioned. In such cases, the concern is not simply with what is asked but with what is asked about. This aboutness constitutes the presupposed background in a mode of questioning. A question will make better sense if such a background is taken into account. In Taylor, this aboutness as the background of his inquiry is the moral or the ethical configuration of ourselves, broadly defined.

Reason as an instrument in the advancement of self toward a higher goal has triumphed. "If rational control is a matter of mind dominating a disenchanted world of matter, then the sense of the superiority of the good life, and the inspiration to attain it, must come from the agent's sense of his own dignity as a rational being" (Taylor 1989, 152). In Kant, rationality explicitly becomes an internal property of modern (Western) subjectivity, though the modern vision of reason was articulated in Descartes (see Taylor 1989, 156). A crucial shift brought about by the Cartesian sense of self is that rationality has lost its substance. "For Plato, to be rational we have to be right about the order of things. For Descartes rationality means thinking according to certain canons. The judgement now turns on properties of the activity of thinking rather than on the substantive beliefs which emerge from it" (Taylor 1989, 156). The social and political background of this shift was embedded in the question of the relationship of humans to God. "The Cartesian proof is no longer a search for an encounter with God within. It is no longer the way to an experience of everything in God. Rather what I now meet is myself: I achieve a clarity and fulness of self-presence that was lacking before" (Taylor 1989, 157). Taylor's point is that the development of the modern conception of self is neither linear nor simple, and this shift in the discursive formation of an disengaged self has practical or real implications in a number of social, economic, and political fields. Taylor discussed "the punctual self" with reference to John Locke, and it is an example of the intensification of the Cartesian disengaged human agent, which intends to create a distance from the objective world, "to identify oneself with the power to objectify and remake, and by this act to distance oneself from all the particular features which are objects of potential change" (Taylor 1989, 171). The significance of Locke is that his self is "the moral agent who takes responsibility for his acts in the light of future retribution" (173). According to Taylor, Locke was a great teacher of the Enlightenment as a result of a combination of two elements in his work: "that he offered a plausible account of the new science as valid knowledge, intertwined with a theory of rational control of self; and that he brought the two together under the ideal of rational self-responsibility" (174).

Taylor refers to Kant only when discussing Descartes; after analyzing Locke's punctual self, Taylor arrives at a conclusion: "This is what distinguishes the classical writers from followers of Descartes, Locke, Kant, or just about anyone in the modern world. The turn to oneself is now also and inescapably a turn to oneself in the first-person perspective—a turn to the self as a self" (1989, 176). Taylor has conjured up a textual image of a thousand plateaus, as Deleuze and Guattari would call it. That is, such a development of modern subjectivity is neither linear nor singular.[12] This is a crucial point: the road to the present is not an evolution of unilinear descent; rather, it is a complex formation of multilineages, each including several segments and a number of extended families, of the same origin but with very different outlooks.

This is only an oversimplified treatment of one of Taylor's three facets of the development of modern (Western) subjectivity, but it illustrates his approach. In saying that his view of the history of modernity can be termed "topographical," I mean that there are not only connections and ruptures on the surface of this topological structure but also continuities and discontinuities underneath it. It is shaped in such a way as to shape the contemporary appearance, although such influences cannot always directly be observed. "For one thing, the three domains don't stay the same; they are continually borrowing from and influenced by each other. For another, there have been attempts to straddle the boundaries and combine more than one" (Taylor 1989, 496). For example, Taylor takes Marxism as a marriage of the Enlightenment naturalism and expressivism. Expressivism in his account is an expression of the spirit of German Romanticism.

Finally, Taylor's approach emphasizes the importance of cultivating an in-depth historical sensitivity in dealing with the problem of identity and self:

> This is one reason why I have had to assemble the portrait of the modern identity through its history. An instantaneous snapshot would miss a great deal. Another reason is that only through adding a depth perspective of history can one bring out what is implicit but still at work in contemporary life: the Romantic themes still alive in modernism, masked sometimes by the anti-Romantic stance of modernists; or the crucial importance of the affirmation of ordinary life, which is in some ways too pervasive to be noticed; or the spiritual roots of naturalism, which modernism usually feels forced to suppress. (1989, 498)

If history holds the key to understanding the horizons of ourselves, there are several different views of what history is supposed to mean. Foucault stands out as a good comparison with Taylor in terms of how such a history of modernity can be (re)written.

Foucault

The significance of Foucault lies in his innovative approach to the history of modernity, which opens up an entirely different channel for our imagination of the past as a foreign country. Foucault's work has been widely discussed and needs no further comment (see, e.g., Dreyfus and Rabinow 1982); I simply wish to draw attention to some common misunderstandings of Foucault's work, particularly among some anthropologists and historians. These misunderstandings have (re)appeared in some recent writings. For example, Lisa Rofel's work on the Chinese experience of revolution and reform (1999) brought up Foucault several times. Apart from charging Foucault with being too focused on European history (see Rofel 1999, 287 n.9)—a very common reaction from scholars working on other parts of the world—Rofel challenges Foucault's genealogical method, which seems to presuppose the discontinuity of history. "While I generally agree with Foucault that invocations of modernity signal a radical break with previous forms of power, I nonetheless found that when memories are involved, the rupture is not as clean as Foucault theorized" (1999, xiii–xiv). Rofel's project, based on her fieldwork among female factory workers in China, looks into the alternative experience of Chinese women struggling with modernity by working through different generations' stories about the Maoist revolution and subsequent reforms, and is itself a very interesting project. However, her reading of Foucault, not unrepresentative of some others, is misleading in that she confuses her own level of analysis with that of Foucault.[13] Foucault's analysis is largely carried out at the level of the conceptual, not specifically concerned with the actual experiences of modernity, which may or may not be continuous. To use actual instances, as some historians have (see Merquior 1985), to argue against Foucault, to charge him with misrepresenting the history of, for example, prison reform, is an error in confusing these two levels of analysis— the conceptual and the actual. This distinction, more or less a conventional one, has largely been transformed, partly as a result of the influence of Foucault himself, into the discursive versus the otherwise (see Foucault 1972; see also Rabinow 1984, 23–27).

It is, of course, legitimate to ask whether it is adequate to work entirely on the discursive formation of an epoch or whether the conceptual is separable from the actual. Anyone associated with the Marxist tradition would have great difficulty accepting the Foucauldian position that begins its analysis from the conditions of possibility of a discursive formation rather than beginning with some sort of understanding, no matter how preliminary, of the real historical or social forces. Precisely for this reason, Foucault charged Marx with being nothing more than a comfortable fish in the water of nineteenth-century thought: "Marxism exists in nineteenth-century thought like a fish in water: that is, it is unable to breathe anywhere else" (1970, 262). That is, what Marx said or what Marx was able to say, was what the bourgeoisie were saying, though from the opposing pole. The post-Marxism debate, invoked by Ernesto Laclau and Chantal Mouffe, is a good example in point. In their response to criticism—for example, by Norman Geras (1990)—Laclau and Mouffe have provided a good model for an approach to the analysis of discursive practice. A serious charge against Laclau and Mouffe (1985) is that they began their analysis from what Marx would have deemed as ideologies—that is, the departure of their analysis is not based on any actual historical or social forces. Rather, it has become discourse itself. According to the classic Marxist view, discourse, no matter how it is supposed to be defined, must be seen as part of the superstructure, part of the representation of the real from a certain class perspective. In a crucial sense, the epistemological question involved in the post-Marxism debate concerns the nature of the real. If the vision of an objective (material) reality as the only source of historical determination is removed, if such a vision is simply taken as a particular construction of the real from a certain epistemological stance, Marxism will collapse. Geras and Laclau (and Mouffe) stand in opposition regarding this question, which reflects the difference between two epistemological stances—those represented by Marx and Foucault. And this difference has become more than a difference in language; it has become a dangerous ditch between the two camps of scholars. This is why Laclau and Mouffe, in responding to Geras, said that "it is simply impossible to use [Geras's] critical account as the framework for our reply" (Laclau 1990, 100), because the departure point for their analysis is "the social space as discursive," shaped by an entirely different intellectual landscape from that of Geras.

The example that both sides in this debate have employed in explaining their position is a classic one with a Wittgensteinian trace: two bricklayers (minimum assumption) building the wall of a house. Bricklayer A asks his coworker to pass a brick to him. Two acts are involved: the first act is asking, which is linguistic; the second is positioning the brick, which is extralinguistic. These two acts, asking and positioning, make up a whole action, which Laclau and Mouffe called "totality" that consists of two partial moments. "Obviously, if this totality includes both linguistic and non-linguistic elements, it cannot itself be either linguistic or extralinguistic; it has to be prior to this distinction. This totality which includes within itself the linguistic and the non-linguistic, is what we call discourse. . . . [W]hat must be clear from the start is that by discourse we do not mean a combination of speech and writing, but rather that speech and writing are themselves but internal components of discursive totalities" (Laclau 1990, 100). But why must this totality—the whole of action—be called discourse? Because anything configured as part of the social formation is always about meaning. To kick a spherical object on the street is different from kicking a ball in a soccer game in that the meaning of the latter is different from that of the former. In a strict sense, there is no such physical object that stands outside the discursive formation that always constitutes this object as an integral part of a social system. "A diamond in the market or at the bottom of a mine is the same physical object; but, again, it is only a commodity within a determinate system of social relations. For that same reason it is the discourse which constitutes the subject position of the social agent, and not, therefore, the social agent which is the origin of discourse—the same system of rules that makes that spherical object into a football, makes me a player" (Laclau 1990, 101). Following such an understanding of the social considered as the discursive, there is little space for conceiving society in terms of a double structure, as in Marx, as the infrastructure versus the superstructure—that is, the actual forces of production versus the ideological representations of them.[14]

This understanding of "the social space as discursive," which shares some crucial features with Foucault's treatment of historical transformation of Europe since the Enlightenment, is also nurtured by the spirit of Wittgenstein's later philosophy.[15] I believe that some significant theoretical aspect of what Laclau and Mouffe have espoused brings the discussion back, for example, to Peter Winch's employment of Wittgenstein in developing "the idea of a social science" ([1958] 1990):

> Our language and our social relations are just two different sides of the same coin. To give an account of the meaning of a word is to describe how it is used; and to describe how it is used is to describe the social intercourse into which it enters.

> If social relations between men exist only in and through their ideas, then, since the relations between ideas are internal relations, social relations must be a species of internal relations, too. (123)

Despite the differences in words, in Winch drawing on Wittgenstein there is a sense that prioritizes the discursive. The classic reaction from a Marxist scholar would be that this stance is trapped in philosophical idealism (see, e.g., Callinicos 1995). In the case of Foucault's work, prioritizing the discursive marked a different intellectual path, paved by French structuralism. Especially in his early works, Foucault showed a very clear influence from structural analysis. The paradigmatic example of his early work is Foucault (1970), in which he set out to map the epistemic shifts in the Western system of knowledge. Although four stages are outlined—the preclassical, until the mid–seventeenth century; the classic, until the end of the eighteenth century; the modern, from the nineteenth century until the mid-twentieth; and the contemporary, which has taken shape only since around 1950; the book hardly touches the episteme of the contemporary world and deals with the episteme of the preclassical age, the Renaissance mode of knowledge, only in passing. Foucault's theoretical novel portrays a series of ruptures in the constitution of the epistemological ground on which Western knowledge is made possible. The point is that this is not about knowledge itself but about the epistemological grounding of knowledge—that is, the conditions of possibility for a certain kind of knowledge to emerge. The story that Foucault told is now well known: Renaissance man thought in terms of similitude, which took four different forms of resemblance: *conventienia*, which connected things near to each other; *aemulatio*, which meant similitude in distance; *analogy*, which indicated the similar relations; and *sympathy*, which likened almost anything to anything else. In the seventeenth century, there was a sudden total collapse of the mode of knowledge based on similitude, and a new episteme, defined as a historical a priori in the configuration of any empirical knowledge, emerged, marking the classical age. Its spirit, so to speak, was representation, of which two main means were *mathesis* and *taxinomia*. Classification therefore became very central to knowledge. In the nineteenth century, the classical mode of knowledge again collapsed, and the modern age brought into the form of knowledge a sense of historicity; within such a mode of knowledge was born the concept of humans as the center of the universe. As is well known, toward the end of his book,

Foucault announced the death of man, to parallel Nietzsche's announcement of the death of God, because the idea of man—that is, the humanist take on history—was itself a historical invention.

The content of Foucault's argument is perhaps arguable; however, I am interested here in addressing some methodological issues invoked by this powerful study of the epistemes of Western knowledge. Foucault assumes an entire break, a sudden rupture, a mutation, from one mode of knowledge to another, a thesis at which some thinkers have frowned. Whatever the case, one should not misunderstand Foucault by reducing him to the level of analysis that he was trying to depart. The episteme of knowledge is the condition of its possibility, not the knowledge itself.

> Quite obviously, such an analysis does not belong to the history of ideas or of science: it is rather an inquiry whose aim is to rediscover on what basis knowledge and theory became possible; within what space of order knowledge was constituted; on what basis of what historical *a priori,* and in the element of what positivity, ideas could appear, sciences be established, experience be reflected in philosophies, rationalities be formed, only, perhaps, to dissolve and vanish soon afterwards. . . . [W]hat I am attempting to bring to light is the epistemological field, the episteme in which knowledge, envisaged apart from all criteria having reference to its rational value or to its objective forms, grounds its positivity and thereby manifests a history which is not that of its growing perfection, but rather that of its conditions of possibility; in this account, what should appear are those configurations within the *space* of knowledge which have given rise to the diverse forms of empirical science. Such an enterprise is not so much a history, in the traditional meaning of that word, as an "archaeology." (Foucault 1970, xxii)

The archaeology of knowledge discovers the conditions of possibility— that is, the historical a priori—for a certain mode of knowledge.[16] For this reason, Foucault looks at three domains of knowledge at the same time—the domains of language, life, and wealth—and argues that from one epistemic epoch to another, there is a systematic transformation in the configuration of knowledge in all three domains. The rupture occurs in the conditions of possibility of knowledge.

Foucault's kinship to the structuralist movement, alongside his affinity with the Annales historical revolution and many other traditions (such as those marked by Nietzsche or Heidegger), seems to be evident, insofar as Foucault (1970) is concerned. Anthropologists or others familiar with the structuralist movement would immediately sense the signifi-cance of the phrase "conditions of possibility" that invokes a series of associations running from Saussure's famous distinction between language (*langue*) and speech (*parole*) to Lévi-Strauss's insistence that myth is language. For structuralists, being able to speak is conditioned by the possibility of a system of signification that may not be conscious to the individual speaker. The conditions of possibility point to the structural qualities of such a system. In the lineage of intellectual kinship, the early Foucault was very much part of this segment of a theoretical clan. The difference is that in Foucault, instead of taking the structure as a structure of signification, he turned to examine the historical a priori as a system of relations. "Every age adopts an image of itself—a certain horizon, however blurred and imprecise, which somehow unifies its whole experience" (Laclau 1990, 3). This fundamental assumption, which may not be entirely new, underlies what the early Foucault tried to discover underneath the surface of human sciences.

Conversely, if one reads Fernand Braudel alongside Foucault, one may also find some interesting parallels. Braudel's notion of *longue durée* constitutes a significant monument of the French historical revolution (the Annales school).[17] By such a theoretical effort, Braudel hoped to reduce the significance of the event and to extend the duration of historical writing to reveal the structure of historical transformation.[18] As Braudel said,

> Life, the history of the world, and all individual histories present themselves to us as a series of events, in other words of brief and dramatic acts. A battle, an encounter between statesmen, an important speech, a crucial letter are instants in history. I remember a night near Bahia, when I was enveloped in a firework display of phosphorescent fireflies; their pale lights glowed, went out, shone again, all without piercing the night with any true illumination. So it is with events; beyond their glow, darkness prevails. (1980, 10–11)

What Foucault termed "empiricities" is more or less how Braudel saw the significance of the event in the *longue durée* historical vision. The event is the most impressive and of the most intense interest; it is also the most superficial. To go beyond the limits of immediate experience is the target of both Braudel and Foucault, in one in terms of *longue durée* and in the other in terms of epistemological breaks. If Foucault is understood as focusing on the discursive formation by a structuralist strategy via the Annales technology, insofar as Foucault (1970) is concerned, it becomes more easily understood why Foucault did what he did: it was an exercise of a new theoretical writing that did not add directly to the existing pool of empirical knowledge but produced an alternative theoretical possibility.

*T*aken *together, these four texts* constitute a tool kit of concepts. According to my reading of these texts, the wholeness of this set of tools is generated for a particular purpose; this wholeness is constructed from my perspective of reading. In Geertz, an interesting conceptual element is his emphasis on a sense of self as a cultural form; the significance of his discussion lies in the understanding that there is a "deep play" of everyday representation of self as a form. The other three texts differ from Geertz's in that they deal with the form of historical difference. Taylor, the most general in scope, focuses on the conflicts—both in terms of ideologies and practices—in the making of modern (Western) subjectivity. Taylor's theoretical stance is implicitly set up against that of Foucault. For in Foucault, according to Taylor, the account of modern transformation in terms of discipline and control is "somewhat one-sided" (Taylor 1989, 159). However, although important, Taylor's insistence on the multisided character of modernity is not fundamental; what is crucial in Taylor, as in MacIntyre and others, is his insistence on an "inescapable framework" that connects the question of self to the question of good. This concern with the moral or ethical configuration of ourselves sits in the background of my own investigation throughout this book. In contrast, an important conceptual dimension in Foucault is his skillful compilation of a genealogy, his ability to create a historical contrast. For him, structural analysis is an analytical strategy, not a substantial ideology. The ruptures in the history of epistemes should be taken as the effects of his writing through which we are able to see ourselves more clearly in a historical mirror. The following chapter will also try to accomplish this end: to stretch things as far apart as possible to allow a different light to shine on the possible differences between three moments of the modern Chinese experience. Comaroff and

Comaroff's work is useful in urging the retention of the historical or cultural specificity of a particular social experience, which represents in some way the classic anthropological tradition. In their discussion, the historical transformation is treated neither as a history of conflicting and/or complementary ideas as in Taylor nor as a history of structural ruptures as in Foucault but always as a field of struggles through concrete social groups and interests. My compilation of a genealogy of the self in contemporary China is to be made within these four analytical dimensions.

Becoming Other

China puzzles those who have tried to understand the significance of its recent past because it is often difficult not to be surprised how oneself is able to become its own Other—not in the sense of changing one's profession or job but in the sense that the character of a person may change entirely within a short period of time—for example, a few years. In the early 1990s, outsiders were commonly surprised to discover that many students whose experience of the antigovernment protests and subsequent crackdown remained very fresh had already turned themselves into successful businessmen and considered the demonstration an unfortunate event that hindered the development of Chinese economy.[19] The image of the demonstration changed in the span of a few years, even among the activists of that heroic movement.[20] This example is representative of a general 1990s tendency for Chinese intellectuals to turn themselves into businessmen, as in the formation of the Beihai Star Group. Given the structural rearrangement of the society, particularly its economic system, it was not unusual for people to change their professions during the years of economic reforms; however, the kind of change, which I intend to discuss, is not simply *external* change—that is, moving to work in a different environment, such as leaving a university position to become a manager in a private company—while the sense of self, defined in terms of the moral configuration in which one lives, remains stable. I intend to discuss the kind of change that is *internal* to the constitution of self as an ethical subject. One's selfhood is determined by such an ethical constitution. This is not change in the sense that a hen wanders around for food and happens to step into the territory of a dog; it is change in the sense that the hen, after a magic rain, turns into a duck—becoming a different animal, as some Chinese entrepreneurs said. This possibility of reconfiguring the moral space within which one(self) dwells is what I call becoming Other. This Other is the otherness of self, stressing the sharp contrast of two moral configurations, one inside the other, invisible, but able to come out of the womb of oneself to create overnight an entirely different outlook on one's moral appearance.

As an ethnographic example, there is Haihun, the general manager of the Beihai Star Group. He was trained in economics in a small college in Taiyuan, Shanxi province, where he was born and grew up. After his graduation in 1982, he became a lecturer at that college and taught there until 1986, when he went on to study for his master's and doctoral degrees at the Sichuan University of Finance and Economics.[21] His research was conducted in the field of Marxism and demography. Through a number of publications while in graduate school, he made himself known in the field, particularly but not only among Marxist scholars and demographers. During these years in Sichuan, he never thought of abandoning his academic career. Though he was studying in another province, his home college in Taiyuan continued to pay his salary in hopes that he would return to teach after he finished his doctoral research. He agreed to this arrangement. Only near the completion of his research, in 1992, did his mind become distracted from what he had always intended to do, teaching. Recalling this critical moment of transition in his life and career, Haihun made specific references to two particular events; and his story about what happened was later confirmed by others.

Although Haihun spent only six years in graduate school, 1986 and 1992 represented two different moments of experience for those in China. The first moment, the mid-1980s, was one in which the meaning of economic reform was still unclear to many who simply wanted to watch—standing outside the currents of the reform—what was going on or what might happen next, hesitating to jump into the stream of new economic experiment, perhaps afraid of getting a cold rather than a cod. The majority of people were waiting for things to change rather than participating in the process of changing things. Economic development was already under way, affecting more people in the countryside than in the cities, but the spirit of reform had not been fully recognized. Academic positions were still considered better than most other jobs; Haihun sought advanced degrees because they would enhance his ability to advance in the academic world. In the early 1990s, however, Deng Xiaoping traveled to South China, signifying the government's determination to come out of the shadow created by the harsh crackdown against the 1989 student demonstrations in Beijing as well as the government's determination to enact further reforms and continued commitment to an open-door policy to the outside world. The spirit of reform subsequently began to penetrate the deeper corners of consciousness of everyday life. Many intellectuals began to think about the kind of fish they might catch by diving into the stream of economic reforms rather than worrying about whether they would drown. In such an environment of difference, in terms of perception and anticipation, in terms of feeling and motivation, Haihun's decision to change his career was conceived.

When asked to explain his decision, Haihun often told the following story: At the end of his tenure in graduate school, Haihun had attempted to publish his doctoral dissertation, more than six hundred pages of a thorough critique of the orthodox reading of Marx and a genuine effort to reread the Marxist theory of labor into a theory of population that might shed light on the Chinese reality. Haihun tried several local presses in Sichuan, but none of the editors showed any interest. Part of the reason for this failure was that his topic was no longer fashionable among younger Chinese intellectuals. "Who wants to read Marxist analysis anymore?" an editor said. "Why don't you write something else? You know, these days are not like those good old days. Whatever we published, we would have been funded by the government. Nowadays, books have to sell. Do you expect people to read your thesis? It is too big a book, in any case."

The publication of academic works had become increasingly difficult as a result of market pressure for commercialization beginning in the mid-1980s, although most publishing houses were still owned by the state. It was a difficult time because the government had just asked most presses to consider themselves independent economic enterprises, responsible for their own profits and debts, a great change from the previous system, under which all publishing houses were government-financed. With much disappointment, Haihun went to see the editor of the People's Press in Shanxi province, where he had been planning to return to teach. The press's academic editor was a high school friend of Haihun's who had failed the national exams to enter college, despite multiple attempts. Through connections, he had come to work for the

People's Press, a major publisher in the province.[22] In a few years, this editor had become known in Shanxi publishing circles because he was excellent at making the press profitable. His success derived from an interesting phenomenon: In China during the 1980s books could only be published with government-assigned publication numbers. These serial numbers, which looked like ISBNs, were distributed only to officially acknowledged publishers, such as the People's Press, which seemed to mean that the government totally controlled the materials published. However, with the increasing pressure for marketization, publishers had to think about what to publish to make a profit. The easiest way of making profits was to sell these official book numbers to entrepreneurs who wished to publish purely commercial materials, such as books on Bill Clinton's sexual behavior in the White House. The manipulation of these book numbers required the talent of a good entrepreneur. Haihun's friend had risen to his post seat by selling book numbers to the right entrepreneurs and thereby earning significant profits for the press.

Academics commonly complained during the early 1990s about the difficulty in publishing. For academic books that would not sell well, publishers often charged authors production fees to guarantee that the press at least would not lose money.[23] In this environment, Haihun went to meet with the editor in Shanxi. The editor was friendly and said that he would like to look at Haihun's manuscript, adding, "You may have to pay for the production costs, but it would be a great favor if I could get you a book number." He did not mean anything ill, but Haihun was terribly offended by the man's willingness to help because it hurt Haihun's pride, nurtured by many years of education. Haihun felt that he should not be in such a position, begging for help from others after so many years of hard work in school. He began for the first time to wonder about the value of his knowledge. On the way back to Sichuan, what stuck in his mind, even in sleep, was the thought, "I must make enough money to be able to publish whatever I wish—*whatever I wish.*"

Whether Haihun realized it or not, this thought was a good indicator of the increasing effectiveness of money as a generalized medium of exchange, filling in all cleavages of the socialist hierarchy that used to define many specific forms of economic or political reciprocity. During the radical years of the Maoist revolution, the socialist system of difference had indeed been a system of hierarchy, but of a different nature. The essential characteristic of the socialist system was the self-denial of its own hierarchical reality. The discursive surface of that system was covered by the language of equality and social justice; however, underneath the surface was a multilayered, complex system of discrimination and differentiation (see Whyte and Parish 1984). Nevertheless, the gaps and cleavages generated in and by this hierarchical system were never supposed to emerge above its discursive surface, to be acknowledged in language and discourse. What was done could not be said. The *said* was considered to be holding some sort of magic power in the transformation of reality, and therefore *saying* was only possible within a particular mode of the *said*—the legitimized, official discourse on revolution and society. In the early 1990s, the socialist discursive surface was collapsing. To what extent such a change has affected or will affect the social infrastructure of Chinese society is arguable, but it is obvious that it is precisely at this level that the image of money comes to function as an essential element in the reconfiguration of a new discursive surface. Two particular images of money were developed: money talks and money walks.

Money talks. Communication in the sense of a dialogue? No. Giving commands and orders? Yes. It is therefore better to say, money orders. The order of things, in the imaginative reordering of reality in contemporary Chinese society, is created by this agent. Order is a hierarchy by force, which means two operations at once: order as a hierarchical arrangement of things, on the one hand, and order as a force that makes things as they are, on the other. Therefore, it is hegemonic in the sense that with or without realizing it, everyone is part of the order of things that conditions the way in which one lives. According to my ethnographic materials, no order in China can be conceived as lying outside the reign of money. Money is seen as the driving force of society.

Money walks. Not in the sense that one goes home with a walking stick, stumbling over a few rotten watermelons in a summer evening, but in the sense that one is able to travel in the newly invented landscape of distinction and difference in wealth. The possibility of movement, of travel, both in the physical and the metaphysical senses, lies in and with the power of cash. Another important reason why Haihun became an entrepreneur initially came from a conversation with a college classmate, Guanmin, who had become a businessman a few years earlier. After graduation, Guanmin worked in a government office for a few years and then opened his own business in Beijing and Shenzhen. By the time he and Haihun talked again 1992, Guanmin was earning a comfortable living, and he invited Haihun to visit Shenzhen for a few days. Consciously or not, Guanmin wanted to show his way of life to Haihun, who was known among his friends as a dutiful son. His mother had died some years earlier; his father was a retired schoolmaster. By going to university and becoming a professor, Haihun had always thought that he was doing well for his father, who had spent all his life teaching in a high school. However, this trip to Shenzhen marked a turning point in Haihun's conception of what being a dutiful son meant. Over lunch in a hotel, Guanmin said, "Open your eyes. Don't be stupid anymore. What is a dutiful son? In today's China, being a professor, you could not even afford to buy your father a good dinner. How can you talk about your sincerity in looking after him? He does not need you to be always by his side; he needs to be able to come to see you or have you visit him in a comfortable way. You have never traveled by airplane because you cannot afford it. If your father wishes to see you here, how can you get him here? By train? Two whole days traveling on dirty trains? Stop being stupid. We hardly need any knowledge at this stage of socialist development. What we need is cash. Things are as simple as this: Make some money first." It was a naked truth. Haihun was shocked but impressed. Soon thereafter, he went to Hainan province to search for business opportunities.

One of these two concrete images of money relates it to the way things are supposed to be, and the other links it to the possibility of traveling in a newly imagined geography of power and wealth. Both images were frequently—though in different forms—invoked in everyday conversations. Money has become an image of everyday life. Money is not always the content of everyday conversation in the sense that it is being discussed or talked about; rather, money has become the code of everyday conversation only by which it is possible to talk about life. Money is the color of everyday life rather than the portrait of it. It is an image, an impression, an impulse, a condition of possibility for speaking.

A couple of further points need to be made. First, this is an ethnographic example, but it is not an isolated case. If an ethnographic account is considered to be, to use a Geertzian term, "a thick description" (1973, 6), it is because it comes out of an experience already based on an understanding that is irreducible to that experience itself.[24] In other words, Haihun's story should be taken as an example of a general trend in today's China; it should not simply be taken as evidence or proof for what is going on. It is an example of illumination with a particular reference to the Beihai story of urban (high-tech) development.

All of the Star Group's managers were well educated, most of them with at least a master's degree. Haihun's case provides an ideal example of the spirit of a general change: the closer linkage between education and business, between intellectuals and cash, between money and society. Second, this ethnographic example shows not simply that someone has changed his profession as a result of the changes in society at large. It also shows the character change, what I have called becoming Other, a radical shift in the understanding of what one is or ought to be. Becoming Other is a process by which a reconfiguration of the self as a moral space takes place. Therefore, it is not simply that one changes what one likes or dislikes, such as in the case of changing T-shirts or lipsticks; instead, it is a rupture in making sense of oneself. Becoming Other is a moral reconfiguration by which oneself turns itself into an Other. If it is defined in such a way, how is it possible to identify the sources of such a radical change? The power of money provides an explanation only for the external conditions for becoming Other. Even if such external conditions are given, could every person become Other in the sense of recasting a moral outlook? What are the internal conditions for such a reconfiguration? As I will argue in the following chapter, what makes becoming Other possible depends on a historically situated, internal reorganization of the moral space of self through a new conception of time. The question of time is a question of the way in which our being in the world is internally shaped, and I now turn to this question.

six ·—

Time, Narrative, and History

As I argued earlier, the human experience itself is narrative in character. This is not simply to say that narrative serves as a form of representation through which human experiences are articulated. Rather, the point is more radical: the human experience itself is structured in the same way as narrative. My analysis in this chapter is based on a further assumption: the understanding of a specific set of historically situated human experiences may be reached by examining how events or characters in the stories told are implicated in the conception of time. What makes a particular kind of narrative structure possible is a certain mode of temporality, for time is the life of narrative. My theoretical assumption is that what is involved in—or, rather, revealed by—such an examination of narrative structure through time is a history-memory complex, a genealogy registering a lineage of things, both authored by and authoring a reading of the past in the light of the present. Such a mode of analysis draws a family tree of historical transformation by which it becomes possible to understand the motivations of one particular group of siblings in relation to—if continuing the kinship metaphor—other "age-groups" in terms of what they want to be. The metaphor of a family tree indeed suggests that all such groups come from a common source of historical and cultural origin, but, in terms of answering the question of what good (life) is, each generation has its own ideology. This chapter examines different conceptions of time as three historical moments (the traditional, the revolutionary, and the modern) of the modern Chinese experience, and shows how a certain kind of story is conditioned by a certain mode of temporality essential to the narrative structure.[1] Before going into a detailed analysis, it is necessary to have a brief discussion of the question of time itself, which is an old question for the discipline of anthropology.

Although some anthropologists may consider the shamans of a

new era to have shifted the foundation of anthropological thought to a higher plateau, as a matter of fact, many of us are still trapped in an older epistemology. When an anthropologist tries to deal with the question of time, a Durkheimian heritage is often—if not always—present in most common cases. What is time? To such a question, Durkheim answers,

> We cannot conceive of time, except on condition of distinguishing its different moments. Now what is the origin of this differentiation? . . . That alone is enough to give us a hint that such an arrangement ought to be collective. And in reality, observation proves that these indispensable guide lines, in relation to which all things are temporally located, are taken from social life. The divisions into days, weeks, months, years, etc., correspond to the periodical recurrence of rites, feasts, and public ceremonies. A calendar expresses the rhythm of the collective activities, while at the same time its function is to assure their regularity. (1915, 23)

Is it not true that many anthropologists still think in this way, though perhaps no longer reading this work? A very basic, by no means unimportant, Durkheimian thesis runs as follows: time is social, social is collective, collective is ritual, and ritual is registered on the calendar. Alfred Gell's insightful critique of the Durkheimian thesis on time is an interesting reaction to a faltering tradition, British social anthropology, that was heavily indebted to this master.[2] Gell argues that Durkheim's theoretical premises have "a fatal defect" that "arises from Durkheim's attempt to promote sociological analysis to the level of metaphysics, by identifying collective representations of time with Kantian 'categories'" (1992, 5). This defect is fatal because it is the origin of all the vices that have led a variety of anthropologists to the labor camp of philosophical relativism. Gell's effort in tracing the influence of Durkheim, particularly with reference to British social anthropology, is indeed useful.[3] Gell's alternative, not in terms of specific studies of (social) time but in terms of searching for a new ontological ground on which a different set of questions may be asked, comes from a universal assumption about human cognition. By taking an anti-Durkheimian, antirelativist position, Gell asserts that time is not vulgarly social; instead, the quality of time depends on the condition of human cognition.[4]

After a somewhat tiresome critique of a number of classic treatments of time in anthropology, Gell moves on, in the second part of his

book, to a discussion of "time-maps and cognition," with its philosophical departure based on a distinction between two fundamental ways of
recognizing events in time by human perception. With particular reference to J. M. E. McTaggart, a Cambridge idealist at the turn of the twentieth century whose work was discussed in Gale (1968), Gell builds his
theoretical foundation on a difference between the two basic modes of
time recognition, respectively called A-series and B-series.[5] The A-
series, as McTaggart put it, consists of events temporally identified or
identifiable according to the chain of past-present-future. A future event
is an event prior to its occurrence; a present event is one that occurs; and
a past event is one after it has occurred. Each event in the A-series
changes its status in relation to the present-ness in which it is supposed
to occur. In the B-series, in contrast, events are identified or identifiable
only with reference to their order in a sequence. One event occurs
before or after another. These two events are recognized by the relation
of after-ness/before-ness. The fundamental difference between these
two series is that in the A-series, the temporal quality of an event
changes according to whether it is present to the presence of human perception. In the B-series, however, such a referential point outside the
order of a sequence of events does not exist. McTaggart's point is that
the A-series is essential to the idea of change because the events in this
series change their status of being events according to the presence of a
moment in the chain of past-present-future. In contrast, in the B-series,
there is nothing but an order of events arranged according to a
sequence—that is, the temporal status of these events themselves does
not change. By saying that the A-series gives events an internal quality
of being temporal, since it is possible to change their status in time,
McTaggart asserts that the A-series is more fundamental than the B-
series or that the B-series is derived from the A-series. Gell disagrees
with this view and has pointed out the logical incoherence of McTaggart's argument, though Gell maintains that this distinction itself is useful. He disagrees with McTaggart only in that it is not logically meaningful to argue that the A-series is more fundamental than the B-series
(Gell 1992, 151–52). I discuss Gell and McTaggart here because this distinction, not taken as a cognitive premise for an anthropology of time
but as a conceptual tool for the analysis of events or characters in time,
is useful for my analysis.[6]

Even if one agrees that events in the A-series obtain a temporal
quality, it is quite difficult to conceive of what that quality is supposed to

mean. Paul Ricoeur revisited the skeptical argument concerning what time is in philosophy: "The skeptical argument is well-known: time has no being since the future is not yet, the past is no longer, and the present does not remain" (1984, 1:7). Or as Augustine cried, "What then is time? If no one asks me, I know: if I wish to explain it to one that asketh, I know not: yet I say boldly, that I know, that if nothing passed away, time past were not; and if nothing were coming, a time to come were not; and if nothing were, time present were not" (1940, 267–68).[7] It is indeed a baffling question, but Augustine found a solution by asserting that the "present of past things is the memory; the present of present things is direct perception; and the present of future things is expectation" (Ricoeur 1984, 1:11). My concern is of course not with the concept of time but with the conditions of possibility of being, as a mode of social existence, which has an irreducible dimension of time. For such a reason, I refer to Ricoeur, to his particular thesis (forcefully argued in Ricoeur 1984 as a continuation of the argument in Ricoeur 1977) that the conventional distinction between fictional and real representations of the actual is itself a fiction. I will implicitly follow this thesis as I develop my analysis of time in contemporary China by reading both ethnography and fiction. In a broad sense, I am following Ricoeur in taking seriously the problem of narrative as a means of getting into the heart of human experience and action (see Ricoeur 1991, 144–67); in a narrow sense, I also follow him in terms of developing a mode of analysis that depends on reading ethnographic or literary accounts of life as a means of understanding it. Materials I have chosen to read are Francis L. K. Hsu's *Under the Ancestors' Shadow* (1948), Haoran's *The Sky of Bright Sunshine* (1964, 1966), and Anyi Wang's *A Song of Everlasting Sorrow* (1995).

Time in and of the Past

There is no better place to begin the discussion of time in and of the past—that is, time conceived by those tied through descent and affinity in the traditional moment of the modern Chinese experience—than Hsu (1948). This is an important monograph in the sense that it occupies a strategic location in a very influential discursive formation in the tradition of writing Chinese society, which is called, in James L. Watson's words (1982, 1986), "the lineage paradigm," a tradition founded by

Maurice Freedman (1958, 1966). This paradigm, which once covered nearly the whole field of anthropological studies of China, indeed lay under the shadow of the category of the ancestor. Hsu's monograph was a monument in this paradigmatic tradition of lineage studies on China, which is an important reason why I choose it as an example.[8] The goal of the kind of writing that Hsu exemplified and for which the functionalist ethnographer always hoped was to reproduce a description of the object under study as the object itself. This is a particular case of the general situation in which one may argue that a careful reading of an ethnographic text may reveal more reality than "being out there." Another reason why I chose this work is that, though written by an anthropologist, it is written in a fictional style. Although it is not a novel, it does retain some narrative features of storytelling that characterize what fiction is supposed to be.

Hsu's monograph is an ethnographic account of a rural community, West Town, near Kuenming, the capital of Yunnan province, in southwestern China. The book contains no map to indicate the location of the community. Is this because, like some other anthropological authors, Hsu does not favor the form of (re)presentation that places everything in maps, tables, or figures? On the contrary, Hsu has prepared many maps, tables, and figures (a total of twenty-six) to illustrate various kinds of social and cultural arrangements within the village. Therefore, this omission simply suggests that Hsu saw ethnography as a practice of observation from within—that is, Hsu believed that the ethnographer's gaze was supposed to be cast from the eyes of an outside insider who did not care about the community's location in the wider geography. This is not simply a habit of an anthropologist of that generation; rather, it reveals an epistemological stance. Each rural community, no matter where it was located in China, carried within itself a depth, a trace of time, a history of family tradition, going back to more than a few hundred years. This and only this depth should be considered as the appropriate object of anthropological analysis. This is what Hsu's book is all about: it is about the depth of a community as an "ideal type" of every community in traditional China. Hsu is not, in any sense, concerned with the relationship of this particular community to other ones in the larger social context of society.

This is precisely what the title of the book, *Under the Ancestors' Shadow*, means: there exists, within each community of this kind, a depth made up by its own multilayered shades, and this depth constitutes a space inside itself as an internal source of energy and reference. This is not to say that even that generation of anthropologists saw no reason to consider any outside influence if a different kind of analysis were to be carried out; rather, this internal depth must be considered shaped in such a way as to absorb any outside forces as part of its own darkness. The point is that Hsu's generation of anthropologists tended to presuppose the power of this internal depth as more essential than anything else in accounting for what a community was, a theoretical assumption that made anthropological research on China entirely dependent on the idea of communal depth as the source of experience and existence. It is not important whether Hsu's representation of rural life in Yunnan was true; instead, his text should be read as a simulacrum of that communal depth.

After a brief discussion of methodology and fieldwork, Hsu begins with a portrait of "worldly and otherworldly residence" that shows that in the everyday language of metaphors, there is in conception a metaphysical resemblance of one world to another. In terms of how they were supposed to be talked about, the world of the living and the world of the dead mirrored each other in a common language of "residence." The idea of family was said to be central to the social organization of cultural life in Chinese society, and the Chinese term for such an idea was *jia*, standing both for the meaning of an elementary kin group and the place that the members of this group shared as home. It is important to note that it is not the family as a kin group that defines the place they share; rather, it is the other way around. The place of residence identifies the members of a family as a group. For this reason, both in the preface and at the beginning of the text, Hsu has discussed the problem of wealth in terms of its symbolic expression in the possession of a good house. As Hsu noted, village houses were often built far more elaborately than was necessary for daily living. Why? Because these houses were not simply places to live but served as a sign of power and wealth, as Hsu writes:

> Within this conformity to tradition the houses give evidence of a high degree of competition for superiority. Worldly residences are not so much places to house the individual members in comfort and ease as they are signs of unity and social prestige for the family group as a whole—the dead, the living, and the generations to come. (1948, 40)

One cannot understand the logic of this kinship practice without understanding the conception of the unity of a family as a whole. This wholeness does not simply mean, as Hsu has shown, the inclusion of everyone related in space; rather, it means that each family as a whole has a depth that goes back to its ancestors and points to the future of posterity. This whole extends in time from a remote past to an infinite future.

One's life, understood in this sense, is a link in a chain of existence that is called family. The crucial difference between the Chinese term *jia* and the English equivalent, *family*, lies not only in that the former implies a strong sense of materiality but also in that the Chinese notion of family belongs to, perhaps more evident in the case of traditional society, a category of time, for it indicates not simply a group of biologically connected individuals but a chain of individuals in time. One's own life runs beyond the time that one lives because it is always part of one's ancestors and descendants in a chain of being. This is what Hugh D. R. Baker calls "the Continuum of Descent":

> By this I mean simply that Descent is a unity, a rope which began somewhere back in the remote past, and which stretches on to the infinite future. The rope at any one time may be thicker or thinner according to the number of strands (families) or fibres (male individuals) which exist, but so long as one fibre remains the rope is there. The fibres at any one point are not just fibres, they are the representatives of the rope as a whole. That is, the individual alive is the personification of all his forebears and of all his descendants yet unborn. He exists by virtue of his ancestors, and his descendants exist only through him. (1979, 26)

Baker's explanation captures an important aspect of what Hsu was trying to portray: a person or a self in the traditional moment was constituted in such a way as to include a great deal more than one's own biological existence. To what extent a person can be called an individual in this context becomes problematic. If the English word *person* is used simply for convenience, it must be understood that the notion of a person, insofar as prerevolution China is concerned, presupposes a sense of time that I will call Time as Descent. A close reading will demonstrate that the purpose of Hsu's book is to show how the various aspects of everyday life in West Town were organized according to Time as Descent.

As Baker's discussion suggests, the idea of descent implies continuation on the one hand and anticipation on the other. A person is a continuation of the family made possible by its ancestors in the past; a person is also an anticipation of possible infinite future reproduction of descendants. Time as Descent therefore encodes the chain of past-present-future as that of ancestor-self-posterity, and vice versa. That is, an equivalence is set up between the relations of time and the relations of descent. Equivalence here means a particular kind of conceptual connection—as A.-J. Greimas and J. Courtés put it, "a relation of reciprocal implications between them" (1982, 108). I emphasize precisely this point: the relation of time to descent, or vice versa, is reciprocal, which means that neither could have been conceived without the other in the practice of everyday life in prerevolution China. Such an understanding creates a sense of time quite similar to what McTaggart said of the A-series: a self or a person changes its status of being in Time as Descent, which means that the status of a person in the family, as that of an event in the A-series, is conceived as essentially temporal.[9]

So far, I have dealt with one side of the central thesis of Hsu's book—that is, with the problem of time itself. I have shown that Time as Descent resembles the characteristics of the A-series in McTaggart. Essentially, this sense of time produces a dynamic conception of the self that is relational and that has a changing status (cf. Elvin 1985). However, another side to Hsu's thesis has not yet been discussed: the past and the future, as the two ends of Time as Descent, have different relations to the present, and the past was essentially used as the symbolic resource for the (re)production of good fortunes for present generations, whose behavior and conduct will in turn affect future descendants.

Continuing to read Hsu's book, it becomes apparent that a practical arrangement of everyday life benefited both the family's old and its young. Each chapter in the main body of the book deals with a theme that is presented as a domain of family practice in relation to the world of the ancestors. For example, the third chapter deals with livelihood but is written from the perspective of "Life and Work under the Ancestral Roof." Chapter 4 discusses marriage but puts it under the heading "Continuing the Incense Smoke." From chapter 6 onward, the book focuses more on how the world of ancestral spirits is perceived and received in everyday life by such phenomena as graveyard performance and how the living depend on the dead as a source of social power and prestige. Children were trained to believe in the significance of "ancestor worship." Thus, toward the end of the book, the reader concludes that a Chinese self or person lived under the shadow of his ancestors not only in a practical sense but also in the metaphysical sense that one was conceived as being part of the ancestors' world. According to Hsu,

> The ancestral spirits will help their own descendants whenever they can. They are the spirits upon which the living may depend without any question and to which the living are related, for better or for worse and without any possibility of change. Their behavior in life, as well as in the world of the dead, exerts influence on the fate of their descendants. In turn, their fate is also influenced by the behavior of their descendants. (1948, 241)

The notion of fate is extremely important in the conceptualization of the Continuum of Descent. As Hsu has shown, this relationship between the dead and the living is functional in the sense that the living depend on the dead for spiritual protection because the fate of the living depends on the behavior of the dead, who must be properly looked after to guarantee the fate of one's descendants. Only very close to the book's end does the significance of the story told at the beginning of chapter 1 become apparent:

> When I was about fourteen years old, I overheard a conversation between my father and my older brother, who was twenty years my senior. They were talking about the rise and fall of some families with whom they were acquainted and about the circumstances involved. My old brother concluded with the following observation: "Wealth is treasure of the nation. Every family can keep it only for a period of time. It must be kept circulating." (Hsu 1948, 3)

The story may contain a tone resembling that of Adam Smith because this was said during the 1920s–30s in China, a country that had been excessively concerned with national wealth since the defeat by the British in the Opium War (1841–42). However, what really drew Hsu's attention was his brother's comment on the nature of family fortune: no family could be wealthy forever; family fortune changed residence from one house to another over generations.[10] Precisely because people believed that wealth would change hands over time, it was important to work hard to convince others that ancestors were being properly looked after. Only with the spiritual protection of one's ancestors might one receive (or deserve) good fortune; otherwise, one's family would be destroyed. This is the practical side of the Continuum of Descent: in the chain of family existence, each generation's conduct affects the fate of the next generation. In some twisted sense, this interpretation somewhat resembles Max Weber's famous argument that good fortune is not guaranteed; nevertheless, it is vital to try hard to prove that one gets what one deserves.

In summary, Hsu reveals a very important aspect of what a person is supposed to be in the traditional moment of the modern Chinese experience: one is always conceived as a link in a chain of existence in time— not physical time measured by a clock but Time as Descent conceived as a genealogical continuum. This mode of time drags because particular weight is placed on the past as a source of spiritual energy for the present; this mode of time lags because the present can and may only be legitimized by making reference to the past; this mode of time nags because the dead curse and bless the life of the living. In short, the weight of the past is heavier than that of the present or the future in this genealogical continuum, because the past rather than the present or the future is conceived as the genesis of both symbolic and material sources of wealth. The heaviness of the past does not simply mean that it is the origin of fortune and wealth but also means that the present is shaped by the shape of the past. In this sense, although physical time as recorded by the clock runs lineally, everywhere and for everyone, a person in the traditional moment of the modern Chinese experience lives in a reversed time, the Time as Descent, that orients toward one's ancestors in and of the past. Future dates of importance are marked on a person's calendar only by the importance of the dates in the world of the ancestors.

Time of the Maoist Revolution

Before turning to a discussion of time in the years of the Maoist revolution, I will again refer to Ricoeur (1984), which provides a good example of how novels may be read to reveal particular modes of human experiences of time. Reading Virginia Woolf's *Mrs. Dalloway*, Thomas Mann's *Der Zauberberg*, and Marcel Proust's *A la Recherche du Temps Perdu* as examples of the effects of fictional experiences of time, Ricoeur refers to A. A. Medilow, who distinguished "tales of time" from "tales about time": "All fictional narratives are 'tales of time' inasmuch as the structural transformations that affect the situations and characters take time. However only a few are 'tales about time' inasmuch as in them it is the very experience of time that is at stake in these structural transformations" (1984, 2:101). The three novels that Ricoeur chose are "tales about time"; however, I wish to twist this distinction by arguing, with reference to Ricoeur's idea of reading as a mode of understanding bearing the potential to create a context of conceptual connections independent of the intentions of the author (see Ricoeur 1991, esp. 105–87), that some tales may be read as "tales about time." Authors may not be conscious of their writing as tales about time, but, in a particular mode of reading, such tales may be taken as being about time. During the radical years of the Maoist revolution (roughly from the mid-1950s to the late 1970s), very few novels were published, and everything published was ideological in the sense that it was an embodiment of some sort of the official ideology, which was in essence a tale about time.

Haoran's 1,785-page novel (1964–66) was very popular. Haoran was a revolutionary writer in the sense that he became a writer only because of the communist revolution (see Haoran 1998). The time of its publication was strategic, because it was often read as a prelude to the storm of the Cultural Revolution in the summer of 1966. In the Cultural Revolution, this novel became an example of the revolutionary (realist) novel, one of the very few available fictional readings for the generation of the Red Guards. I believe that this novel also opened up the heroic dead-end path of Chinese socialist realism, in which fictional characters became purely ideological constructs or, as Chinese critics put it, had bones without blood or flesh. In contrast to Haoran's later works, this novel has characters of moderate ideology—that is, they were still portrayed as people rather than simply incarnations of communist ideologies. The significance of this novel to the generation of the Red Guards may be demonstrated by asking them whether they still remember it: my sense is that few have forgotten its opening sentence: "Three years after the death of Xiao's wife, he remained single."[11]

This novel indeed contains a thread of personal life—more precisely, some examples of revolutionary friendship, love, and marriage—but this line of development is allowed only when it is useful in showing how the emotional world of a true revolutionary is supposed to be shaped. According to the logic of the novel, true revolutionaries would sacrifice their personal lives to achieve the higher values of the Communist Party in its struggle for the future of socialist China. In so doing, the revolutionaries would receive respect and love from their comrades of the opposite sex. Nevertheless, to some degree, the existence of this thread of personal life proves that the characters were not yet totally ideologized.[12]

The novel is long but lacks a complicated plot: it is a well-structured tale organized around a number of themes. The central theme is the struggle between Xiao, a village party secretary, a good revolutionary who tries to lead poor peasants along the road of socialist collective production, and Ma, a traitor who pretends to be good, cheats the government, and represents the interests of former landlords who hate socialism and collectivization. The struggle centers on whether peasants should be organized to work collectively. Although the author does not specify the year in which the story takes place, it must be set during the mid-1950s, when the Maoist government began to organize peasants into collective economic operations. The nationwide storm for the organization of people's communes was in 1957–58, and this story, as the author indicates, takes place a couple of years earlier, because the peasants in this village, Dongshanwu, had not yet been organized into a people's commune. The novel concerns how they were trying to move in the direction of collectivization by pooling together land and other production means. At this stage, cooperation in some degree was still based on voluntary participation. In Dongshanwu, everyone began to be organized to work in a village cooperative.[13] The novel shows how poor peasants welcomed the socialist policy of collectivization as a result of their class backgrounds and consciousness; conversely, a group of middle peasants were reluctant to join the village cooperative because of their class roots. Thus, the struggle between Xiao and Ma is represented as a class struggle between poor peasants willing to follow the party for socialism and selfish middle peasants and former landlords who represent the old values of feudalism and exploitation, struggling against collectivization. The main plot of the novel is about how the wheat harvest should be distributed among the members of this village cooperative. According to Xiao, the representative of socialism and the party, it should be distributed only according to the labor contributed to the cooperative by each member of the village. However, Ma and his followers believe that the wheat should be distributed according to the amount and quality of land that each person had brought to the cooperative. During the early 1950s land reform, all properties belonging to landlords and rich peasants were confiscated and redistributed to poor peasants, but middle peasants' property was not taken away.[14] Therefore, even after land reform, many places retained an observable degree of difference in wealth between the poor peasants and the middle peasants. Middle peasants often continued to possess more land and better productive means, such as draft animals, than did poor peasants. As a result, middle peasants were reluctant to join cooperatives, which required pooling together all productive means, including land, into a pond from which one was supposed to receive "income" only in proportion to one's contribution of labor. Some middle peasants believed that they deserved more than the poor peasants because the middle peasants contributed more material means of production. However, the Marxist principle, as it was read during the Maoist revolution, was that labor was the sole source of wealth, and wealth accumulated in any form of private property was the result of exploitation of labor; therefore, collectivization must be oriented toward distributing earnings entirely according to the contribution of labor.

The struggle between Xiao and Ma can be read as one between a revolutionary hero and a representative of the "old society" (*jiu shehui*), as it was called during the Mao years, vaguely equating "old" (before the arrival of Maoist society) with "bad." As in the typical Chinese communist story of a revolutionary hero, Xiao is tested on several grounds, including his personal life. The first stage of the battle shows that Xiao could sense—true revolutionaries were supposed to be able to smell good and evil through class awareness—everything by listening and talking to his comrades and to poor peasants, because these people were close to the party in the habits of their hearts. Ma's attempts to deceive Xiao soon fail. Ma then gathers a group of middle peasants under the name of the masses and encourages them to challenge Xiao's authority as the party secretary and the head of the village cooperative, of which Ma, also a party member, is vice director. As a revolutionary hero, Xiao controls himself and distinguishes his real enemy. Xiao takes the middle peasants one by one, educates them, and finally convinces them that it was both right and good for everyone, including the middle peasants, to distribute wheat according to the contribution of labor because the increased productivity resulted from the collective operation of the village economy. Ma desperately attempts to use his wife's connections to persuade a young woman to seduce Xiao; if successful, this lapse would have been a deadly weapon against Xiao's authority. During the radical Mao years, "immorality" centered almost entirely on sex. Even choosing the "wrong" spouse was a risk to one's future. This effort, like Ma's earlier ones, fails, and Ma subsequently kills Xiao's only son via the hands of a landlord who hates not only Xiao but the entire society under Mao. Xiao pays little attention to his son's disappearance, believing that the class struggle taking place in Dongshanwu is more important than his own son. The future of socialism demands his attention. Xiao knows that Ma has taken away the son simply to distract Xiao from the struggle between the two forces. As a hero, Xiao sacrifices his son for the sake of a socialist victory. Finally, Ma lies to a higher-level party official who did not personally like Xiao very much, but this official soon is proved wrong, and Ma is shown to be a traitor who joined the party because he wanted power, not because he wanted to serve the people. The communist hero, Xiao, wins the battle with blood and loss of life. At the end of the novel, Xiao receives a copy of the *Selected Works of Mao Zedong* and is told that the only way to victory is to understand Mao's teaching.

Although very long, the novel describes events taking place over only a few days. For example, the first volume—627 pages—covers only a day and a half. Why is there no specific reference to the year in which the story takes place? Because it assumes a metaphysical presence of the present as it was understood by everyone in that society during that time. In other words, in an anticipated mode of addressing an audience of Chinese readers whose actual experience of the revolution was still fresh, the novel assumes the presence of the reader in the present time of the characters: *The Sky of Bright Sunshine* was written for Xiao's contemporaries, and their sense of the present-ness did not differ from that of the hero. The notion of "contemporaries" is borrowed from Geertz, who defines it as "persons who share a community of time but not of space: they live at (more or less) the same period of history and have, often very attenuated, social relationships with one another, but they do not—at least in the normal course of things—meet" (1973, 365). In the Chinese socialist realist tradition, this technique of writing presupposes a sense of the present (time) that unites the characters of the story and the world of the audience.

This sense of a present-ness is extremely important because it sets a metaphysical ground on which the communist ideology could be built. If one reads *The Sky of Bright Sunshine* as a tale about time, it is fair to argue that it is in fact a tale about the present, because time for Xiao and his contemporaries was no longer what it had been, as it were, "under the ancestors' shadow," where the present was a continuation or an extension of the past. Under "the sky of bright sunshine," the past, whenever it came into view, always appeared only in the background of the present: that is, a past event or character could be understood only from the perspective of a present one. For example, the story of Ma's past is told in a way that informs readers that he was never a true believer in communism. He was an opportunist when he joined the party. The book reads as if Ma's personal history, like other such personal histories in the novel, were a present past—not a past of the past but a past of the present, a past subject to the domination of the present.

Borrowing a metaphor from Malinowski, one may say that the way an ethnographer enters another culture is like someone joining an ongoing conversation of another people. The conversation bears several layers of a past, such as the existing modes of relations among those people involved, topics discussed, and so on. The functionalist assumption is that although one does not belong to what has been said by this group of people, one can still step into the middle of a conversation, precisely because the past and the present are in the present, from which perspective an ethnographic observation is supposed to be produced (see Bloch 1977). This idea of a conversation is very interesting, but it is important to note that the content of a conversation does not have to be about the present: it may be about the past. That is, "the past and the present in the present" does not have to mean that the conversation in the present can only be about the present; on the contrary, as Hsu's work illustrates, it may be a conversation of the past *in* the present. In other words, in Hsu, this conversation in the present is a dialogue of and about the past. In terms of the content of the conversation through which the changes taking place in Maoist society are understood, the revolutionary conversation, as represented in *The Sky of Bright Sunshine*, was always of and about the present. Through the censorship of the present, past events or characters were made ideologically meaningful. By "ideologically meaningful," I mean that the present was driven by the orientation toward the future.

To use McTaggart's language to compare Haoran's mode of time with Hsu's, both assume a certain kind of conception of time that resembles the A-series, where events or persons are conceived in the chain of past-present-future and change their status of being according to changes in time. However, the difference is that in the case of a lineage, the wholeness of the family grounds the conception of time that shapes the understanding of a person as an embodiment of the temporal chain. During the Maoist revolution, in contrast, the temporal constitution of a self goes beyond a person's immediate circle of livelihood to link his or her existence to the larger context of society. Consequently, Haoran's novel constantly reminds readers that Xiao was not struggling for his own good but for the benefit of many others who did not belong to his family. The breakdown of the family as the grounding for the novel's conception of the chain of past-present-future reinforces community at another level—the level of society—progressing from the past as "the old society," through the present of collectivization, to the future of "bright sunshine," communism's final victory. By saying that this conception of time resembles what McTaggart said of the A-series, I am emphasizing that a clear sense of change is still envisioned in the idea of persons and events. The past, present, and future were still lived by Haoran's characters, but the internal force that drove them was no longer the past.

The difference—a crucial one—between *The Sky of Bright Sunshine* and *Under the Ancestors' Shadow* is that during the Maoist revolution, the present was no longer heavily implicated in the past; rather, the present was freed from the prison house of the past and oriented toward the future. As a result, in Haoran's novel, Xiao and his comrades never used the past to authorize their actions for the present; instead, they always denied the value of the past and presented the present as an unavoidable step toward the future of a mature socialism. In *Under the Ancestors' Shadow*, the present could not have existed without being part of the past, whereas under *The Sky of Bright Sunshine*, it is the other way around: the past exists only as part of the present, which is in turn determined by the future of communism. In both the traditional and revolutionary moments of the modern Chinese experience, both texts conceive of the temporal as the chain of past-present-future, resembling McTaggart's A-series, but the difference is that, in one, everyday life is oriented toward the past as the weight of this chain, whereas, in the other, it is oriented toward the future. Present-ness during the Mao years was detached from its reliance on past-ness as its source of existence and became oriented toward the future. The temporal conceived in this way is Time as Anticipation.

Time after Revolution

Vincent Descombes asked an interesting question at the beginning of his short history of modern French philosophy (1980): "Can the color of time be described?" He was inquiring about the shifting ground in an intellectual history that has greatly affected the Western social sciences in the latter half of the twentieth century.[15] I ask, What is the shape of time in today's China? Before examining ethnographic details to show how Beihai's entrepreneurs have developed a peculiar set of temporal practices, I will first discuss Anyi Wang's tale about time (1995).[16] Wang is an eminent young writer whose novels are very widely read in today's China. This novel may be read from different angles, for example, as a story about women and emotion; I read it as a tale about time because I am primarily interested in the conception of time, implicitly rather than explicitly presented in the novel, although the author may not be entirely conscious of this conception.

The story concerns a woman's life in Shanghai over half a century, roughly from the mid-1940s to the late 1980s.[17] Wang Qiyao is a pretty young woman brought up in an ordinary Shanghai family. While attending high school, a photographer picks her as a model, and one of those pictures appears on a magazine cover with the label "a lovely young lady of an ordinary Shanghai family." Later on, encouraged and assisted by the photographer and a close friend from school, Jiang, Wang Qiyao enters the Miss Shanghai competition, taking third place. By this time, the photographer, Mr. Cheng, has been in love with her for a while, but Jiang, from a better-off family, is in love with Mr. Cheng. Because of her status as "Miss Shanghai no. 3," Wang is picked by a powerful man as his mistress, a condition that she accepts quite willingly. This man buys her a place and supplies her with everything she needs except enough time together with him. By the time Wang moves into her new home, she has cut off all connections with her friends, including Mr. Cheng, spending her life waiting for the man. Although he truly likes her, the man cannot come very often because of his job obligations. The author suggests, but does not state, that he holds a powerful position in the nationalist government. He dies in a mysterious air crash just before the communists come to power, but the last time he sees Wang Qiyao, he gives her a little antique box containing some gold, the best kind of valuable during that period of Chinese history.[18]

The death of this mysterious man is the end of the first part of the novel, indicating the birth of a different social order in the book's second part. In communist Shanghai, Wang Qiyao becomes a nurse, working entirely on her own, using her small apartment as a clinic for those who need simple treatment. She presents herself as a widow, and her neighbors introduce her to some men considered appropriate for her remarriage. She cannot accept any of them because their taste is nowhere close to her past lifestyle. As "Miss Shanghai no. 3," Wang resists the lifestyle in communist Shanghai, which often represents peasant life as an ideal for ordinary people. She retreats into her own world of memory and has only one friend, a slightly older woman, Yan, a housewife from a bourgeois family. They become good friends because of their common stylistic tastes. This friendship expands to include Yan's cousin, Kang, who falls in love with Wang Qiyao. The second part of the novel touches on almost nothing outside this small circle of friends, talking to each other while sitting together in front of an oven and cooking dinner or preparing dessert. The novel mentions no political events. A large portion of the second part of the book concerns the friendship and, later, love between Wang and Kang. One day, Kang brings to the gathering a friend, Sasha, who is half Russian and half Chinese and was brought up in Shanghai. The group's peace comes to an end as a result of Wang Qiyao's pregnancy. She initially decides to have an abortion. Because Kang cannot marry a widow several years older than he and exposure of the pregnancy would dishonor him, Wang sleeps with Sasha to make him the scapegoat for the pregnancy. Although Sasha knows that the child is not his, he takes Wang to the hospital for an abortion, but at the last minute she decides to keep the baby. The situation for a single mother at the time was extremely difficult, with everything, from food to thought, under tight government control. Just before Wang is to give birth, she meets Mr. Cheng on a street corner. The photographer has remained single, and he looks after Wang until her child is safely born.

The second part of the novel ends when Mr. Cheng leaves Wang Qiyao when she, in an attempt to return his kindness and passion, tells him that she would be happy to marry him if he still wants to marry her. Mr. Cheng kills himself at the beginning of the Cultural Revolution (1966–76). The novel's third section covers the period of economic reforms that began with Mao's death in 1976. The third part of the novel describes Wang Qiyao's life through her interaction with her daughter, Weiwei, as well as with her friends. Unlike her mother, Weiwei is a very plain girl, but she has a girlfriend, Zhang, who—though from a very poor family—is pretty and has a good sense of fashion. After learning that Wang Qiyao was once "Miss Shanghai no. 3," Zhang befriends Wang. Zhang dates a large number of boys and dumps almost everyone. On one occasion, Zhang brings Weiwei along on a date but does not continue to see this man. Weiwei takes over Zhang's boyfriend and later marries him. Through a relative, Weiwei's husband soon receives an opportunity to study in the United States, and Weiwei leaves Shanghai. The city of Shanghai in the 1980s experienced a peculiar combination of things, at once new and old, traditional and modern. Some forms of entertainment that had been forbidden during the Maoist revolution, such as dancing parties, came back but were distorted because few young people knew how to dance properly. Wang Qiyao is often invited to teach at dancing parties at private houses, and she is interviewed by a local newspaper about her experiences as Miss Shanghai— people sometimes forget to mention that she only came in third. She is flattered by the attention, but like everything else in the 1980s, the attention soon goes away; and she once again becomes the lonely widow. At one of the dancing parties, Wang meets a young man, nicknamed Old Color, who is tremendously interested in everything old—from the 1930s and 1940s. Old Color is attracted to Wang Qiyao, whose manner and style are far superior to those of members of his own generation. After a long period of resistance, Wang sleeps with Old Color, who is more than twenty years her junior. Although it looks like it will last forever, the good feeling between them ends very quickly when Old Color leaves Wang Qiyao for someone else, unexpectedly disappointing this old woman pretending to be young. Wang desperately even tries to bribe the young man to stay with her for a few more years by presenting him with the antique box, which still has most of its gold, although Wang had sold a small amount of it during difficult times. Dismayed, hopeless, sick, and abandoned, Wang takes to her bed. Zhang's latest boyfriend comes to see Wang, but his real purpose is to borrow money because he is in debt. She refuses, telling him that she has no money, but he does not believe her. He claims that everyone in Shanghai knows that she was Miss Shanghai and an extremely rich man's concubine and that she had been given a great deal of gold. He begs but does not succeed. He returns during the night to steal the antique box, but Wang, unable to sleep, is watching. She threatens to call the police, and at the end of the story, he decides to strangle her to leave no trace of his crime.

This novel is indeed a tale about time, not because time is always explicitly discussed but because, as Ricoeur would have said, the experience of time is at stake in the narrative structure that produces the novel's characters. Time is essential to the narrative structure on three levels. First, the story is structured according to three different periods of time in twentieth-century Chinese history—prerevolution, the Maoist revolution, and economic reforms of the 1980s—that serve as an explicit frame of reference for Wang Qiyao's three different life stages. Wang Qiyao's story does not simply take place with these periods as a background. If it did, any novel set during the second half of the twentieth century in China could be said to be a tale about time. *A Song of Everlasting Sorrow* employs historical periodization as a plot of time to situate Wang Qiyao's life outside the internal clock of history. The character of Miss Shanghai can only be revealed in the juxtaposition of two modes of time: historical time and the personal time of Wang's life. This leads to my second point: the novel treats each character as essentially temporal, which means that, for example, not only does the character of Wang Qiyao live *in* time, but, more importantly, her existence as a person is made *of* time. Time itself plays a central role in the formation of such a character. Finally, by questioning the nature of time, this novel forces the reader to consider the question of what time is in general and the relation of time to existence in particular.

The Sky of Bright Sunshine contains almost no references to time except when it reminds the reader that an event took place in the afternoon or the following morning, and its bridges between sections or chapters rely on internal logic in the development of a character or a plot. In contrast, in *A Song of Everlasting Sorrow* the author constantly brings time to the reader's awareness. For example, there is a seeming contradiction in Wang Qiyao's experience of two forms of time: her growing old, on the one hand, and her frequent feeling that nothing has changed, on the other. Growing old is a physical fact that links to an understanding of time as lineally moving to a finite future. In various ways and on different occasions, the novel repeatedly describes this fact of life. Conversely, however, despite the drastic social and political changes taking place in society, the novel quietly but persistently brings the reader to Wang's experience of time as unchanging. For example, even during the Cultural Revolution, the reader feels as if nothing has changed. Wang Qiyao and her friends meet every other day, in front of an oven, cooking the same kinds of dessert and soup, making the same kinds of jokes, as if time has changed nothing in life. Of course, this mode of time is not historical time outside the character: it is the experience of time inside a person, unchanging, as the author forces the reader to experience through the experience of Miss Shanghai. Why did the author portray Wang Qiyao in this way, not experiencing change despite the context of drastic social and political changes? This is not a question about how Wang experienced time but about how the novel came into existence as an expression of a particular conception of time in the last decade of twentieth-century China. The novel has posed a paradox: what has actually changed in the course of a history full of violence and blood? Because of this seeming contradiction in the experience of time, the novel portrays Wang as doubting change in time. Even when having a child, which is the most evident mark of change for a woman, Wang remains suspicious of any changes in time: "If it were not for seeing the child grow bigger day by day, it would seem that nothing moved in time" (A. Wang 1995, 246).[19]

These doubts constitute the characters' experiences as they are often allowed to return to the past from a present moment in time, as if they could travel backward in history. There is a brilliant love scene between Wang Qiyao and Old Color, who was passionate for Miss Shanghai as the ultimate sign of the old city, for which he lived. Holding each other, often in darkness, Wang Qiyao would tell Old Color stories about her past, but the listener would take these stories as possibilities for the present according to which he designed his life. From time to time, the author informs the reader that Wang would hesitate in her storytelling because there was no longer any distinction between the past and the present.[20] Wang would momentarily feel that Old Color were someone from the 1940s, such as Mr. Cheng. This blurred vision that makes the past indistinguishable from the present for Wang Qiyao is the reality of Old Color. He has great difficulty in conceiving anything as arranged according to the chain of past-present-future because everything in his life—past or present, old or new—exists at the same time. When, after hearing the same story many times, he tells Wang Qiyao that he feels that as if he were from her generation, forty years earlier, running after her on her way to school, asking whether she would like to go to a movie with him, Old Color did not mean that he wished this to be so; rather, he meant that he could identify the past as the present. The difference exists only in terms of who was in the 1940s—that is, a before-ness—but there is no such thing as an internal temporal change. This is precisely what the novel delivers: the breakdown of the chain of past-present-future as a metatemporal coordinate in the organization of events or persons in time. To return to McTaggart's language, the breakdown of this metatemporality means that events in time are now conceived as in the B-series, in which there is only an identification of before-ness/after-ness, a sequence in time rather than the status of being in change. Three identifiable time periods can be used to situate Wang Qiyao's life externally; however, there is no way to conceive her life internally as organized through a chain of past-present-future. What happened in her life is simply a happened that does not determine or even link to the happening. That is, the happened is not a link in the chain of past-present-future but simply a before-ness, recognized only in external time. This novel has introduced a different understanding of the question of change, whether the author has done so consciously or otherwise. In terms of the conceptualization of time and change, the fundamental difference between this novel and *The Sky of Bright Sunshine* or *Under the Ancestors' Shadow* is that in this work, events or persons in time are only identifiable as in the B-series—as events (or persons) arranged according to "after" or "before" one another. They cannot be considered as constituent elements of the chain of past-present-future that accommodates change. Change implies a direction of the movement in time. The B-series lacks such a character in the organization of events (or persons) and, therefore, signifies no change but a sequence measured in the physical flow of time.[21]

I will now turn to a specific set of business practices in Beihai to see how the reading of Wang Qiyao's story is grounded in an ethnographic understanding of the conception of time in today's China. I will consider the example of how Beihai entrepreneurs used time to schedule their meetings and appointments. There was, as everywhere else, a common sense about what should be done next, but there was no such system of time scheduling in Beihai—that is, nothing was supposed to be planned out in advance according to a time schedule.[22] The total absence of any sense of scheduling, as my ethnographic materials show, is a key feature of South Chinese business practice in general. None of the Beihai entrepreneurs with whom I worked or whom I interviewed kept a schedule book or had their secretaries keep one, a sharp difference from Western practice, in which everyone is supposed to keep a date book that records appointments in the near future and traces events attended in the recent past. In the West, it is common to hear someone say, "Oh, I forgot to bring my schedule book with me. I will make an appointment with you later." If one is familiar with such a life, one will likely be surprised upon arriving in Beihai. Beihai's business world runs in the fast lane, and its participants have a full schedule of meetings: how do they manage without an appointment book?

Few meetings were scheduled in advance, and when such meetings were needed, they would commonly be planned over the cellular phone. Part of the reason is that Beihai's businesspeople traveled a lot and sometimes did not know where they would be in the next few days. During the summer of 1998, when I was with him, the Star Group's general manager traveled quite frequently across the country. More than a few times, I heard him respond to requests for meetings, and the requests often began with questions about where he would be over the next few days. He often responded, "How can I know where I am tomorrow?" Then he would ask the person to call him again a bit later in the day or the next morning to see where he would be staying. If someone did call again later, he would do the same thing again to this person. Several times, when I looked a bit puzzled by his reaction, he repeated to me what he had just said: "How can I know where I am tomorrow?" For a Western mind, one needs to plan these things, to create a schedule, precisely because of the uncertainty of future happenings; in contrast, in the Beihai business world, everything was left open to the challenge of time.

There is a sense of irony in his response to other's requests for meetings, but it does not mean that he was joking. He was not making fun of other people; his actions may be understood, at least partly, as a reflection on the ironic situation in which his business was practiced. In 1998 the Beihai Star Group was listed on the Shenzhen stock market, a privilege accorded only to a select few companies. Not all companies would have the same opportunity, and the state administered a strict selection procedure (see Hertz 1998, 44–70). Companies chosen for listing would have very little difficulty in accumulating capital, but being listed required a lot of work. One of the most important tasks involved was dealing with the officials in charge of the selection process. To prepare the Star Group to be listed, the general manager, Haihun, stayed in a Beijing hotel for more than six months to, as he put it, "work" on the officials in charge of determining which companies would be selected. Like many other businessmen, Haihun believed that drawing the officials' attention to the Star Group's case was a necessary first step toward success. To attract this attention, Haihun attempted to get to know each official, which was not always easy because he lacked personal connections with them.²³ It took many weeks for Haihun to accomplish this task. Haihun tried to visit the officials on Friday afternoons, just before they left the office for home, to suggest that they spend the weekend in Beihai, two hours away by airplane. The officials could look at the company itself, thereby providing an appropriate excuse for the trip and avoiding the arousal of superiors' suspicions. Dinners and other forms of entertainment had been tried many times before, but Haihun believed that the most important tactic was to get the officials away from Beijing, where they were timid because of their familiarity with the political environment and where it was difficult to make friends with them. After a long period of persuasion, some officials finally agreed to visit Beihai. Haihun immediately urged them into taxis to the airport, denying them any time for second thoughts, although married men would usually call their wives to tell them about the business trip. After arriving at the airport, Haïhun would see whether the officials would prefer to spend the weekend somewhere else—Shanghai or Shenzhen or Hainan. All wishes were granted. Nobody really cared to go to Beihai to see the company: everyone knew that the real reason for traveling was to take a pleasure trip to South China, a region considered economically more developed and politically less controlled. Most officials simply chose the next flight leaving for South China. Who wanted to waste time at the airport? Was there any plan for such trips? No. Everything was decided right at the moment of *now*. Imagine the scene: A group of middle-aged men, some bald and many wearing glasses, jumped out of a taxi and impatiently stood in front of a huge electronic board listing all departing flights, eagerly searching for the next flight to South China. A decision was soon reached; Haihun hurried to the ticket counter, and the men quickly disappeared into one of the many gates.²⁴

These junkets were purely pleasure trips, and the officials would be entertained, as described in the first part of this book, by the golden production line of entertainment—a banquet of turtles or other rare animals, singing in a karaoke bar with hostesses, and finally a sensual massage by the "invisible hands." The golden production line was the norm in the treatment of the official guests; however, their other desires would also have to be satisfied. On one occasion, I met Haihun and an official at the airport in Haikou, the capital of Hainan province, and noticed that the official was carrying a plastic bag full of live crabs and shrimp in water. He was really fond of steamed crabs but wished to eat only the freshest ones, which meant that they had to be alive when they went into the pot. Hainan is famous for its sea products, and whenever he went there, he would bring fresh seafood back to Beijing. These animals should be able to survive the journey. However, as was often the case, the airplane was delayed for a couple of hours. Some of the animals must have died, because they began to smell. It was a hot and sticky July day, and the air-conditioning did not seem to work in Hainan's very small old airport, which used to be occupied by the military force. Flies began to hover around the plastic bag and people looked suspicious. We finally boarded the airplane, but two of the flies followed us. The airplane was not fully booked, and we changed seats a couple of times, but wherever we sat, the flies followed. We asked the flight attendant to bring us ice and put it into the plastic bag to keep the crabs comfortable. I don't know how many of them remained alive when we finally arrived at the Beijing airport. Before we parted company, the official said to me, "You know why I did this, despite all the trouble? Freshness—the freshness of these crabs. If they are not fresh, there is no point in having them. To keep them fresh, time is crucial. Damn the delay!"

Time is crucial. But this sense of time has nothing to do with what may be understood as "schedule." This sense of time, either in the case of pleasure trips or in that of carrying crabs back to Beijing, is the time of urgency. In contrast to "schedule" as a sequence of events or appointments arranged according to time as an external frame of reference recorded on a calendar, this sense of time is internal to business practice. In a sense, it is strategic, because time itself is part of the activity carried out in time. Friday is marked out not because a sequence of events leads to it but because it is a strategic moment for action. What are the effects of such business practices on those who engage in them? Will their sense of time be affected by such temporal practices? Or the other way around?

A very important factor that needs to be taken into account is the use of cellular phones, which is the technological base for a new mode of communication that allows people to be instantly connected without appointments. When I was in China, the use of such telephones often frustrated me. A typical attempt to meet with a businessman began with my calling to make a dinner appointment. He said, "Why don't you call me later—I mean, before I leave my office—to see whether we can meet sometime, perhaps today?" I waited until 5:00 and called again, only to find out that the man was no longer in his office. I then tried his cellular phone. He answered in his car and told me that he was on his way to see whether he could meet with a business partner for dinner. But this appointment was not definite, and he suggested that I call again five minutes later. When I tried again, he said that the other meeting would not be taking place and he would be happy to have dinner with me. He was kind enough to offer to come to my hotel to pick me up, but he did not want to know my room number; instead, he said that he would call when he arrived in about five minutes. Twenty minutes passed with no phone call, so I called again but got a busy signal. I tried again after a few minutes, and he said that he had been waiting downstairs in the reception area for a while, making a few more phone calls.

This possibility of instant connection relies on mobile communicational means, which constitute the condition of doing business in today's China. This may be called a mobile-phonic space, which differs both from virtual space, where the boundary between the real and the unreal in the conventional sense is blurred, and from communal space, where communication is largely carried out face to face. In some way, the existence of this mobile-phonic space reinforces the conventional understanding of what is real as a result of the reliance on electronic technology. But the reality of mobile-phonic space is out of the immediate physical contact required for the kind of communication in a communal space. In China, many people had no home telephones before acquiring their cellular phones. During the Maoist revolution, only a few officials had private telephones; in the vast countryside, face-to-face contact was the only means of communication, and in the cities, telephones were only available in workplaces. To call someone during those years was an experience with a fixed place or time. The reality of that experience was secured by the identities of real places. However, with mobile-phonic space, such identities of real places no longer play a significant part in the constitution of the experience of communication. Communication is still real—that is, one person hearing another over the phone—but the experience in terms of a shared sense of real places is no longer a condition for this kind of communication. This is the technological base for Beihai's business practices.

As for the question of how people are supposed to be related in such a space, it is quite understandable that those involved in such a mode of communication may develop a different sense of time. The root of this difference lies in the constancy of being able to be reached and the immediacy of possible contact. The constancy means that this is a community of contemporaries—that is, they belong to the same time, which is the time of the present, the moment in which one speaks to another in space. The immediacy allows people in this mobile-phonic space to get instant access to other people, which may explain, at least partly, why scheduling is not terribly important to South Chinese business life. Those with whom I worked or whom I interviewed were always on the phone. For them, time has lost its depth, and the world has become one of constancy and instantness.

The Today-ness of Today

If the genealogy of the self in contemporary China may be sketched, even tentatively, an analysis of the everyday conception of time is necessary. My preliminary analysis suggests that it is possible to view the three moments of the modern Chinese experience in terms of three different conceptions of the temporal. My analysis assumes that the differences in the conception of time may be recognized by taking the temporal as relations of events (or persons) in time. McTaggart's distinction between two basic modes of time recognition, the A-series and the B-series, is used only as a vocabulary for my analysis. The A-series consists of events arranged in time according to the chain of past-present-future. Because each event in the A-series changes its status in relation to the present-ness in which it is supposed to occur, time thus conceived of is essential to understanding change. The B-series consists of events arranged in time identifiable only within the order of these events in a sequence. One event occurs before or after another, which does not measure change, for there is nothing but a sequence in the B-series, and the temporal status of an event does not change. As I said at the beginning of this chapter, I am not concerned with whether McTaggart is right; instead, I use his distinction to show a possible difference in historical shifts in the constitution of the self in contemporary China.

In the traditional moment of the modern Chinese experience, as exemplified in the lineage organization of everyday life, time was recognized as the A-series, in which a person was conceived of as a link in a chain of family existence. There was an equivalence between the chain of past-present-future and that of ancestors-self-descendants. The essence of a person in the lineage self was supposed to change from one status of being to another, and the fundamental source for the direction of change was believed to lie *Under the Ancestors' Shadow.* In the revolutionary moment of the modern Chinese experience, exemplified in the Maoist years, time continued to be recognized as the A-series, but the domain of the temporal was rearranged to be oriented toward the future. The self was no longer imprisoned by the shadow of the ancestors; a new equivalence was created between the chain of past-present-future and that of old society—the Maoist present—communism. An event or a person was conceived as not only changing but also orienting toward the future, a promised future of communism. The past was denied its value and the future was valorized. The present moment of the modern Chinese experience has a conception of time whose fundamental character is to deny the possibility of change in time—that is, to recognize time as the B-series, where the temporal is only marked by after-ness or before-ness. For example, to those inhabiting the Beihai business world, events in time are only recognizable as the arrangements of before or after one another: there is no conception of an internal logic of temporal change.

The word *today* offers an illustrative example of this phenomenon. When *today* is used, it is supposed to express a sense of present-ness. This present-ness, understood in the sense that it indicates the relations of the present to the past and to the future, is pregnant with meaning, by which I mean that this utterance carries within itself—in its womb, if one likes—another connotation. A pregnant word has a double meaning, one overt and the other latent. When *today* is uttered by a person *Under the Ancestors' Shadow,* the utterance, although pointing to a present-ness, is pregnant with a yesterday-ness in its womb. In such cases, the utterance *today* is always "yesterday's today." The today-ness of this utterance is implicated in the yesterday-ness. For those *Under the Ancestors' Shadow,* "today" was always implicated in a "yesterday," and the meaning of *yesterday* was always inside the body of the utterance of *today.* Therefore, the present-ness is, in this case, a presence of the past as the present.

For a person under *The Sky of Bright Sunshine*—that is, during the Maoist revolution—the utterance *today* carried in its womb a connotation of a "tomorrow." Whenever such an utterance occurred, as in the case of Xiao, the novel's protagonist, its latent meaning was always implicated in what it would become. This "what it will become" dwelled in the womb of the utterance *today* for those under *The Sky of Bright Sunshine,* and it was always "tomorrow's today." There was no "today" without being pregnant with "tomorrow;" the today-ness of *today* was implicated in the tomorrow-ness—the future of communism. This tomorrow-ness is, I would argue, inside the utterance *today* as an internal determination of its meaning. The present-ness under *The Sky of Bright Sunshine* is therefore a presence of the future as the present.

For those whose life is part of *A Song of Everlasting Sorrow* or is spent on those pleasure trips, the utterance *today* seems no longer pregnant with either "yesterday" or "tomorrow"; instead, the utterance has become "today's today." In other words, the today-ness of today seems to have become nothing else but today itself. It is no longer burdened by the world of ancestors or driven by the promised communist final victory. This possibility of uttering *today* as "today's today" has brought a very different orientation to everyday life. *Under the Ancestors' Shadow,* the everyday-ness of everyday life was implicated in the presence of the past in the present; under *The Sky of Bright Sunshine,* the everyday-ness of everyday life was implicated in the presence of the future in the present. In contrast, with *A Song of Everlasting Sorrow,* the everyday-ness of everyday life suggests the presence of the present in and as itself. In an ironic sense, one may say that it is pregnant with itself—that is, one is one's own child, which means that nothing comes from outside the present. On those pleasure trips, the game of everyday life is played out within the space of the present.

Of course, my observation here is only tentative, in the sense that I am trying to grasp a historical emergence in the constitution of the self. By no means do I suggest that this new character, portrayed in my ethnographic account of Beihai's business practices, represents the general picture of what is going on in (South) China. It is a truism to acknowledge the diversity of local knowledge or to assert that modern power works as a mechanism that in fact accommodates a dispersed field of strategies and tactics in everyday life. It is also a commonplace to claim that ethnography is partial (Clifford 1986). Given all these restrictions on my argument, however, I still emphasize that a new character demarcated by his ability to utter *today* as "today's today" arises from the historical horizon of contemporary China.

seven

The Being of Becoming

"Being and Nothingness"

One Saturday afternoon in July, a few of Haihun's friends and some of their wives got together at the house of one of his college classmates in Beijing, and after a delicious meal at a luxurious hotel around the corner, they began to play cards. It was a very common form of gathering: when people got together, they tended to play games, most commonly *majiang* (mah-jong) or cards. Haihun's friends rarely played *majiang* but often played a card game, which was said by some to be learned from Hong Kong. The game, *cuodadi*,[1] was simple and closely resembled a card game, *zhenshangyou* (literally, trying to be in the upper stream), widely played in China for many decades. In both games, the winner was the first person to discard all his cards. Four people usually played. In *cuodadi*, points were counted and recorded according to how many cards remained in each player's hand after the winner's hand was empty. A game would be over when one person accumulated one hundred points; the winner was the person with the fewest points. It was a simple game for gambling, though the gambling could be symbolic rather than real. When Haihun and his friends played, each point was worth one yuan, and the winner would make a few hundred yuan in a couple of hours. On one occasion, I talked with a friend of Haihun's who was known as a keen gambler. When he played, each point was often worth fifty yuan, which meant that the winner could make a few thousand yuan or even more in a few hours. He told me that in 1998 he made no business profit, and the only money he earned was through playing *cuodadi*. I hesitantly asked, "How much are we talking about?" "Not much," he replied, "a little more than a quarter of a million"—about $30,000. This may have been a rather unusual case, but I observed that for Haihun and his friends, as for many other businessmen, this card game served as a very popular form of entertainment. As discussed earlier, when entertaining officials or business guests, these businessmen would have to arrange elaborate dinners and visits to karaoke bars, saunas, and massage parlors; when a few friends got together, however, they preferred to play *cuodadi*.

This afternoon was such an occasion. The host, Wenying, had been a college classmate of Haihun two decades earlier, and he was the only one who did not become a businessman, working for the state statistical bureau. His wife, Xiaoying, was away, taking their daughter to a music lesson, a popular practice among a generation of young Chinese parents in the 1990s. In addition to Wenying and me, there were three couples and two more men, Haihun and Laosun. Not everyone joined in the card game. Xiaoying returned and greeted everyone, but she hesitated slightly when she greeted one young woman, the wife of a well-built man, Quanyou. Quanyou's wife, Lanlan, was the most fashionable, perhaps slightly younger than others, properly dressed in a gray suit and wearing carefully applied makeup, unlike the other women. She also wore a pair of glasses of a new design without frames. At first, I thought that Xiaoying had hesitated because of this woman's different dress and makeup, a mark of economic and social status, or because she did not know Lanlan. However, both my guesses were wrong; Xiaoying had held back in greeting Lanlan because Xiaoying thought she knew this woman but could not tell who she was. Like everyone else in the room, they had known each other since they attended college in Taiyuan almost twenty years earlier, although Lanlan was one year younger than Xiaoying. Why didn't Xiaoying recognize her friend? Lanlan looked different. They had not seen each other for about a year, and during this time some changes had occurred in the life of Lanlan. After her graduation, she had worked in a government office in Beijing for more than fifteen years. Recently, however, she had been assigned to invest government funds in the new Chinese stock markets. Her job had changed for two reasons: first, there were too many people working in her office; and, second, the office had some government funds that needed to be invested but no one knew how to do so. She was chosen. Stock market investment was new to everyone, especially in Beijing; it had only become popular among ordinary citizens after the mid-1990s. She learned and became quite successful, making a considerable profit for her office and thereby surprising some people. The profits did not belong to her, but her boss was more than happy to reward her success with a car and a house. Although these things were supposed to belong to the government, she could drive the car wherever she wanted to go, doing business or meeting with friends. Because of her extraordinary investment talent, other people asked her to invest for them, and in so doing, she had made a fortune for herself. About a year before the gathering, Lanlan had begun to frequent beauty parlors, getting manicures and facials. As a result, she looked quite different—younger, her friends said—and Xiaoying had not recognized her old friend. The two women later talked about the benefits of visiting a beauty parlor and how much it cost. Xiaoying agreed with her friend on the efficacy of such visits but withdrew her opinion after hearing that one visit would cost a few hundred yuan, nearly her whole monthly salary.

After a while, Quanyou went to have a nap, and his wife took over his cards. Lanlan was very good at the game, not because she always won but because she was determined to win. Her calculation was accurate, but more impressive than anything else was her decisiveness. She did not hesitate in the slightest. When playing, her countenance was soft, but her decisions were always resolute. The game went on for about another hour, and the players chatted and joked with each other. A main topic of the conversation was whether they should buy shares in Haihun's company, which had been just listed on the Shenzhen stock market. "Shall we give it a go?" Lanlan said, in language difficult to translate into ordinary English. Haihun replied, "Why not? We could use it. We still have room." "Yes, why not?" "So how much can you get?" "Well, a couple of million." "That's all?"—Haihun was discarding a crucial suit—"it is not worth doing it. How much can you make with that amount?" "I can probably get a little more, perhaps four or five million." "Still, it is a small fish. If we want to do it, let us do it well." "How much do you have in mind?" "Don't you see it? A few million can do what? In the end we would get only twenty or thirty thousand for each of us. What is the point of doing it? If we want to do it together, we should at least get ten million. Then we get something for everyone; otherwise, let us just play cards. It is your turn." "Phew, Haihun is now making big money, ah." Wenying, his wife, and others kept silent during this conversation. A few thousand for them would be a good fortune.

The topic was dropped, and everyone concentrated on the game. In the end, when everyone looked a bit tired, Laosun suggested going out. Wenying had kept score, and Haihun had won the most. Lanlan was also a winner. Wenying and another man lost, but no more than two hundred yuan. Those who lost paid the right amount to the winners. And everyone began to say that it was time to leave. While they were talking to each other, Lanlan was alone, sitting on a sofa, watching a cartoon television program for children. For about ten minutes, she did not change her position, sitting almost still on the sofa, her face expressionless. During a silence, she suddenly said, to no one in particular, "There is nothing worth living for." The Chinese word she used was *meijin*, whose meaning is ambiguous, a combination of boredom and meaninglessness.

There is nothing worth living for. The woman who said this was a great business success, able to send her child to a private suburban boarding school that was costing more money than most people could afford. A few minutes earlier, the same woman was so decisive while playing cards and was discussing investing millions. What suddenly changed her mood? Wenying's wife, Xiaoying, was perplexed and kept repeating, "If your life is boring and meaningless, what about ours?" She may have missed the point, because having "nothing worth living for" did not necessarily mean that Lanlan was bored. She may indeed have been bored, but the reason for this boredom was not itself boring. She had fun. She went to the beauty parlor, she had lunch with her husband's friends, she played *cuodadi*, she was happy, she was busy. But she still said this amazing thing: "There is nothing worth living for." To impose my own interpretation on this situation, she was indicating a loss of direction in her life. Life exists only as a road to pleasure, perhaps more than ever before in the history of the People's Republic. Making money and enjoying oneself were possibilities of a new order of social things. Everyone was busy with economic activities and investments, to a greater or a lesser degree depending on their own opportunities and chances. But—let me emphasize this *but* as a reversal of meaning in anticipation—where is one going? Or, more precisely, where are we going? The speed of movement is evident, but its direction is not at all clear. The question of the We—that is, the question of the relationship of oneself to Ourselves within which one's location is supposed be found—is no longer clear. I do not contend that there is no longer any *we*, but the significance of the small *we* cannot be articulated through any *We*. One can still say what we are doing in terms of business, for example, but it is difficult for anyone, at least among those entrepreneurs in Beihai, to imagine any Ourselves. Because of this impossibility in articulating the relationship of oneself to Ourselves, people find it difficult to orient themselves toward anything. Any sense of direction has been lost. People can conceive of what to do next, but they cannot conceive of the significance of what should be done. Life goes on, but the perspective and orientation of life have begun to disappear.

The title of this section, "Being *and* Nothingness," borrowed from Jean-Paul Sartre (1956), means something quite different from what he meant. As Vincent Descombes pointed out (1980), Sartre's work can be seen as an effort to develop a dualist ontology that Alexandre Kojève specified (1969, 214).[2] A dualist ontology, to put it simply, is an ontology of the duality of being—that is, Nature on the one hand and Man on the other.[3] I will now present this complicated enterprise in a simplified version to see why it is useful to borrow this pair of words from Sartre. Kojève expressed the basic idea of this dualist ontology in a powerful metaphor in a footnote to his reading of Hegel:

> Let us consider a gold ring. There is a hole, and this hole is just as essential to the ring as the gold is: without the gold, the "hole" (which, moreover, would not exist) would not be a ring; but without the hole the gold (which would nonetheless exist) would not be a ring either. But if one has found atoms in the gold, it is not at all necessary to look for them in the hole. And nothing indicates that the gold and the hole *are* in one and the same manner (of course, what is involved is the hole as "hole," and not the air which is "in the hole"). The hole is a nothingness that subsists (as the presence of an absence) thanks to the gold which surrounds it. Likewise, Man *is* Action and could be a nothingness that "nihilates" in being, thanks to the being which it "negates." And there is no reason why the final principles of the description of the nihilation of Nothingness (or the annihilation of Being) have to be the same as the principles of the description of the being of Being. (1969, 214–15 n.15)

Rather than writing in words, this is writing in image. Or, as Roman Jakobson might say, it is poetry, for poetry is thinking in image. In this image, so vivid an impression, there is a duality of Man versus Nature as the hole versus the gold. Neither would exist, as a ring, without the other, but the difference is that the gold would exist as something else without the hole, and this statement cannot be reversed. This is a fundamental difference between what is Nature and what is Man. The existence of the hole is a negation of the existence of the gold—that is, the presence of an absence. Thus, nothingness is positive in the sense that it negates. This idea of negation, coming from Kojève's reading of Hegel's dialectics, is an essential quality of Man that is Action. Action negates. Nature does not. This is the "humanization of nothingness" (see, e.g., Descombes 1980, 23–54).

I am not concerned here with whether Sartre's lengthy work has achieved the task it set for itself—to posit an "and" between these two terms. I borrow this pair of words for a particular purpose, not entirely loyal to the author's intended meaning. My writing deals with the question of being understood as a historically situated mode of social existence. It is an ethnography with a message: it is time to suspend the unstoppable urge to move into a domain of politics, where power relations dominate consciousness; it is time, with patience and perhaps some hesitance, to pose the question of being itself to understand *what there is*. The phenomenon of China has posed a basic question: What is the being of this becoming?

To pose the question in such a way reflects my reading of current trends in Western social sciences. As Anthony Giddens wrote,

> Most of the controversies stimulated by the so-called "linguistic turn" in social theory, and by the emergence of post-empiricist philosophies of science, have been strongly epistemological in character. They have been concerned, in other words, with questions of relativism, problems of verification and falsification and so on. Significant as these may be, concentration upon epistemological issues draws attention away from the more "ontological" concerns of social theory, and it is these upon which structuration theory primarily concentrates. Rather than becoming preoccupied with epistemological disputes and with the question of whether or not anything like "epistemology" in its time-honoured sense can be formulated at all, those working in social theory, I suggest, should be concerned first and foremost with reworking conceptions of human being and human doing, social reproduction and social transformation. (1984, xx)

The best example, accommodating or perhaps anticipating Giddens's call, is Pierre Bourdieu's attempt to construct a theory of practice (1977, 1990). His idea of habitus, as I discussed elsewhere (2000, 22–24), is an effort to redraw a picture of what there is (see also Taylor 1993). The recent "practice approach" to social theory intends to rework the ontology of ourselves. Consequently, I have borrowed Sartre's phrase because it points to the same theoretical horizon. My ethnographic account is not oriented toward a revelation of power relations, however defined; instead, I seek to show the meaning of being in the Beihai business world, in which I found a loss of direction in the business of being in the world. This is what I meant by borrowing Sartre's phrase.

Studies of Chinese society often contain questions about the power of the state, and it is common to view the social space as being constituted by state institutions and agents. By no means do I deny the significance of the state in the formation of both discursive and actual practices in China. But I do object to the theoretical vision that makes no distinction between what the state does and what the state effects. For example, Comaroff and Comaroff have made it clear that the term *state* should be understood as both an institutionalized political order and a condition of being: "Consequently, colonialism has been as much a matter of the politics of perception and experience as it has been an exercise in formal governance" (1991–, 1:5).

What is the *state* of being in today's China? This ethnographic account is intended to answer this question. As I have shown, any sense of direction seems to have disappeared. Without any direction in time, it is difficult to utter a clear *We*. This difficulty in the pronunciation of *We* also suggests that the relation of the past to the present and of the present to the future is conceived no longer as temporal but rather as spatial. It is not that it is not possible to hear the sound of *we* but that there is a difference in today's utterance of *we* and yesterday's pronunciation of *We*. The difference is that *We* as a particular form of collectivity presupposes a direction in time, whereas *we* is simply a pronoun. In both the traditional and revolutionary moment of the modern Chinese experience, any utterance of the pronoun *we* was already and always implicated in a *We* as its condition of possibility of being able to be uttered. What lies at the background of my ethnographic focus is the image of the lineage-village organization and the work-unit organization of everyday experience, made through the anthropological lens into a contrast to the practice of business life in Beihai. There is obvious continuity in the shaping of this entrepreneur as a character in the Beihai story of urban (high-tech) development; however, my writing strategy is to defamiliarize the familiar appearance of the face of everyday experience in Beihai. My ethnographic account suggests that it seems no longer to be the case that when *we* is uttered, there is always an implicated *We*. The *We* is blurred; the relation of *we* to *We* is difficult, if not impossible, to articulate. This is the state of being in today's China.

Now, unlike in Sartre, this nothingness may indicate the impossibility of a relationship—that of *we* as a pronoun, signifying a specific social group, to *We* as the imaginary concept of a social totality. Or perhaps nothingness here means the disarticulation of *we* to *We*. This is how I understood what Quanyou's wife, Lanlan, said: there is nothing worth living for. She was not saying that there were not many things ahead of her, waiting for her to deal with them; nor was she saying that she would give up making more money. Rather, she was saying that there was no way to imagine a unity of Ourselves among manifold individual experiences. This is how I borrowed the phrase, "Being *and* Nothingness," by which I intend to draw attention to the question of the state of being in today's China as well as the impossibility of the relations of oneself to Ourselves. An *and* must appear between the two words, signifying a separation rather than articulation of one to the other. The double meaning linked by the *and* is being in the Beihai business world *and* the inability to figure out the business of being in the world.

Subject, Subject Position, and Subjectivity

It is now time to draw some general significance from what has been said—to move on to an analytical plain, to a *terra firma* of theory in which ethnographic details are cultivated. The question of the *We* must be posed from a perspective outside the Beihai story. The perspective that I introduce here is rooted in recent social theory's larger concern with the problem of subject, which has been marked by a number of intellectual footsteps, such as feminism, Lacanian psychoanalysis, and so on. On this matter, anthropologists are perhaps most familiar with the Foucauldian notion of subject as the effect of power/knowledge (see, e.g., Dreyfus and Rabinow 1982, 208–26; Rabinow 1984, 7–12);[4] instead, I hope to take a turn in this forest of theory by invoking Ernesto Laclau and Chantal Mouffe's work (mentioned in chapter 5), which consists of a reevaluation of the Western Marxist tradition in search of a new vision on the revolution of our time.[5] The relevance of their work, insofar as the modern Chinese experience is concerned, is that their discussion is cast from the perspective of "after the revolution," to borrow a term from Arif Dirlik (1994). My discussion will focus on Laclau and Mouffe's understanding of subject and subject position, but first I will reformulate the question of the *We* as a conceptual preparation.

This pronoun is commonly uttered with an emphasized connotation; this emphasized *we* should be understood as a suggestion for a certain social or political position, presupposing a collectivity essential to the utterance as such.[6] For example, the word was often heard in the context of "To resist evil aspects of capitalist global expansion, *we* must act in such and such a way." Or, similarly, "To protect *our* environment, *we* have to fight against the selfish interests of transnational corporations." Different intentions may lie behind the use of the pronoun, but it is undeniable that its employment signifies a political desire for collective action of some sort, and *we* is most commonly uttered these days in reaction to various "local" struggles against the penetration of transnational capital.[7] In such a theoretical orientation, which stresses the significance of *a* people, there lies both the meaning and function of the *we*, from which two questions arise. First, onto what intellectual horizon is or was projected the significance of this emphasized *we?* Second, is this intellectual horizon still an adequate understanding of the contemporary world in which such struggles are reconstituted?

A careful reading of Laclau and Mouffe's work suggests that the implicit connotation of this emphasized *we* points to an old kind of intellectual horizon, deriving its theoretical justification and conceptual energy from the struggles in and of the past. It is practically dangerous and theoretically unproductive without a critique of its inadequate association with a set of old problems projected from a dying horizon of our theoretical conventions. The definition and meaning of this emphasized pronoun must be enriched.[8] Several layers of the meaning of this pronoun relate, in a very complex way, to its functions in various social groups' struggles. In specific, the struggles of an older kind brought three different but related senses of the term: "*we* are," "*we* must," and "*we* know (what/who) *we* are." I will briefly detour to laying out what they are supposed to mean and how they are related to the problem of subjectivity. First, and most commonly, such an emphasized pronoun was intended to indicate the existence of a collective identity as an entity of collectivity. That is, this collectivity was defined as and by the property of a *we*. Its utterance connotes an essence. Uttering such an emphasized *we* was supposed to achieve a political or social solidarity, which would demand some sort of action implied in the second sense of its meaning—"*we* must." This emphasized pronoun was supposed to give the collective agency for the *we*. Third, such an emphasized pronoun further implicated a sense of self-awareness of the position from which it was uttered—that is, an emphasis on the self-consciousness of the *we* as a collective group: "*we* know (what/who) *we* are." In this sense, the *we* was meant to emphasize that *we* were conscious of our subject position clearly shaped against a *they*.

In a way, these three senses of meaning correspond to the triple question of subject, subject position, and subjectivity, for which Laclau and Mouffe's theoretical practice may provide an answer. Unlike Jacques Derrida, on whose work they rely, Laclau and Mouffe's deconstruction of the classic Marxist tradition reconstructs a theoretical landscape by taking up the intellectual challenge of the present. One of the key questions raised by intellectuals in recent decades is whether deconstruction simply leads to nihilism, which provides no answer to the political struggles of various kinds on the ground. Laclau and Mouffe answer,

> The intellectual climate of recent decades, on the other hand, has been dominated by a new, growing and generalized awareness of limits. Firstly, limits of reason, as has been pointed out from very different intellectual quarters—from epistemology and the philosophy of science to post-analytical philosophy, pragmatism, phenomenology and post-structuralism. Secondly, limits, or rather slow erosion of the values and ideals of radical transformation, which had given meaning to the political experience of successive generations. And finally, limits arising from the crisis of the very notion of "cultural vanguard" which marked the different moments and stages of modernity. . . .
>
> An initial reaction to this new intellectual climate has been to become entrenched in the defence of "reason" and attempt to relaunch the project of "modernity" in opposition to those tendencies considered "nihilistic." The work of Habermas is perhaps the most representative of this attitude. Our position, however, is exactly the opposite: far from perceiving in the "crisis of reason" a nihilism which leads to the abandonment of any emancipatory project, we see the former as opening unprecedented opportunities

for a radical critique of all forms of domination, as well as for the formulation of liberation projects hitherto restrained by the rationalist "dictatorship" of the Enlightenment. (Laclau 1990, 3–4)

The devastating reaction to Laclau and Mouffe's position, especially from the conventional Marxist camp, can be imagined, because the alternative space of political representation, set against the bourgeois liberal tradition of democracy and symbolized by Marxism for the Western Left, would likely vaporize if such a position was accepted.[9] For example, Norman Geras attacked Laclau and Mouffe as ex-Marxists trying to be fashionable in an intellectual climate no longer in favor of the Marxist spirit. The nature of this exchange between these authors, which offers a good example of the shifting intellectual climate, is clearly visible in their essay titles: Geras, "Post-Marxism?" (1987); Laclau and Mouffe, "Post-Marxism without Apologies" (1987); Geras, "Ex-Marxism without Substance: Being a Real Reply to Laclau and Mouffe" (1988).

Substance is a word with strong implications of the origin of the Western metaphysical tradition, going back to such thinkers as Plato and Aristotle. In dealing with the character of Greco-Roman historiography, G. R. Collingwood wrote, "Now a substantialistic metaphysics implies a theory of knowledge according to which only what is unchanging is knowable" ([1946] 1994, 42). Conscious or not, many of us are still trapped in this metaphysical tradition, to which Marxism was a good representative (Foucault 1970, 261). This is precisely what Laclau and Mouffe have targeted as a central problem of the intellectual fallacy inherent in the development of the Marxist tradition in the West. For example, according to Laclau and Mouffe, the collective identity of the working class—that is, the proletariat—cannot be taken as a substantial entity defined by an essence of its inherent qualities, simply because it is historically untrue and logically incoherent; instead, the unity of (the working) class must be seen as a theoretical construction of a collective identity, responding to the structure of dislocation and antagonism brought about by classic capitalism as a hegemonic reading of a particular historical situation (see Laclau and Mouffe 1985, esp. 7–41; Laclau 1990, esp. 36–37). Laclau and Mouffe's deconstruction of the Marxist notion of class can be seen as a good example of their overall effort to project their understanding of the contemporary world onto a new theoretical horizon marked by the problem of subject as a central question: given the contemporary conditions of life penetrated by transnational capital and capitalism, how is it possible to locate the subject position of a social group whose subjectivity is always overdetermined and open to question? To quote from Laclau,

> *Any subject is mythical subject.* By myth we mean a space of representation which bears no relation of continuity with the dominant "structural objectivity." Myth is thus a principle of reading of a given situation, whose terms are external to what is representable in the objective spatiality constituted by the given structure. The "objective" condition for the emergence of myth, then, is a structural dislocation. The "work" of myth is to suture that dislocated space through the constitution of a new space of representation. Thus the effectiveness of myth is essentially hegemonic: it involves forming a new objectivity by means of the rearticulation of the dislocated elements. Any objectivity, then, is merely a crystallized myth. The moment of myth's realization is consequently the moment of the subject's eclipse and its reabsorption by the structure—the moment at which the subject is reduced to "subject position." If the condition for the mythical character of a space of the dominant structural objectivity (a distance which is only made possible by the latter's dislocation), the subject is only subject insofar as s/he mediates between two spaces—a mediation which is not itself representable since it has no space of its own. (1990, 61)

"Any subject is mythical subject."[10] This is a strong statement against any essentialist argument on the constitution of the *we*, because "structural objectivity," necessary for defining any subject in substantial terms, cannot be anything other than a myth—that is, a mechanism of suturing dislocated elements into a whole to be considered as an objective reality.[11] Subjectivity is an effect of the structural dislocation; subject position is a moment of fixation in a "crystallized myth"; subject is an act of mediation between the crystallized myth and the effect of structural dislocation: it has no objectivity in itself.

Following such an argument, a couple of points may be made with reference to the question of the *We*. First, it is necessary to address the problem of action. When the utterance *we* is emphasized, as I said, a certain mode of action is often called for. This way of uttering this pronoun presupposes the solidarity of a social group as a collective agent being objective, most commonly conceived in terms of communities defined by geographic locations. Partly as a result of the technological innovations of late capitalism, particularly in the sphere of telecommunication, the conventional definition of a local community, which used to be largely constituted on the basis of real geography, has begun to lose its significance as a natural ground for collective action.[12] However, in this case, there is a misrecognition of the subject position as if it were an objective reality; in fact, it is simply a crystallized myth. What is misleading in this emphasized *we* is the recognition of the subject as substantial in itself. This does not mean that the emphasized *we* should not or cannot be employed in calling for collective action; rather, it means that it must *not* taken for granted; it must *not* be taken as a subject identifiable by its essence. The social contexts of suturing the structural objectivity shift, as do the identities of subject positions.[13] The question is, in what way can this pronoun still be uttered as in the past? Apart from anything else, it is necessary to learn from Laclau and Mouffe to strip off the word's essentialist tails. To put it bluntly: *we* has no objectivity in itself.

Such a reading of Laclau and Mouffe may help provide an understanding that recent theoretical trends lead away from the humanistic conception of history and society. This is not to deny that such a conception might have been effective as a reading of the myth in the past, but one should be aware of the historical conditions under which such a humanistic conception emerged. Such an awareness is a necessary first step in understanding the making of subjectivity as the act of reading or the effect of structural dislocation; it is itself made in history. Therefore, to understand history not only means to understand it from the perspective of the *We* but also means to understand how the *We* is constituted in history. The globalizing process taking place now should be understood as a historical force in itself, in and through which new kinds of human subjectivities are constituted. I contend that without such a recasting of the intellectual horizon, it is quite impossible to utter an emphasized *we* effectively for today's struggles.

This discussion of the problem of the subject, via Laclau and Mouffe, leads to a stance outside the Beihai story of urban (high-tech) development for a theoretical reflection. There are three levels of analysis in this book. The first is the level of ethnographic description, which, like any other ethnographic account, sketches a portrait of the lived world of business practice in Beihai. The second level of analysis tells the story of development from a *we* position to understand a particular vision of the (business) world and its possible future trajectory. The third level of analysis, which is rooted in the current intellectual effort in reworking the social, warns against taking the subject position, the temporary moment of a fixation, as if it were of substance or essence. This is why I have called what I have described "characters." Characters understood in this way are the images of a reading of the reality. This treatment of the problem of subjectivity is not a treatment in its own right; instead, it is a brief but necessary movement to come outside the Beihai story of urban (high-tech) development to show its limits of objectivity.

Conclusion: Memories of the Future

One evening during the last summer of the twentieth century, Haihun was entertaining a group of guests in his Beijing hotel room. The purpose of this gathering was to introduce Haihun's new friends to his old ones. The group members had finished their dinners and returned to the room for a rest. Since there were no particular topics on which to concentrate, conversations were slow and casual. Someone asked where Haihun had been during the past few days. Haihun did not answer immediately and, after a pause, said that he could not remember where he had been. He added, "Well, my memory has gotten very bad over the past few years—since I went to Beihai. I cannot remember anything. Where was I? Where have I been? I don't even remember." He laughed at himself, and others joined him. Everyone laughed, and it didn't really matter. As one friend said, "As long as you don't switch off your cellular phone, I don't care where you are. You were on the phone, weren't you?"

I later talked to Haihun about the conversation. He seriously believed that his memory had deteriorated: "I cannot remember anything these days, though it does not mean that I forget things. There is nothing there in my brain. I have nothing to forget. Nothing. Do you know? Nothing stays there in my brain. When I was in college, I was known for my good memory." Someone told me that Haihun was weak in mathematics in college but that his grades were always good. He studied math much like a foreign language, trying to remember all the examples given in the books and then matching them with similar questions on exams. That was how he managed to get good grades for math and other related subjects. Why could Haihun not remember where he had been during the past few days? Perhaps a better question is not whether he has lost his memory but whether memory (of this kind) has lost its significance for him? By asking this question, I do not mean to generalize about whether Haihun is representative of other Beihai entrepreneurs. I am not concerned with the extent to which Haihun's loss of memory should be explained by his individual character and personal capability. What came out of this striking ethnographic experience is an impression that this sort of memory seems to have little significance for those in the Beihai business world. Whether my feeling is statistically verifiable or not, I believe that Haihun's loss of memory was indeed a sign of the disappearance of any sense of yesterday-ness in everyday business life, which is oriented entirely toward the present—that is, "today's today." This, of course, does not mean that connections or networks of relations do not have histories: old friends indeed have a special value for business. It does means that the life of everything is its here and now. Things no longer have any tails of the past: everything is on the cellular phone; time has lost its temporality.

I will juxtapose this example with another of a very different kind. In the autumn of 1998, Jiang Zemin, the president of the People's Republic of China, visited Japan, a trip that both sides took as a significant event in a relationship troubled by the memory of World War II.[1] In a particularly interesting incident, Jiang, representing the Chinese government stance, insisted that Japan should make an official apology to China, as Japan did to South Korea, to acknowledge the damages caused by its invasion of China. For some reason, the Japanese government refused to do so. Hence, when Jiang was invited to attend the emperor's reception, he wore a Mao suit as a gesture of anger and distrust.[2] Jiang was known to enjoy speaking English and to prefer the Western style of dress.[3] Throughout his Japanese visit, he wore a Western suit; only on this occasion did Jiang wear a Mao suit. This outfit was a sign of a historical sentiment. Dressing in this way strongly criticized the Japanese invasion of China during the war. I do not believe that Jiang's choice of dress was a coincidence. There was an ideological connection between the strong criticism of Japan and the Mao suit that might be taken as a signifier of a particular historical sentiment. This sentiment prioritizes the significance of the past by saying that one must not forget history. By correctly understanding what happened in the past, China and Japan may be able to develop a good future relationship.

This is only the tip of a huge iceberg of difference. This incident invoked two different senses of the past. First, there is a sense of the past taken as an essential moment of the chain of past-present-future. As discussed in chapter 6, this sense of the past is recognized as an inseparable link in the whole temporal chain. Furthermore, it is conceived that within this whole, a force of determination runs from the past to the present and then to the future. The past has a weight, so to speak, of and on its own. The other sense of the past differs because it takes the past only as a piece of a whole. In a similar way, the present and the future are also taken as pieces of the same whole, which can be composed and recomposed according to the needs of situation or perspective. The past in this understanding has lost its weight and become slender. When Jiang was in Japan, whenever he referred to history, he was employing the first sense of the past, whereas the Japanese officials often used it in its other sense. This was the main reason why both groups were puzzled by the other's ignorance. For Jiang, without a "correct" understanding of the past, there is no possibility of talking about the present or the future. Conversely, the Japanese take the stance that it is proper to look into the possibilities of a future to deal with the current relationship between China and Japan, even if there is disagreement about how to reevaluate the past. The difference was not a difference of opinion in the sense that they disagreed on a commonly held subject; rather, it was a difference in presupposition. They stood on two different planes of historical presuppositions.

This difference is not reducible to the domain of geopolitical analysis. The difference between Jiang and his Japanese counterparts, to put it simply, is one between two forms of historical sensitivity. To borrow a distinction from Joseph R. Levenson, for Jiang, the war and violence of the past were "historically (really) significant." In contrast, the Japanese officials saw the war as "(merely) historically significant." "We may describe an item in the human record as historically (really) significant or as (merely) historically significant. The distinction is between an empirical judgement of fruitfulness in time and normative judgement of aridity in the here and now" (Levenson 1965, 85). That is to say, the history of war and violence was merely *historically* significant (a dead subject for the here and now) for the Japanese officials, but for Jiang it was really historically *significant* (the point of departure for any understanding of the present and the future). These two forms of historical sensitivity, representing two families of views, shape and are shaped by two different modes of memory as different ways of being in history. Memory's significance lies in its function in enabling people to relate themselves to what actually happened. Put another way, memory is the vehicle by which to travel in history.[4]

What is the meaning of this juxtaposition of two examples of memory? It is quite clear that, in terms of relations of oneself to the past, Hai-hun's case is closer to the Japanese officials' indifference to history. In other words, Jiang's historical sensitivity was perhaps more distant from Haihun than was the Japanese one, although this does not mean that Haihun would not when necessary take up the official stance against the Japanese invasion of China. In both the Beihai business world and the Japanese official world, the utterance *today* does not carry within its womb a *yesterday*. It is important to note that I am dealing with two dis-cursive formations of sentiments, not the individual adoption of either of these possibilities as a situational practice. Further, in today's China, what is taken as really historically *significant* in the official world is con-sidered as merely *historically* significant in the Beihai business world. As a result, all the official slogans and ideologies were turned into jokes, often sexual ones. By saying this, I intend to suggest that there is an increasing gap between what is going on in the lived world of business practice and in the official world. I see an emergence of two modes of memory as two different ways of being in history. The official story of Ourselves, whenever it is needed to be told, has remained somehow old-fashioned and mirrors nothing in the Beihai business world.

For an entrepreneur, the difficulty is that he is unable to tell a story about himself in relation to any Ourselves. That is, he knows what he wants to do only for the reason of doing it. Apart from the practical sense of doing business, the hero (*laoban*) in the Beihai story of urban (high-tech) development is losing his perspective on himself. In a metaphor, he could not see the (moral) ground on which he is standing. As MacIntyre put it,

> Man is in his actions and practices, as well as in his fictions, essen-tially a story-telling animal. . . . [T]he key question for men is not about their own authorship; I can only answer the question "What am I to do?" if I can answer the prior question "Of what story or stories do I find myself a part?" We enter human society, that is, with one or more imputed characters—roles in which we have been drafted—and we have to learn what they are in order to be able to understand how others respond to us and how our responses to them are apt to be construed. (1984, 216)

"Of what story or stories do I find myself a part?" Human animals should be able to articulate a relationship of oneself to Ourselves. This does not mean that each person in society has the same relationship to the larger forces of that society; rather, it means that there is always this question of the *We* that must be answered for us to know where we are in a moral or an ethical sense. In today's China, there is a great difficulty in answering the question "What am I to do?" or "What am I doing?" because the question "Of what story or stories do I find myself a part?" cannot be answered. That is, today's China is characterized by a conjuncture between the impotence of the official world and the inability of (Beihai's) entrepreneurs to tell stories about Ourselves.

Notes

Preface and Acknowledgments

1. Marshall Sahlins used the phrase "the structure of the conjuncture" to mean "the practical realization of the cultural categories in a specific historical context, as expressed in the interested action of the historic agents, including the microsociology of their intention" (1985, xiv). This is different from—as Sahlins himself was referring to—Braudel's use of a similar phrase, "a history of conjuncture." I am using this term here in a way that is closer to Braudel's meaning. For an original account of the meaning of the term, see Braudel 1972, 2:892–900; see also Braudel 1977, 1980. For a general discussion of the French historical revolution by the Annales school, particularly Braudel's place in it, see P. Burke 1990.

2. That the village should be the most appropriate site for anthropological investigation in China was first formally announced by Radcliffe-Brown, a founding father of structural functionalism, when he visited Beijing in the mid-1930s. For a brief discussion of Radcliffe-Brown's proposition and an example of such research, see Fei's influential monograph on peasant life in China (1939, esp. 4–5). Western missionaries had written a number of much earlier works on village life in China; see, e.g., A. H. Smith 1899.

3. For the anthropological debates on fieldwork and writing in the past two decades, see, e.g., Rabinow 1977, 1986; Boon 1982; Fabian 1983; Sperber 1985; Marcus and Fischer 1986; Clifford 1986, 1988a, 1988b, 1988c; Sangren 1988; Geertz 1988; Fardon 1990; Stocking 1992; James, Hockey, and Dawson 1997; Gupta and Ferguson 1997.

4. Geertz later referred to Wittgenstein in a footnote (1973, 405 n.45). See Taylor 1985 for a general account of the theories of meaning.

5. Geertz indeed said that "culture is public because meaning is" (1973, 12).

6. For example, Mintz struggles in arguing against Mary Douglas's semiological approach to the question of meaning in food by saying that "social eating is precisely that: *the social*, involving communication, give and take, a search for consensus, some common sense about individual needs, compro-

mise through attending to the needs of others" (1985, 201). Here my concern is not with who is more acceptable in the analysis of meaning in food; I would like to point out the simple fact that the definition of the social in Mintz is too vague to be useful.

7. Lyotard defined the postmodern as "incredulity toward metanarratives. The narrative function is losing its functors, its great hero, its great dangers, its great voyages, its great goal" (1984, xxiv). I argue that this condition of life poses a moral or an ethical question for those in (South) China. As I will show, this does not mean that they do not hope to say something about their place in society but simply that they cannot.

8. For some recent examples of interesting research on South China's economic development, see Lee 1998 (on Shenzhen women factory workers); Hertz 1998 (on the Shanghai stock market); Hsing 1998 (on Taiwanese investment in South China); Wank 1999 (on Xiamen's entrepreneurs).

Chapter 1. The Dance of a Nissan

1. It is useful to compare Guangxi with its neighbor, Guangdong. In 1998 Guangxi had a population of 46.75 million; a GDP of just over 0.19 trillion yuan; and per household expenditures were 2,040 yuan. Guangdong's population numbered 71.43 million; GDP was just over .79 trillion yuan; and per household expenditures were 4,686 yuan (National Bureau of Statistics 1999, 62–63, 72, 113).

2. For a brief account of the events taking place during these early reform years and the reason for having "coastal open cities," see *Zhonghua* 1996, esp. 1234–35.

3. The illusion that the central government would invest heavily in Beihai to make it another Shenzhen was generated by a chain of important visits by the highest officials from Beijing: President Jiang Zemin came in November 1990; Wan Li, chair of the People's Congress, in November 1991; Vice Premier Wu Xieqian in November 1992; Premier Li Peng in December 1992; Vice Premier Zhu Rongji in January 1993; and Li Ruihuan, chair of the Congress of Political Alliances, in April 1993. This list includes almost every important top political leader. Either during or before their visits, all the leaders except Zhu Rongji wrote blessings for the city, and all these writings were painted on huge posters erected at major intersections between the airport and the city center. Jiang's blessing, "A latecomer with great expectation" (*houqizhixiu qiantuwuliang*), was most interesting, indicating that Beihai had not developed as much as other cities but would catch up in the future.

4. In an irony, Beihai's streets contained very few Chinese cars. Most cars came from other countries, such as Japan, despite the high taxes on and strict rules for importation of foreign cars.

5. In a strict sense, the first generation of students returning to Chinese universities after the Cultural Revolution should be the class of 1977, but their exams were organized by each province. Because of the chaos in the educational system, the 1977 class did not attend college or university until the spring of 1978, which means that year was the true historical marker for this dramatic change.

6. For the story of how Haihun became a businessman, see chap. 5. Here I hope to clarify a point with reference to the idea of an informant. A significant characteristic of this project is that it truly constitutes multisited field research spanning more than three years, roughly 1998–2000. In collecting ethnographic materials, I went to several cities, including Beihai, Nanning, Haikou, Shenzhen, and Beijing, where the past of the Beihai Star Group lingers. As articulated by Marcus (1995), "multisited fieldwork" means more than simply traveling to different places. I agree with Marcus's view, but I mean to stress something quite different. For such a project as this, it will be very difficult to produce a coherent account if one is lost in often redundant collections of interviews and notes. It is very important to construct a number of referential loci, such as making some key characters appear at the foreground of the description, through which some sort of coherence of an ethnographic account may be achieved. Haihun will be used as such a referential locus. The choice of some of these "informants" in my writing must be understood in this sense because they produce a space for the concentration of descriptive details.

7. I knew none of the love songs that people enjoyed singing. The few songs that I knew were from the Maoist revolution. I was asked what I would like to sing, and I hesitantly mentioned the name of a revolutionary song. Everyone looked at me as if I were an extraterrestrial.

8. The literal meaning of *shi* is "thing." Normally, to say that this (thing) is done, a verb, *zuo* (make or finish) is needed. When Tu used the word *shi*, he usually left out the verb.

9. A possible danger of invoking Goffman's work here in this way is that one may be misled into thinking that the situation into which a businessman communicates with an official is like a face-to-face encounter in everyday life. Although it is a face-to-face experience, it should not be considered "the presentation of self in everyday life" (Goffman 1959), because what is involved in this encounter is not two individuals in the strict sense of the term; instead, they are characters given birth by two different social forces. Therefore, what needs to be analyzed is not strategies or tactics involved in the "interaction ritual" or "behavior in public places" (Goffman 1967, 1963) but the characteristics of these forces in specific situations. The difference is how we wish to consider the significance of these situations. They are not, in my treatment, the end but the means of analysis.

10. Such ideas as social or symbolic capital are not alien to Chinese people. For example, during the years of the Cultural Revolution (1966–76), a most

popular phrase was "political capital" (*zhengzhi ziben*), and many people, consciously or not, indeed envisioned the political or the social world through the metaphors derived from the theory of political economy. Bourdieu's theoretical contribution, in my view, lies in his insistence on the importance of distinguishing the intellectual relation to the object—that is, the observer's relation to practice, from the practical relation to practice (see esp. Bourdieu 1990, 34). To do so, one must first be aware of the possibilities of transgressing metaphorical boundaries established in our disciplinary traditions.

11. The way that they asked this question about my earnings was very much like the way that I was interrogated when doing fieldwork in a northern Shaanxi village in the early 1990s. The villagers were very direct in their questioning and distrusted me when I told them how much I earned as a university teacher in Beijing. They thought I was lying about my income, which was a few hundred yuan (less than fifty U.S. dollars). My point is that there was no difference between these two categories of people in terms of asking this question, though they believed that they belonged to two entirely different worlds.

12. A few days after Nee and Tu left Beihai, I heard some interesting stories about their visit. Tu was said to be unhappy about the massage girl chosen for him, but he did not complain because he thought that the girl was selected particularly for him and, therefore, he should not express his dissatisfaction. But just before he left Beihai, he told Haihun that the girl had some skin problems that looked unhealthy and scary. In relating the story, Haihun laughed: "This man is a bit stupid. If he had told us, we would have been happy to get him another girl he liked. Look at Nee Chuzhang, who is a clever man. He specified the girl from Shandong, whom he knew from his last visit here. The girl was brought to his room. What a clever man!"

Part I

A note on the epigraphs. Both translations are mine. Mao's words were known to everyone who grew up during the Cultural Revolution, and this was probably the most famous quotation from Mao, printed at the beginning of his little red book. When the entrepreneurs made fun of the official ideology in the late 1990s, they kept the structure of the sentence exactly the same but changed *Communist Party of China* to *Bank of China* and *Marxism and Leninism* to *chihepiaodu* (literally, "banqueting and getting drunk and having sex with prostitutes and gambling"). For a better English expression, I translated *chihepiaodu* as "sex, money, and consumerism," which I believe captures the spirit of the original purpose of the linguistic twisting.

Chapter 2. Characters of the Story

1. For three examples of such a writing strategy, see Firth 1936; Abu-Lughod 1986; Liu 2000.

2. For a discussion of the characteristics of the Malinowskian type of field-work, see Kuper 1996, 22–28; Stocking 1984, 1986.

3. The recent interest in invoking Mikhail Bakhtin's work is a good example. Bakhtin has paid particular attention to the problem of a special class of discourse, "indirect speech," as constituting a special layer of social reality signified by the quotation marks. See Bakhtin 1986; Volosinov 1973, esp. pt. 3, chap. 3.

4. In the field of anthropological studies of China, a recent example is Anagnost 1997, which is theoretically challenging but has little ethnographic coherence.

5. For commentaries on MacIntyre's work, see Horton and Mendus 1994; Knight 1998.

6. See, e.g., Benedict 1934; Wallace 1961.

7. For a brilliant critique of functional anthropology that created the image of fieldwork as walking in a village, see Boon 1982, 3–26.

8. Readers should not consider mentions of individual officials as referring to their personal qualities. Instead, using them as examples, I seek to reveal the qualities of the official as a character in the story of development.

9. I will address the question of corruption later. It suffices to say here that corruption is a cultural category, and the full meaning of it must be revealed in its own historical context, to which this entire book is devoted.

10. For some theoretical reflections on the question of postmodernity, see Lyotard 1984, 1997; Jencks 1986; Habermas 1987; Hassan 1987; Jameson 1991, 1998; Anderson 1998.

11. For a discussion of the problem of model, see, e.g., Lévi-Strauss 1976.

12. In terms of the content of their research, Schram (1987) differs from Shue (1988). Schram brings together European studies of the similarities between imperial and subsequent China with particular reference to the symbolic representations of power. Shue focuses primarily on the process of the reconfiguration of rural society into the web of the state power during the Maoist revolution.

13. Anthropologists and philosophers have devoted considerable attention to the problem of implicit meaning or practical knowledge—that is, meaning as assumed and knowledge as embedded. For a range of discussions on this subject from different theoretical perspectives, see Douglas 1975; Polanyi 1962; Polanyi and Prosch 1975; Bourdieu 1977; Giddens 1984.

14. See Gates 1996 for a discussion of what she called "a tributary mode of production," managed by the state, that runs parallel to "the petty capitalist mode of production" that characterizes the Chinese capitalist spirit in everyday life. Hsing 1998 provides an interesting example of how the Taiwan connection has affected economic development in the coastal areas of South China.

15. Weber became quite fashionable among Chinese intellectuals in the 1980s and 1990s, and a large number of his works were translated into Chinese.

Weber's rise on the Chinese intellectual horizon is both an indication and a result of the decline in the interest in Marxist theory. For a discussion of intellectual trends in postreform China, see Cao and Wei 1992; J. Wang 1996.

16. For a recent collection of essays discussing the significance of the idea and organization of the work unit in China's economic transition, see Lu and Perry 1997. For an account of everyday experience in urban China during the Maoist revolution, when everyone was working for and within a work unit, see Whyte and Parish 1984.

17. For a discussion of the trends in the development of a private sector in China since the late 1970s, see Zhang, Xie, and Li 1994.

18. For an anthropological account of the image of the peasant in the 1990s, see Liu 2000, esp. chap. 1.

19. A Chinese friend of mine from London told me about an embarrassing experience when he went back to China in 1993. He went to Hainan for a conference with a group of old friends who had become businessmen. It was a rather formal meeting, with local officials present, and whenever the group had a meal, he was asked to choose a *xiaojie* to accompany him to drink and eat. He had been in Britain for six or seven years prior to the trip and was not accustomed to being fed by a young girl. His friends laughed at his embarrassment and called him uncivilized.

20. I read a similar story in a Chinese novel (see Q-H. Wang 1997, 32). I cannot be certain that the story I heard from this young man was not a rehearsal of his reading of the novel. The source of this story does not affect my argument, however. My point is that there is a narrative structure that conditions the way in which stories about business and society may be told.

Chapter 3. A Theater of Desires

1. This is the second time that I have invoked this sense of newness, which deeply impressed me. See chap. 1 for a discussion of this sense of newness when traveling in Beihai for the first time. The significance of it will be fully discussed in chap. 6.

2. For a discussion of different theories of power, see Lukes 1986.

3. A careful reader may find that this language somewhat resembles Kojève's reading of Hegel: "Therefore, to desire the Desire of another is in the final analysis to desire that the value that I am or that I 'represent' be the value desired by the other: I want him to 'recognize' my value as his value" (1969, 7). The difference is that, in my analysis, the substantialist tone is removed because I am dealing with how people envision society and business by telling stories about them. Desire is a quality of the character.

4. The smallest rooms in such establishments would be for only two persons—lovers, perhaps—and would not be larger than a few square meters. Most rooms would accommodate small groups of people.

5. It is difficult to generalize about how much the *xiaojie* earned. But some extremely detailed and interesting examples of their earnings were provided in Pan 1999, which was based on his heroic fieldwork (i.e., participant observation) in two prostitute communities (see esp. 239–46). Pan's impression was that it was not easy to make money because of the intense competition among the many available sex workers.

6. All of these names consist of three Chinese characters, with only one character different: *xian-yu-dian* (Fresh Fish), *xian-rou-dian* (Fresh Meat), *xian-pi-dian* (Fresh Beer), *xian-hua-dian* (Fresh Flowers). *Xian* means "fresh"; *dian* is "shop." By changing the middle character, an entirely different name is formed.

Chapter 4. A Grammatology of Pleasure

1. For some classic examples of literary studies of narrative, see Booth 1961; Scholes and Kellogg 1966; Kermode 1967; Burke 1969.

2. See, e.g., Gallie 1964; M. G. White 1965; Danto 1965. See also Mandelbaum 1967; Goldstein 1976.

3. See also H. V. White 1978, 1987; Attridge, Bennington, and Young 1987; Certeau 1988.

4. The choice of memory as an example is not random. There has been great interest in the studies of memory as a new approach to our experiences of the past. There have been some very interesting pieces of writing on memory (e.g., Nora 1989); however, I do not think that the theoretical foundation for such discussions has been properly built. It is too easy for the anthropologist to slide into the slope of thinking about *How Societies Remember* (Connerton 1989), with little or no knowledge of the nature of memory itself. A discussion of memory via time will be the main theme of the second part of this book.

5. See, e.g., Merleau-Ponty 1962 for a discussion of the significance of perception for the phenomenologist as well as of the difference between the objective space of geometry and the space as lived experience. For a clear and short introductory treatment of the basic phenomenological concepts, see Sokolowski 2000. For a detailed discussion of the phenomenological movement's twists and turns over the past century, see Spiegelberg 1994.

6. Schutz's general theoretical undertaking by bringing Husserl and phenomenology to the social sciences and his particular engagement with Weber's theory of action (via the debate with Parsons) are relevant in a double sense: on the one hand, the common-sense world is taken for granted, and its unconscious, habitus structure is not transparent to the actors involved; on the other hand, in challenging Weber's individualistic approach to the question of meaningful action, Schutz tried to develop a more systematic treatment of meaning in everyday life by introducing a whole set of phenomenological tools (see Schutz 1967). For a general discussion of Schutz's work in relation to German

philosophy, see Bubner 1981, 40–43; for short, good introductions to these two aspects of Schutz's work, see Natanson 1967; Walsh 1967. For a critique of Schutz's phenomenology of social action, see Carr 1986, 37–38.

7. See Radcliffe-Brown 1952, 1957. Returning to these classic writers on human action and social structure is not beating a dead horse, because the problem is that we sometimes cannot even see our own feet, let alone the ground on which we stand. It is in this sense that I have said that the objective of this inquiry is to find out *what there is*. This statement should not be read as if I am totally rejecting the critical impulse of the contemporary inquiry; the point is to strengthen it. For me, this strengthening cannot be done without constructing a genealogy—in the Foucauldian sense—of *a longue durée* of our theoretical visions.

8. With Parsons and Schutz setting the background of social theory, one is able to see much more clearly the reason and motivation for some recent reflections on the problem of action and agency. The best example of such reflections is Bourdieu's notion of habitus and practice (1977, 1990); for an ethnography of the logic of practice in rural China, see Liu 2000.

9. See, e.g., Anagnost 1997; Rofel 1999.

10. Paul Ricoeur is one of the theorists against whom Bloch was arguing.

11. I am moving into a theoretical lane of narrative and time because I believe that some recent studies on China have been weak in terms of theoretical formulation. In a very broad sense, there are two approaches to the studies of contemporary Chinese society, one historical and the other comparative. The historical approach, which is not taken simply by historians, is based on an assumption that an understanding of China relies on a reading of the present in the light of a unique shape of its recent past, the Maoist revolution. The question of the past and memory is an interesting one (see, e.g., R. S. Watson 1994; Jing 1996); however, the problem, it seems to me, is not what people remember or forget for political reasons but the forms of memory that cultivate our different ways of being in history. The weakness of this approach is that it often takes for granted what is supposed to be meant by memory. To deal with the problem of memory, as I have argued, one must take up the question of time.

The comparative approach is of a particular flavor—that is, it tends to place China together with other former socialist countries, mainly in Eastern Europe, and to focus on the transition of these societies from socialism to "postsocialism." This link, this possible comparison, between China and other former socialist countries in transition relies on an assumption that similar organizations of social and political life existed under different modes of socialism. To compare, however, they must also differ. Hence, this comparison requires specific historical and cultural knowledge of these countries in their own contexts. Therefore, one may say that the comparative approach presupposes the necessity of some historical understanding. Thus, one comes back to history, which—to me—means coming back to the ways in which different stories are being told. This is why I see as necessary a discussion of the problem of narrative, time, and subjectivity.

12. In terms of the density and popularity of the gamelands, there is no comparison between the United States or Europe and Japan. In Japan (Tokyo in particular), almost every street corner has a gameland, just as every London corner has a pub or every San Francisco intersection has a gas station. A special kind of gameland, Pachinko, is more like low-stakes gambling and is quite different from the normal gameland discussed here.

13. In the United States in particular, the term *virtual reality* is more associated with the cyberspace generated on a computer. However, if a distinction is needed, I would argue that Japanese virtual reality is more public or collective, whereas in the United States, it is private or individual.

14. The sharp difference between urban and rural China in all aspects of life, especially during the Maoist revolution, has been extensively commented on. However, such discussions often focus on the issue of inequality and the system of control installed by the Maoist revolutionary government (see Potter and Potter 1990, 296–312; Cohen 1993). It is much less mentioned that, as a result of such governmentality, two different ways of being emerged in society.

15. Some clarifications may be needed regarding the problem of anthropological methodology. I have been trying to show not only the dilemma for anthropology as an academic discipline but also a crucial shift in the condition of contemporary life—crudely put, there is no longer a natural association between truth and actuality. This concern differs in theoretical orientation from the 1980s debates on ethnography and writing, which were very much about the question of power, for example, asking questions about who was able to write about whom under what kinds of power relations (see, e.g., Fabian 1983; Clifford and Marcus 1986). My concern is different: I want to look into the body of experience to understand what reality means today and how it may be reconceptualized.

16. Propp's work was published in Russia in 1928 but was not translated into English until 1958. For general discussions of the formalist movement, see Erlich 1955; Jameson 1972, pt. 2.

17. Following François Dosse, I am inclined to view so-called poststructuralism as part of the structuralist movement. Nevertheless, Foucault said, "Structuralism is not a new method, it is the awakened and troubled consciousness of modern thought" (quoted in Dosse 1997, 1:vii). This work marked a turning point in his intellectual development as well as the end of his early period. Of course, this statement does not mean that there is no conceptual rupture between what is now customarily viewed as the early Foucault and the later Foucault, the early and the later Barthes, and so forth. The point is that there were continuous flows of concerns and themes yet conceptual breaks

and theoretical departures. For this reason, I believe that *post* should be in parentheses: (post)structuralism.

18. By saying this from a perspective "after the revolution" (Dirlik 1994), I do not mean to suggest that there was no reason, embedded in a historical sentiment and rationality, for the socialist ideology of art and literature to have taken the form it did. The socialist state encouraged realism and censored other forms of art and literature. If, for example, the question is why the modernist impulse had to be censored or why realism was important to socialism, Lukács 1962 may provide some illumination. Lukács was trying to define how socialist realism differed in nature from bourgeois art or literature, and he made a number of distinctions that may be useful in thinking about the mentality of the socialist state in censoring other forms of art and literature.

The first distinction he draws is between modernism and realism or, more precisely, between bourgeois modernism and socialist realism. Modernism includes a large number of different contemporary forms, and the wide range of authors Lukács discussed includes Thomas Mann, Musil, Kafka, Joyce, O'Neill, Proust, Becket, Faulkner, and Sholokhov. The fundamental difference, according to Lukács, is that modernism deprives literature of a sense of perspective. In contrast, socialist realism always entails a perspective. What does this mean? First, literature as a whole is determined by its subject matter, content. It is not simply a play of forms, detached from what is written about. Bourgeois modernist writing, which developed particularly in the late nineteenth and the early twentieth centuries, was often simply a play of artistic or literary forms. As a result, the organic relationship between literature's form and content was cut off. The socialist movement was a reaction to this phenomenon. Second, "perspective" implies a correct understanding of the historical development toward socialism, which certainly presupposes a historical destiny outside literature. Socialist realist writers were therefore supposed to capture the trace of this historical necessity.

The other distinction Lukács made concerns different forms of realism. One of them is what Lukács called "critical realism"—for example, in the writing of Balzac or Dickens. Lukács used the term *critical* in a manner very different from how it is used today. In his use, it means more a sense of criticizing the existing order of capitalist societies. Critical realism criticizes but lacks a clear vision of the direction in which history travels. The difference between critical realism and socialist realism is that the critical vision in the former is cast from outside—that is, the former does not see the form of literature as an integral part of the historical necessity of socialism. Critical realism can show the irony or the exploitative nature of capitalism but cannot tell where the future lies. In terms of capturing the direction of human society and history, socialist realism describes it from inside. Literature is part of human emancipation. Today, we feel extremely uncomfortable with a deterministic tone or a teleological notion of history, but we must understand that the socialist revolution was possible only by projecting a totalizing vision of history.

19. For a discussion of history and theory of folklore, see Propp 1968, 3–18; 1984.

20. As Propp said, "This work is dedicated to the study of fairy tales. The existence of fairy tales as a special class is assumed as an essential working hypothesis" (1968, 19). For his further discussion of the unique status of fairy tales as a literary genre, see Propp 1984, 3–15.

21. Propp's example illustrates this point:

> A tsar gives an eagle to a hero. The eagle carries the hero away to another kingdom.
>
> An old man gives Súcenko a horse. The horse carries Súcenko away to another kingdom.
>
> A sorcerer gives Iván a little boat. The boat takes Iván to another kingdom.
>
> A princess gives Iván a ring. Young men appearing from out of the ring carry Iván away into another kingdom, and so forth. (1968, 19–20)

The characters in each of these tales differ. The gifts presented also differ. However, in terms of the function that these gifts serve and of the relation by which characters are organized, these tales tell the same story. This is the morphology of the fairy tale.

22. For a concise discussion of the difference between Propp's morphological analysis of folktale and Lévi-Strauss's structural analysis of myth, see Dundes 1968.

23. Anthropologists, by inclination or by nature, tend to feel hostile toward the structuralist approach to culture, because—among other reasons—they feel that structuralism as demonstrated in Lévi-Strauss entirely defies the agency of the people under study. The problem of agency is complicated, but it suffices to say that, particularly in Anglo-Saxon academic circles, viewing people as actors is a basic presupposition in the study of cultures. See Ortner 1984 for an account of the insignificance of structuralism's influence in American anthropology and an example of the strong assertion for people as the agents of history. In my view, structural analysis does not automatically deny human agency but simply stresses that agency is the effects of structural dislocations.

24. The term *moral* is used here, as well as in the previous chapters, as a broad category that defines the foundation of our judgment on what good life is supposed to mean. It should not be used narrowly to mean whether a specific mode of behavior is good or bad (see Taylor 1989, 25–52).

25. I have previously commented about this region's relative lack of industrial development. The province of Guangxi is often noted for its geographic beauty and diversity of ethnic cultures but is often considered backward in economic terms. When mentioned in daily conversations, "South China" often means Guangdong or the Shanghai area. When people talk about South China's rapid development, they do not intend to include Guangxi. As earlier

ethnographic descriptions have shown, my discussion has little to do with the minority groups in Guangxi; instead, I have focused on the growth of a high-tech company in this relatively less developed area. In so doing, I seek to reveal the complex investment structure that involves, first and foremost, the accumulation of social and political capital rather than economic or technological input. In terms of the complexity of the investment structure, it is no less striking—if not more striking—than any other cases in any other Chinese regions.

26. The question of luck and chance deserves a full study of its own. In my view, it holds some sort of key for understanding the modern Chinese experience in the second half of the twentieth century. In my earlier work on everyday life in rural Shaanxi, I also found that by attributing success to luck or chance, farmers downplayed the role of individual innovation or hard work. They would rather explain the increasing economic differentiation, a fact of social life in the 1990s, in terms of luck (see Liu 2000, 157–60). The logic of the practice in everyday reasoning seems to resemble the case under discussion here.

27. Ten thousand yuan is a little more than one thousand U.S. dollars.

28. For a detailed discussion of the workings of the Shanghai stock market, see Hertz 1998, 50–54.

29. He did not know how to sign his name and used a thumbprint in place of a signature.

30. See, e.g., Q-H. Wang 1997, 126–32. It is possible that those who told me this story had read this novel; however, it is also possible that the process took place the other way around. The author of the novel may have heard the story from the businessmen and incorporated it into his novel. I tell this story simply to show the significance of luck and chance in the conception of success in the Beihai business world.

31. For an earlier experience, see Kristeva 1977; for a most representative ethnographic experience, see M. Wolf 1985, in which she constantly invokes this idea that the government brainwashed Chinese women to make "untrue" statements. Wolf's impression is a complete mistake, confusing discourse with speech. *Speech* is the language of everyday life that a particular individual may choose to employ; *discourse* is the condition of possibility of speaking, which should and can be divided into the official and the nonofficial region. One can certainly speak the language of the state by choice or for its particular effects, but doing so does not necessarily mean that a person is brainwashed.

32. The literal translation of *she-jing-ban* would be "Ejaculation Office." To catch the meaningful equivalence in English, particularly in consideration of readers who do not understand Chinese, I have translated it as "Sucking Cock Office."

33. I heard several different versions of this story, the first in Beihai in 1999.

34. It is, in my view, important to understand the meaning of sex in the historical development of Maoist morals, which seem to have centered entirely on sexual behavior as a negative significance construed in opposition to the revo-

lutionary discourse of virtues. A genealogy of this system of morals is yet to be written, although there have been a number of promising works on the question of prostitution in Chinese society, often focusing either on the pre–Cultural Revolution period or after it. See, e.g., Hershatter 1997; Pan 1999. Early works on the formation of the Maoist revolutionary morality, such as that by Madsen (1984), were often shadowed by the experiences of the revolutionaries of that time and missed the discursive qualities that can be discovered only from a later perspective. A genealogy of the morals during the Maoist revolution cannot be written by following the ideological landscape marked out by the revolutionaries themselves.

Chapter 5. The Structure of the Self

1. A relativist tone is apparent in Geertz, who, in my view, represents two key features of the tradition of American cultural anthropology since Franz Boas (see Geertz 1973, 2000). The first feature of this tradition is its cultural relativism, and the second is its emphasis on the symbolic aspect of cultural process.

2. Volume 2 of Comaroff and Comaroff 1991–, published in 1997, is subtitled *The Dialectics of Modernity on a South African Frontier.* The introduction to the second volume contains a response to criticism of the first volume and mentions that the authors are working on the third volume.

3. Comaroff and Comaroff 1991–, 1:xi, opens with a very suggestive metaphor that corresponds to Sahlins's remark on the relationship between history and culture.

> In 1818 the directors of the London Missionary Society sent a mechanical clock to grace the church at its first station among the Tswana in South Africa. No ordinary clock—its hours were struck by strutting British soldiers carved of wood—it became the measure of a historical process in the making. [The clock was c]learly meant to proclaim the value of time in Christian, civilized communities. . . . In the face of the clock they had caught their first glimpse of a future time, a time when their colonized world would march to quite different rhythms.

This powerful metaphor not only indicates the central theme of this book—that is, how the European idea of history gained a universal value in the colonizing process—but also shows the authors' methodological concern with focusing on Europe's symbolic dominance. The clock is a symbol of time, a particular mode of time that marks progress in history, a sense of time that dwells on evolution or development.

4. Comaroff and Comaroff's work can, or should, be located in a chain of writing that may be called historical ethnography (or anthropology) and that characterizes a turn in the discipline as a moment of theoretical renovation.

Among other works, this chain includes Asad 1973, 1993; Rosaldo 1980; E. Wolf 1982; Mintz 1985; Sahlins 1985; Jean Comaroff 1985; Taussig 1987; Dirks 1993; Ohnuki-Tierney 1993; Pemberton 1994.

5. As they ask, "How, precisely, is consciousness made and remade? And how is it mediated by such distinctions as class, gender, and ethnicity? How do some meanings and actions, old and new alike, become conventional, while others become objects of contests and resistance? How, indeed, are we to understand connections, historical and conceptual, among culture, consciousness and ideology?" (Comaroff and Comaroff 1991–, 1:xi–xii). Of course, this is not to deny that the colonization of southern Africa was bloody and violent. However, their point is that the making of modern South Africa has involved a long battle for the possession of implicit meanings, signs, and symbols. Class struggle is at the same time a struggle over the means of signification. "Colonizers everywhere try to gain control over the practices through which would-be subjects produce and reproduce the basis of their existence. No habit is too humble, no sign too insignificant to be implicated" (5).

6. The Comaroffs' mode of writing is largely metonymical. For example, they often start with a character or a story as a clue to what they will write about later. One story or character leads to another, which in turn serves as a clue to a larger picture of the context of writing. For example, chapter 2 begins with Jane Eyre, particularly her relationship with a priest, St. John Rivers. The portrait of St. John Rivers as an ambivalent figure, on the one hand a kind of cold nonhuman being and on the other a hero of sacrifice and devotion, brings us to the social or sociological background of Brontë, whose father was a vicar. From Brontë's father, the reader is led to this excellent portrait of the class background of the Nonconformist Christian missionaries:

> Patrick Brontë had come from Irish peasant stock. . . . He raised his children in the vicarage at Haworth, Yorkshire, where their small circle was made up largely of clergy and their families, where much of their reading matter was church literature then full of discussion of mission work abroad. Even more significantly, Haworth was in the West Riding, one of the regions of England most affected by the industrial revolution. It was also an area in which Christian revivalism gained a firm hold and from which many Protestants departed for Africa to extend the Empire of Christ and, no less, of Great Britain. . . . Haworth, in short, was not far from the center of the social and economic, and religious upheavals of the age. By coincidence, too, it was the home of one James Broadbent, the brother of the first Methodist evangelist among the Tswana. (Comaroff and Comaroff 1991–, 1:50)

7. Literacy played an important role as a means of self-improvement, as Comaroff and Comaroff argue. It was the best way for the newly cultivated self to both look out on the world and watch itself in silence—in silent dia-

logue with itself. There were of course technological and other reasons for the boom of literacy in the late eighteenth and early nineteenth centuries. "But its social impact was closely tied to the ascendance of the reflective, inner-directed self: a self, long enshrined in Protestant personhood, now secularized and generalized as bourgeois ideology" (Comaroff and Comaroff 1991–, 1:63).

8. Although the engagement with Foucault is often implicit in Taylor's work, it is quite clear that Taylor writes not as "a historian of discontinuity" (see, e.g., Foucault 1972, 21–30).

9. Taylor uses the term "modern identity" to refer to this history. As he says, "I want to explore various facets of what I will call the 'modern identity.' To give a good first approximation of what this means would be to say that it involves tracing various strands of our modern notion of what it is to be a human agent, a person, or a self" (1989, 3). For a discussion of his idea of human agency (and the significance of language in making it), see Taylor 1985.

10. Taylor's discussion of inwardness is grounded on his treatment of the history of reason. However, I am concerned primarily with the historical emergence of an inner space as the house of modern subjectivity. If my account of Taylor is somehow distorted, it is because my reading of his text is oriented toward a purpose outside that textual space, toward my own objective in explaining the sense of self that emerged in postreform China.

11. For a discussion of why this inquiry differs from the conventional inquiry in moral philosophy, see also MacIntyre 1984, esp. chap. 2.

12. To show the complexity of the evolution of modern subjectivity, for example, Taylor contrasted Montaigne with the Cartesian notion of self:

> Descartes is a founder of modern individualism, because his theory throws the individual thinker back on his own responsibility, requires him to build an order of thought for himself, in the first person singular. But he must do so following universal criteria; he reasons as anyone and everyone. Montaigne is an originator of the search for each person's originality; and this is not just a different quest but in a sense antithetical to the Cartesian. Each turns us in a sense inward and tries to bring some order in the soul; but this likeness is what makes the conflict between them particularly acute.
>
> The Cartesian quest is for an order of science, of clear and distinct knowledge in universal terms, which where possible will be the basis of instrumental control. The Montaignean aspiration is always to loosen the hold of such general categories of "normal" operation and gradually prise our self-understanding free of the monumental weight of the universal interpretations, so that the shape of our originality can come to view. Its aim is not to find an intellectual order by which things in general can be surveyed, but rather to find the modes of expression which will allow the particular not to be overlooked. (1989, 182)

The contrast between Descartes and Montaigne is only one of a large number of examples in Taylor, which shows the structural shifts taking place in the making of the Western notion of self.

13. For a classic discussion of the level of analysis (in linguistics), see Benveniste 1971b.

14. Laclau and Mouffe's language may have returned to the philosophical distinction between meaning and action. However, they did not intend to return to such a distinction in any old fashion. Their argument is that, with reference to Wittgenstein's notion of language games, such a distinction has been increasingly blurred and should not be considered the equivalent of the linguistic versus the extralinguistic because the extralinguistic is also meaningful in the sense that it is part of a system of social relations defined as and in discourse. Following such a logic, Laclau and Mouffe have taken the view that the natural phenomenon in a strict sense is also discursively determined insofar as such phenomenon enters the social space (see Laclau 1990, 101–3).

15. See Wittgenstein 1958b, 8–10, for his discussion of the example of the bricklayers; see also Wittgenstein 1958a for his idea of a language game.

16. See Rabinow 1986, 237–41, for a discussion of Foucault and Hacking on the question of a historical a priori and its relevance to today's anthropological inquiry.

17. For a discussion of the French historical revolution, see Braudel 1980; P. Burke 1990.

18. Whether Braudel has achieved such a goal is arguable. For example, see Ricoeur 1984, 1:206–25, for a discussion of the fate of the event in Braudel 1972.

19. I had a friend who used to work in the Academy of Social Sciences and was known as an influential figure in the field of sociology because he translated the works of a number of leading Western scholars, including Max Weber. I once stayed in his house overnight; when I got up at about six o'clock the next morning, he had been sitting at his desk for more than an hour, doing translation work. Talking with him was often difficult for me because his mind focused more on sociological literature than on anything else. I was (and remain) very impressed by his sincerity and his dedication to his research. In 1989 he received a scholarship to study for his doctorate at the University of California at Los Angeles, and shortly thereafter I went to London to pursue my degree in social anthropology. When I returned to China for fieldwork in 1991, I met him in a Beijing restaurant: he was dressed in a suit, driving a brand-new car, and constantly talking on a cellular phone. He had been in the business world for about a year. Max Weber was perhaps no longer on his notebook computer, but the spirit of capitalism was surely now in his body.

20. For an ethnographic study of the movement, see Pieke 1996.

21. In China, both master's and doctoral degrees require three years of study.

22. Each province has its own People's Press, which in most cases is the most important provincial press and which is always located in the provincial capital.

23. There are many stories about how difficult it is to publish academic works. The experience of my graduate-school supervisor at Beijing's Renmin University in the 1980s offers one example. He spent about fifteen years working on a book examining Marx's, Engels's, Lenin's, Stalin's, Mao's, and other revolutionary thinkers' understanding of statistics. But no publisher would take the book because it would not be profitable. Just before his retirement, with much dismay and little hope, my adviser asked one of his students, Wangying, who had been working for the State Statistics Bureau, to see whether the bureau's press would publish the book. The press agreed but only if my supervisor would pay two thousand yuan in cash because the editor knew that this book would not make any profit. This sum represented four months of my supervisor's 1993 salary, and he could not afford it. Wangying found half of the money in his office budget, and the rest was finally provided by another former student who was working in a provincial statistical bureau. The book finally came out in 1996, two years after my adviser's retirement, as a mark of half a century's effort in searching for the truth of statistical reason from the perspective of the revolutionary leaders. The price for publication of academic works is now at least five times higher.

24. The idea of understanding, with its trace in the tradition of hermeneutics and, in particular, with reference to Dilthey (1989; see also Ricoeur 1991), is that experience can only be meaningful when it is already part of the understanding by which such an experience is brought into focus. One may even say that understanding highlights a certain kind of experience in the field notes of memory.

Chapter 6. Time, Narrative, and History

1. Some explanation is needed for the phrase "three historical moments of the modern Chinese experience." By using "the modern Chinese experience," I am trying to avoid any periodization that fixes this experience according to the actual dates of historical events. The history-memory complex, with which I am dealing here, is not the kind of history that can be divided into the republican period, the Maoist revolution, the reform period, and so forth. In China, overlapping motivations always exist at any given period of history. Therefore, "the modern Chinese experience" indicates a whole history-memory complex that consists of three moments: the traditional, the revolutionary, and the modern. What is traditional? What is revolutionary? And what is modern? Each person can have individual interpretations or answers to these questions. For example, *revolution* can mean the Maoist revolution (1966–76); it can also

mean the republican revolution, and so on. However, whatever specific connotations are given to each of these moments, there are certain stabilities in the
structural relations between the three moments constituted into a whole. I
specifically use the word *moment* to describe the quality of each part of this
whole, because there are two kinds of parts. "*Pieces* are parts that can subsist
and be presented even apart from the whole; they can be detached from their
wholes. Pieces can also be called *independent* parts. . . . *Moments* are parts that
cannot subsist or be presented apart from the whole to which they belong; they
cannot be detached. Moments are *nonindependent* parts" (Sokolowski 2000,
22–23). For example, acorns taken away from a tree will stand on their own
and become wholes in themselves. In contrast, the color yellow cannot be separated from some surface or spatial expanse. The latter is a moment of a whole,
whereas the former is a piece of a whole. For the original discussion of part-
whole relations, see Aristotle 1979, books 25 and 26, 97–98.

2. For discussions of the British social anthropological tradition, see, e.g.,
Bloch 1977; Leach 1982; Kuklick 1991; Moore 1994; Goody 1995; Stocking
1995; Kuper 1996.

3. Gell 1992 (esp. chaps. 2, 3, 4, 8) provides a good discussion of a number of classic treatments of time by leading anthropologists such as Evans-
Pritchard, Leach, Lévi-Strauss, and Geertz.

4. For a different approach, Benveniste's work (1971a) on three senses of
time may be useful. Benveniste identifies three forms of time: linguistic, physical, and chronological or "event" time. Linguistic time is marked by tense,
and its center is the present of the act of speaking—that is, the time of the
speaker. Physical time is continuous, uniform, infinite, and linear and can be
segmented as one wishes. Chronological or event time is social time that is
recorded on the calendar.

5. Gell is not uncritical of McTaggart's philosophy, but in terms of the
articulation of these two series, Gell believes that McTaggart was the most
clear philosopher (see Gell 1992, 151).

6. I may have taken McTaggart's argument out of its context, where he
was trying to figure out what was the essential quality of time. My reason for
mentioning him here is not that he provides a good answer to the problem of
time; rather, it seems to me that he suggests an interesting path for considering
the quality of time. As Richard M. Gale said, "McTaggart's argument is fallacious, but it is fallacious in such a deep and basic way that an adequate answer
to it must supply a rather extensive analysis of the concept of time, along with
a host of neighbouring concepts that are themselves of philosophical interest,
such as change, substance, event, proposition, truth, etc." (1968, 6).

7. The translation of the first part in Ricoeur's text is, "What, then, is
time? I know well enough what it is, provided that nobody asks me; but if I am
asked what it is and try to explain, I am baffled" (1984, 1:7).

8. The village Hsu studied may not be a typical Chinese village, although

the text reads as if it were. Either way, I do not think that my analysis is affected. Hsu's work was read by anthropologists of China as a significant monument in the tradition of lineage studies opened up by Maurice Freedman. This is my reason for choosing it.

9. McTaggart was dealing with the perception of event in time, whereas I have switched to a discussion of the Chinese understanding of a person or a self in relation to the family. I do not think that I can defend my free use of McTaggart, but I still think that even though partially and perhaps superficially, the distinction between the A-series and the B-series is helpful in clarifying my points, though I understand that there are conceptual dangers in using McTaggart's distinction in such a way.

10. That family fortune changes hands over time seems to be a popular point of view among Chinese anthropologists writing in English in the 1940s. Three major works on family life in China, published roughly at the same time (M. C. Yang 1945; Hsu 1948; Lin 1948), shared such a view, with few differences.

11. All the translations from this novel, including the title, are mine.

12. It became a joke during the later years of the Cultural Revolution that all the communist heroes in revolutionary dramas, operas, and novels were single—no parents or partners, let alone more distant relatives. They stood firmly with the party and other revolutionaries.

13. In the relevant literature, this is called a co-op, a kind of collective economic organization prior to the organization of the people's communes. For a general discussion of the land reform and the subsequent process of collectivization, see Shue 1980; for an inside view of the process, see Friedman, Pickowicz, and Selden 1991.

14. For two classic descriptions of the land reform in Chinese villages, see Crook and Crook 1959; Hinton 1966.

15. For an account of this intellectual history, see Dosse 1997, which provides a thorough treatment of the paradigmatic shift from structuralism to poststructuralism in France. For an account of the intellectual scene in France in the past two decades, see also Dosse 1999.

16. The title of this novel is borrowed from a famous Tang Dynasty poem by Bai Juyi.

17. The novel does not give any hint on the condition of life under the Japanese occupation, and the reader may therefore assume that what is described happened after the surrender of the Japanese military in 1945.

18. For a general account of the civil war period (1945–49), see Fairbank 1992, 331–37. During this period, inflation was skyrocketing, and as a result, Wang received gold.

19. All translations from this novel are also mine.

20. See, e.g., A. Wang 1995, 325–42.

21. Once again, I must emphasize that I use McTaggart's language for the

sake of convenience. The point has been made very clear: given the explicit framework of historical time used as a periodization in A. Wang's novel, her point is to stress that there is no longer any sense of an organic time, internally linking events or persons in time to a chain of past-present-future. Time is externalized and has become a clock outside the self experience. This seems to me something similar to the B-series, where there is only before-ness and after-ness but no internal logical connections between events (or persons) in time.

I realize that my treatment of these three moments of the modern Chinese experience may appear to be too neat to be true. However, I am not dealing with the actual experiences of time but with time as a discursive condition though which actual experiences are made possible. To enable the differences to be seen more clearly, I have stretched the contrasts between these moments of temporal experiences as far as I can. Since I am not claiming that reality is supposed to be so, I have brought these conceptual contrasts to their extreme forms.

22. The idea of a time schedule has not only become an intrinsic part of business management in industrial societies but once served as an important instrument in the historical development of disciplinary power in the West. See Thompson [1967] 1993; Foucault 1977.

23. For a discussion of the significance of personal connections in China, see M. M-H. Yang 1994; Yan 1996; Kipnis 1997.

24. In the late 1990s, most airplanes were not fully booked, and last-minute passengers were always welcomed. Haihun said that for a couple of months, he did nothing but take these officials for pleasure trips whenever possible or convenient for them.

Chapter 7. The Being of Becoming

1. No one could provide an adequate explanation for the meaning of the term *cuodadi*. I was unable to determine the words of three Chinese characters in this phrase. The image this term invokes is, at least in my mind, quite unclear.

2. The subtitle of Sartre 1956 is "an essay on phenomenological ontology."

3. However, Sartre's later work is "immense, pedantic, repetitious, and essentially formless and unreadable" (Levi 1969, 376, discussing Sartre 1976, which was translated into Chinese in 1998; it was a late arrival on the Chinese intellectual scene, when Marxism had lost its territories to other theories).

4. Mentioning Foucault has become a commonplace in anthropological writings. As some commentators have pointed out (see Certeau 1984, 45–49; Baudrillard 1987; Deleuze 1988), the theoretical beauty of Foucault's writing lies in the fact that his style resists any freezing. Theory has become, in Fou-

cault's adept hands, a novel, a novel marching in a history whose life is created by this movement itself. That is, Foucault has provided a brilliant example to show how to detheorize theoretical concepts by compiling a genealogy from the present point of view. This style of a theoretical novel in Foucault has both a flavor of deconstruction as in Derrida and an ingredient of defamiliarization as in Viktor Sklovskij, a father of Russian formalist movement. To deconstruct is to jeopardize the foundation on which thought happily rests; to defamiliarize is to recreate a critical distance between habits of the heart and the heart of habits. Foucault has shown how to defamiliarize what used to be conceptual habits. After Foucault, theory can no longer be considered a frozen space of concepts but must be seen as a genealogy of traces. In other words, Foucault destabilizes frozen theoretical concepts (as in his marvelous accounts of the history of madness [1973], archaeology of knowledge [1972], discipline and punishment [1977], the technique of self [1988], and the uses of pleasure [1985]) to produce a theoretical fiction.

5. By "Laclau and Mouffe's work," I mean Laclau and Mouffe 1985; Laclau 1990, 1996; Mouffe 1993. See also A. M. Smith 1998 for a general introduction to the movement of their thought.

6. I was selected as an Asia Leadership Fellow (1998–99), a program sponsored by the Japan Foundation (Asia Center) and administered by the International House of Japan. This allowed me the opportunity to work with five other fellows from Southeast Asian countries. A series of discussions and exchanges among the fellows and between the fellows and Japanese scholars brought to my awareness of this question of the *We*. I thank Janadas Devan of Singapore, Sylvia Mayuga of the Philippines, Suwanna Satha-Anand of Thailand, Endo Suanda of Indonesia, and Diana Wong of Malaysia for their encouragement and stimulation during the period of fellowship.

7. For two anthropological approaches to the problem of transnationalism, see Appadurai 1996; Ong 1999.

8. Two propositions are implicit in my inquiry here. First, an adequate understanding of the theoretical horizon of our presuppositions and assumptions is a precondition for employing the emphasized *we* as a political strategy, either for or by any social group that intends to do so. Second, the change of the conditions of life in the contemporary world has made it clear that it is impossible to go on with such a use without a redefinition of this emphasized pronoun.

9. For an overview of the Western Marxist tradition, see Anderson 1976.

10. Laclau's discussion on the question of subject extends to include three further points. For a full discussion of these points, see Laclau 1990, 62–67.

11. Anthropologists are familiar with the idea of myth, which is central to the work of a great master, Claude Lévi-Strauss. Perhaps not everyone agrees with his interpretation of the Oedipus myth as a double opposition of the overestimation/underestimation of blood relations paralleling the affirmation/

denial of the autochthonous origin of man (Lévi-Strauss 1967, 213–16); however, some understanding of his definition of myth may be useful here. According to Lévi-Strauss, myth is language, which means that, following Saussure, language as simultaneously a system of signification, a social institution, and a system of values differs from speech, which is the individual actualization of communication. Such communication, either in conversation or in writing, relies on the structural qualities of language as a precondition for making sense, and such a precondition is not always conscious to those who communicate. What is unconscious in everyday life is not the contents of saying or the said, nor is it the anticipated effects of saying; rather, it is the way in which one is able to speak. Understanding of what Laclau means by "any subject is mythical subject" must take place in this sense.

12. In the case of China, the translocal experience should be understood in two senses. First, in an actual sense of the term, travel and migration have provided people experiences of a different kind—that is, in an empirical sense, people have crossed various kinds of regional and local boundaries. Second, in a symbolic sense, electronic media, such as television and the Internet, have penetrated local life in such a way that the distinction between real experience and its simulacrum has become blurred.

13. Life goes on and people continue to fight against various kinds of exploitation, real or imagined. But the difficulty that arises from this discussion concerns the form of collective action rather than its content. The form of collectivity means the way in which collective actions are possible, rather than the actual manifestations of collective activities.

Conclusion: Memories of the Future

1. I was doing research in Tokyo during the period of Jiang's visit to Japan and followed the media representations of his visit.

2. There is a slight difference in the style of the Mao suit and the Sun (Yat-sen) suit. Moreover, I suppose that by changing into a non-Western suit, Jiang was invoking the spirit of Mao Zedong rather than that of Sun Yat-sen. For this reason, I have called the garment the "Mao suit."

3. On most occasions, Jiang wore a Western suit, only occasionally dressing in the Mao suit. His mind was Western in some very interesting ways. According to a Chinese newspaper report, when Jiang went to visit Dalian, a northern seaside city, in the summer of 1999, he remarked, "Oh, this is a beautiful city." He paused and then added, "It almost feels like walking in San Francisco."

4. When such an example is brought up, it is hardly possible to avoid a discussion of the question of social memory, for which Connerton 1989 may serve as a good starting point. In Connerton's treatment, memory is assumed

to belong to either an individual's capacity or a society's function; of this opposition, his interest lies with the latter. According to Connerton, social memory is performative in nature, and therefore his key question concerns public ceremonies. Connerton's account of the historical transformation, primarily in Europe, of how societies remember through documents, monuments, and public celebrations is informative and illuminating, but however exciting his analysis is, he has remained trapped in the wreck of the sociological dualistic premise: individual versus society. In my view, the importance of the rise in interest in the study of memory is precisely that it has brought hope for transcending such a dichotomy. It is not so much a question of whether societies remember differently from individuals; rather, the point is whether it is possible to recast a conceptual space, centered on the notion of memory (or imaginary), as a departure from the prison house of society always considered as the opposite of the individual.

References

Abu-Lughod, L. 1986. *Veiled sentiments: Honor and poetry in a Bedouin society.* Berkeley: University of California Press.

Anagnost, A. 1997. *National past-times: Narrative, representation, and power in modern China.* Durham: Duke University Press.

Anderson, P. 1976. *Considerations on Western Marxism.* London: NLB.

Anderson, P. 1998. *The origins of postmodernity.* London: Verso.

Appadurai, A. 1996. *Modernity at large: Cultural dimensions of globalization.* Minneapolis: University of Minnesota Press.

Aristotle. 1979. *Aristotle's Metaphysics.* Trans. with commentaries and glossary by H. G. Apostle. Grinnell, Iowa: Peripatetic Press.

Asad, T., ed. 1973. *Anthropology and the colonial encounter.* New York: Humanities Press.

Asad, T. 1993. *Genealogies of religion: Discipline and reasons of power in Christianity and Islam.* Baltimore: Johns Hopkins University Press.

Attridge, D., G. Bennington, and R. Young, eds. 1987. *Post-structuralism and the question of history.* Cambridge: Cambridge University Press.

Augustine, Saint. 1940. *The Confessions of St. Augustine.* Intro. by C. van Doren. New York: Literary Guild of America.

Austin, J. L. 1962. *How to do things with words.* Cambridge: Harvard University Press.

Baker, H. D. R. 1979. *Chinese family and kinship.* London: Macmillan.

Bakhtin, M. M. 1986. The problem of speech genres. In *Speech genres and other late essays,* ed. C. Emerson and M. Holquist, trans. V. W. McGee, 65–102. Austin: University of Texas Press.

Baudrillard, J. 1987. *Forget Foucault and forget Baudrillard.* New York: Semiotext.

Benedict, R. 1934. *Patterns of culture.* Boston: Houghton Mifflin.

Benveniste, E. 1971a. The correlations of tense in the French verb. In *Problems in general linguistics,* trans. M. E. Meek, 205–16. Coral Gables, Fla.: University of Miami Press.

Benveniste, E. 1971b. The levels of linguistic analysis. In *Problems in general linguistics,* trans. M. E. Meek, 101–12. Coral Gables, Fla.: University of Miami Press.

Bloch, M. 1977. The past and the present in the present. *Man,* 13, no. 2:21–33.

Bloch, M. 1993. Time narratives and the multiplicity of representations of the past. *Bulletin of the Institute of Ethnology,* Academica Sinica, Taiwan, no. 75.

Boon, J. A. 1982. *Other tribes, other scribes: Symbolic anthropology in the comparative study of cultures, histories, religions, and texts.* Cambridge: Cambridge University Press.

Booth, W. C. 1961. *The rhetoric of fiction.* Chicago: University of Chicago Press.

Bourdieu, P. 1977. *Outline of a theory of practice.* Trans. R. Nice. Cambridge: Cambridge University Press.

Bourdieu, P. 1984. *Distinction: A social critique of the judgement of taste.* Trans. R. Nice. Cambridge: Harvard University Press.

Bourdieu, P. 1990. *The logic of practice.* Trans. R. Nice. Cambridge, Eng.: Polity; Oxford: Blackwell.

Braudel, F. 1972. *The Mediterranean and the Mediterranean world in the age of Philip II.* Trans. Sian Reynolds. New York: Harper and Row.

Braudel, F. 1977. *Afterthoughts on material civilization and capitalism.* Trans. P. M. Ranum. Baltimore: Johns Hopkins University Press.

Braudel, F. 1980. *On history.* Trans. S. Matthews. Chicago: University of Chicago Press.

Bubner, R. 1981. *Modern German philosophy.* Trans. E. Mathews. Cambridge: Cambridge University Press.

Burke, K. 1969. *A grammar of motives.* Berkeley: University of California Press.

Burke, P. 1990. *The French historical revolution: The Annales school, 1929–89.* Cambridge, Eng.: Polity.

Callinicos, A. 1995. *Theories and narratives: Reflections on the philosophy of history.* Durham: Duke University Press.

Cao, W.-J., and C.-S. Wei. 1992. *Zhongguo bashi niandai renwen sichao* (China's 1980s: Trends in humanities and social sciences). Beijing: Xuelin.

Carr, D. 1986. *Time, narrative, and history: An essay in the philosophy of history.* Bloomington: Indiana University Press.

Carrithers, M., S. Collins, and S. Lukes, eds. 1985. *The category of the person: Anthropology, philosophy, history.* Cambridge: Cambridge University Press.

Cassirer, E. 1946. *The myth of the state.* New Haven: Yale University Press.

Certeau, M. de. 1984. *The practice of everyday life.* Trans. S. Rendall. Berkeley: University of California Press.

Certeau, M. de. 1988. *The writing of history.* Trans. T. Conley. New York: Columbia University Press.

Chang, K. C., ed. 1977. *Food in Chinese culture.* New Haven: Yale University Press.

Clifford, J. 1986. Introduction: Partial truth. In *Writing culture: The poetics and politics of ethnography,* ed. J. Clifford and G. E. Marcus, 1–26. Berkeley: University of California Press.

Clifford, J. 1988a. Introduction: The pure products go crazy. In *The predica-ment of culture: Twentieth-century ethnography, literature, and art,* 1–18. Cambridge: Harvard University Press.

Clifford, J. 1988b. On ethnographic authority. In *The predicament of culture: Twentieth-century ethnography, literature, and art,* 21–54. Cambridge: Har-vard University Press.

Clifford, J. 1988c. On ethnographic self-fashioning: Conrad and Malinowski. In *The predicament of culture: Twentieth-century ethnography, literature, and art,* 92–113. Cambridge: Harvard University Press.

Clifford, J., and G. Marcus, ed. 1986. *Writing culture: The poetics and politics of ethnography.* Berkeley: University of California Press.

Cohen, M. L. 1993. Cultural and political inventions in modern China: The case of Chinese peasants. *Daedalus* 122, no. 2:151–70.

Collingwood, R. G. [1940] 1998. *An essay on metaphysics.* Ed. with an intro. by R. Martin. Oxford: Clarendon.

Collingwood, R. G. 1942. *The new Leviathan, or, Man, society, civilization, and barbarism.* Oxford: Clarendon.

Collingwood, R. G. [1946] 1994. *The idea of history.* Ed. with an intro. by J. van der Dussen. Oxford: Oxford University Press.

Comaroff, J. 1985. *Body of power, spirit of resistance: The culture and history of a South African people.* Chicago: University of Chicago Press.

Comaroff, J., and J. Comaroff. 1991–. *Of revelation and revolution.* 2 vols. to date. Chicago: University of Chicago Press.

Comaroff, J., and J. Comaroff. 1992. *Ethnography and the historical imagina-tion.* Boulder: Westview.

Connerton, P. 1989. *How societies remember.* Cambridge: Cambridge Univer-sity Press.

Crook, I., and D. Crook. 1959. *Revolution in a Chinese village: Ten Mile Inn.* London: Routledge and Kegan Paul.

Danto, A. C. 1965. *Analytical philosophy of history.* Cambridge: Cambridge University Press.

Davis, D. S. 1995. Introduction: Urban China. In *Urban spaces in contemporary China: The potential for autonomy and community in post-Mao China,* ed. D. S. Davis, R. Kraus, B. Naughton and E. J. Perry, 1–19. Washington, D.C.: Woodrow Wilson Center.

Dawkins, R. 1976. *The selfish gene.* Oxford: Oxford University Press.

Deleuze, G. 1988. *Foucault.* Trans. and ed. S. Hand. London: Athlone.

Deleuze, G., and F. Guattari. 1987. *A thousand plateaus: Capitalism and schizo-phrenia.* Trans. B. Massumi. Minneapolis: University of Minnesota Press.

Descombes, V. 1980. *Modern French philosophy.* Trans. L. Scott-Fox and J. M. Harding. Cambridge: Cambridge University Press.

Dilthey, W. 1989. *Introduction to the human sciences.* Ed. R. A. Makkreel and F. Rodi. Princeton: Princeton University Press.

Dirks, N. B. 1993. *The hollow crown: Ethnohistory of an Indian kingdom,* 2d ed.

Ann Arbor: University of Michigan Press. Original edition, Cambridge: Cambridge University Press, 1987.

Dirlik, A. 1994. *After the revolution: Waking to global capitalism.* Hanover, N.H.: University Press of New England for Wesleyan University Press.

Dosse, F. 1997. *History of structuralism.* 2 vols. Trans. D. Glassman. Minneapolis: University of Minnesota Press.

Dosse, F. 1999. *Empire of meaning: The humanization of the social sciences.* Trans. H. Melehy. Minneapolis: University of Minnesota Press.

Douglas, M. 1975. *Implicit meanings: Essays in anthropology.* London: Routledge and Kegan Paul.

Dreyfus, H., and P. Rabinow. 1982. *Michel Foucault: Beyond structuralism and hermeneutics.* Chicago: University of Chicago Press.

Dundes, A. 1968. Introduction to the second edition. In *Morphology of the folktale,* by V. Propp, trans. L. Scott, rev. and ed. with a pref. by L. A. Wagner, xi–xvii. Austin: University of Texas Press.

Durkheim, E. 1915. *The elementary forms of religious life.* Trans. J. W. Swain. New York: Free Press.

Elias, N. [1939] 1994. *The civilizing process.* Trans. E. Jephcott. Oxford: Blackwell.

Elvin, M. 1985. Between the earth and heaven: Conceptions of the self in China. In *The category of the person: Anthropology, philosophy, history,* ed. M. Carrithers, S. Collins, and S. Lukes, 156–89. Cambridge: Cambridge University Press.

Erlich, V. 1955. *Russian formalism: History-doctrine.* Pref. R. Wellek. The Hague: Mouton.

Evans-Pritchard, E. E. 1939. Nuer time reckoning. *Africa* 12:189–216.

Evans-Pritchard, E. E. 1940. *The Nuer: A description of the modes of livelihood and political institutions of a Nilotic people.* Oxford: Clarendon.

Fabian, J. 1983. *Time and the other: How anthropology makes its object.* New York: Columbia University Press.

Fairbank, J. K. 1992. *China: A new history.* Cambridge: Belknap Press of Harvard University Press.

Fardon, R., ed. 1990. *Localizing strategies: Regional traditions of ethnographic writing.* Edinburgh: Scottish Academic Press.

Fei, X.-T. 1939. *Peasant life in China: A field study of country life in the Yangtze Valley.* London: G. Routledge and Sons.

Firth, R. W. 1936. *We, the Tikopia: A sociological study of kinship in primitive Polynesia.* London: Allen and Unwin.

Foucault, M. 1970. *The order of things: An archaeology of the human sciences.* London: Tavistock.

Foucault, M. 1972. *The archaeology of knowledge.* Trans. A. M. Sheridan-Smith. New York: Pantheon.

Foucault, M. 1973. *Madness and civilization*. Trans. R. Haward. New York: Vintage.

Foucault, M. 1977. *Discipline and punish: The birth of the prison*. Trans. A. Sheridan. New York: Pantheon.

Foucault, M. 1985. *The history of sexuality*. Vol. 2, *The use of pleasure*. Trans. R. Hurley. New York: Vintage.

Foucault, M. 1988. *The history of sexuality*. Vol. 3, *The care of the self*. Trans. R. Hurley. New York: Vintage.

Freedman, M. 1958. *Lineage organization in southeastern China*. London: Athlone.

Freedman, M. 1966. *Chinese lineage and society: Fukien and Kwangtung*. London: Athlone.

Friedman, E., P. G. Pickowicz, and M. Selden. 1991. *Chinese village, socialist state*. New Haven: Yale University Press.

Gale, R. M. 1968. *The language of time*. London: Routledge and Kegan Paul; New York: Humanities Press.

Gallie, W. B. 1964. *Philosophy and the historical understanding*. London: Chatto and Windus.

Gates, H. 1996. *China's motor: A thousand years of petty capitalism*. Ithaca: Cornell University Press.

Geertz, C. 1973. *The interpretation of cultures*. New York: Basic Books.

Geertz, C. 1983. *Local knowledge: Further essays in interpretive anthropology*. New York: Basic Books.

Geertz, C. 1988. *Works and lives: The anthropologist as author*. Stanford: Stanford University Press.

Geertz, C. 2000. *Available light: Anthropological reflections on philosophical topics*. Princeton: Princeton University Press.

Gell, A. 1992. *The anthropology of time: Cultural constructions of temporal maps and images*. Oxford: Berg.

Geras, N. 1987. Post-Marxism? *New Left Review* 163: 40–82.

Geras, N. 1988. Ex-Marxism without substance: Being a real reply to Laclau and Mouffe. *New Left Review* 169:34–61.

Geras, N. 1990. *Discourses of extremity: Radical ethics and post-Marxist extravagances*. London: Verso.

Giddens, A. 1984. *The constitution of society: Introduction of the theory of structuration*. Berkeley: University of California Press.

Goffman, E. 1959. *The presentation of self in everyday life*. Garden City, N.Y.: Doubleday.

Goffman, E. 1963. *Behavior in public places: Notes on the social organization of gatherings*. New York: Free Press of Glencoe.

Goffman, E. 1967. *Interaction ritual: Essays in face-to-face behavior*. Chicago: Aldine.

Goldstein, L. J. 1976. *Historical knowing*. Austin: University of Texas Press.

Goody, J. 1995. *The expansive moment: The rise of social anthropology in Britain and Africa, 1918–1970*. Cambridge: Cambridge University Press.

Greimas, A.-J. 1983. *Structural semantics: An attempt at a method*. Trans. D. McDowell, R. Schleifer, and A. Velie. Lincoln: University of Nebraska Press.

Greimas, A.-J., and J. Courtés. 1982. *Semiotics and language: An analytical dictionary*. Trans. L. Crist, D. Patte, J. Lee, E. McMahon II, G. Phillips, and M. Rengstorf. Bloomington: Indiana University Press.

Gupta, A., and J. Ferguson, eds. 1997. *Anthropological locations: Boundaries and grounds of a field science*. Berkeley: University of California Press.

Habermas, J. 1987. The philosophical discourse of modernity. Trans. F. Lawrence. Cambridge, Mass.: MIT Press.

Haoran. 1964–66. *Yanyangtian* (The sky of bright sunshine). 3 vols. Beijing. People's Literature Press.

Haoran. 1998. *Yuanmeng* (Realizing a dream). Beijing: People's Literature Press.

Harris, M. 1968. *The rise of anthropological theory: A history of theories of culture*. New York: Crowell.

Harvey, D. 1989. *The condition of postmodernity: An enquiry into the origins of cultural change*. Cambridge, Mass.: Blackwell.

Hassan, I. H. 1987. *The postmodern turn: Essays in postmodern theory and culture*. Columbus: Ohio State University Press.

Hershatter, G. 1997. *Dangerous pleasures: Prostitution and modernity in twentieth-century Shanghai*. Berkeley: University of California Press.

Hertz, E. 1998. *The trading crowd: An ethnography of the Shanghai stock market*. Cambridge: Cambridge University Press.

Hinton, W. 1966. *Fenshen: A documentary of revolution in a Chinese village*. New York: Monthly Review.

Horton, J., and S. Mendus, eds. 1994. *After MacIntyre: Critical perspectives on the work of Alasdair MacIntyre*. Notre Dame, Ind.: University of Notre Dame Press.

Hsing, Y.-T. 1998. *Making capitalism in China: The Taiwan connection*. New York: Oxford University Press.

Hsu, F. L. K. 1948. *Under the ancestors' shadow: Chinese culture and personality*. New York: Columbia University Press.

Husserl, E. 1964. *The phenomenology of internal time-consciousness*. Trans. J. S. Churchill. Bloomington: Indiana University Press.

James, A., J. Hockey, and A. Dawson, eds. 1997. *After writing culture: Epistemology and praxis in contemporary anthropology*. London: Routledge.

Jameson, F. 1972. *The prison-house of language: A critical account of structuralism and Russian formalism*. Princeton: Princeton University Press.

Jameson, F. 1991. *Postmodernism; or, The cultural logic of late capitalism*. Durham: Duke University Press.

Jameson, F. 1998. *The cultural turn: Selected writings on the postmodern, 1983–1998*. London: Verso.

Jencks, C. 1986. *What is post-modernism?* London: Academy Editions.

Jing, J. 1996. *The temple of memories: History, power, and morality in a Chinese village*. Stanford: Stanford University Press.

Judd, E. R. 1994. *Gender and power in rural North China*. Stanford: Stanford University Press.

Kermode, F. 1967. *The sense of an ending: Studies in the theory of fiction*. New York: Oxford University Press.

Kipnis, A. B. 1997. *Producing Guanxi: Sentiment, self, and subculture in a North China village*. Durham: Duke University Press.

Knight, K. 1998. Introduction. In *The MacIntyre reader*, ed. K. Knight, 1–27. Notre Dame, Ind.: University of Notre Dame Press.

Kojève, A. 1969. *Introduction to the reading of Hegel: Lectures on the phenomenology of spirit*. Assembled by R. Queneau, ed. A. Bloom, trans. J. H. Nichols Jr. New York: Basic Books.

Kristeva, J. 1977. *About Chinese women*. Trans. A. Barrows. New York: Urizen.

Kuklick, H. 1991. *The savage within: The social history of British anthropology, 1885–1945*. Cambridge: Cambridge University Press.

Kuper, A. 1996. *Anthropology and anthropologists: The modern British school*. 3d rev. and enl. ed. New York: Routledge.

Laclau, E. 1990. *New reflections on the revolution of our time*. London: Verso.

Laclau, E. 1996. *Emancipation(s)*. London: Verso.

Laclau, E., and C. Mouffe. 1985. *Hegemony and socialist strategy: Towards a radical democratic politics*. London: Verso.

Laclau, E., and C. Mouffe. 1987. Post-Marxism without apologies. *New Left Review* 166:97–106.

Leach, E. R. 1954. *Political systems of highland Burma: A study of Kachin social structure*. Boston: Beacon.

Leach, E. R. 1961. *Rethinking anthropology*. London: Athlone.

Leach, E. R. 1982. *Social anthropology*. New York: Oxford University Press.

Lee, C. K. 1998. *Gender and the South China miracle: Two worlds of factory women*. Berkeley: University of California Press.

Levenson, J. R. 1965. *Confucian China and its modern fate*. Vol. 3, *The problem of historical significance*. Berkeley: University of California Press.

Levi, A. W. 1969. *Humanism and politics: Studies in the relationship of power and value in the Western tradition*. Bloomington: Indiana University Press.

Lévi-Strauss, C. 1966. *The savage mind*. Chicago: University of Chicago Press.

Lévi-Strauss, C. 1967. *Structural anthropology*. Trans. C. Jacobson and B. G. Schoepf. New York: Basic Books.

Lévi-Strauss, C. 1969. *The raw and the cooked: Introduction to a science of mythology*. Vol. 1. Trans. J. Weightman and D. Weightman. New York: Harper and Row.

Lévi-Strauss, C. 1976. The meaning and use of the notion of model. In *Structural anthropology*, trans. M. Layton, 2:71–81. Chicago: University of Chicago Press.

Lin, Y.-H. 1948. *The golden wing: A sociological study of Chinese familism*. London: K. Paul, Trench, Trubner.

Liu, X. 2000. *In one's own shadow: An ethnographic account of the condition of post-reform rural China*. Berkeley: University of California Press.

Lu, X.-B., and E. Perry, eds. 1997. *Danwei: The changing Chinese workplace in historical and comparative perspective*. Armonk, N.Y.: M. E. Sharpe.

Lukács, G. 1962. *The meaning of contemporary realism*. Trans. J. Mander and N. Mander. London: Merlin.

Lukes, S., ed. 1986. *Power*. Oxford: Blackwell.

Lyotard, J.-F. 1984. *The postmodern condition: A report on knowledge*. Trans. G. Bennington and B. Massumi. Minneapolis: University of Minnesota Press.

Lyotard, J.-F. 1997. *Postmodern fables*. Trans. G. Van Den Abbeele. Minneapolis: University of Minnesota Press.

MacIntyre, A. C. 1984. *After virtue: A study in moral theory*. 2d ed. Notre Dame, Ind.: University of Notre Dame Press.

Madsen, R. 1984. *Morality and power in a Chinese village*. Berkeley: University of California Press.

Mandelbaum, M. 1967. A note on history as narrative. *History and Theory* 6:416–17.

Marcus, G. E. 1995. Ethnography in/of the world system: The emergence of multi-sited ethnography. *Annual Review of Anthropology* 24:95–117.

Marcus, G. E., and M. M. J. Fischer. 1986. *Anthropology as cultural critique: An experimental moment in the human sciences*. Chicago: University of Chicago Press.

Merleau-Ponty, M. 1962. *Phenomenology of perception*. Trans. C. Smith. London: Routledge and Kegan Paul; New York: Humanities Press.

Merquior, J. G. 1985. *Foucault*. London: Fontana.

Mintz, S. W. 1985. *Sweetness and power: The place of sugar in modern history*. New York: Viking.

Moore, S. F. 1994. *Anthropology and Africa: Changing perspectives on a changing scene*. Charlottesville: University Press of Virginia.

Mouffe, C. 1993. *The return of the political*. London: Verso.

Natanson, M. 1967. Introduction. In *Collected papers*, vol. 1, *The problem of social reality*, by A. Schutz, ed. M. Natanson, xxv–xlvii. The Hague: Nijhoff.

National Bureau of Statistics, PRC. 1999. *Zhongguo tongji nianjian* 1999 (China statistical yearbook 1999). Beijing: China Statistics Press.

Needham, R., ed. 1971. *Rethinking kinship and marriage*. London: Tavistock.

Nora, P. 1989. Between memory and history. *Representations* 26 (spring): 7–25.

Ohnuki-Tierney, E. 1993. *Rice as self: Japanese identities through time.* Princeton: Princeton University Press.

Ong, A. 1999. *Flexible citizenship: The cultural logics of transnationality.* Durham: Duke University Press.

Ortner, S. 1984. Theory in anthropology since the sixties. *Comparative Studies of Society and History* 26, no. 1:126–66.

Pan, S.-M. 1999. *Cunzai yu huangmiu: Zhongguo dixia xingchanye kaocha* (Existence and absurdity: Observations of China's underground sex industry). Beijing: Qunyan.

Parsons, T., and E. A. Shils, eds. 1951. *Toward a general theory of action: Theoretical foundations for the social sciences.* Cambridge: Harvard University Press.

Pemberton, J. 1994. *On the subject of "Java."* Ithaca: Cornell University Press.

Pieke, F. N. 1996. *The ordinary and the extraordinary: An anthropological study of Chinese reform and political protest in Beijing, 1989.* London: K. Paul.

Polanyi, M. 1962. *Personal knowledge: Towards a post-critical philosophy.* London: Routledge and Kegan Paul.

Polanyi, M., and H. Prosch. 1975. *Meaning.* Chicago: University of Chicago Press.

Potter, S. H., and J. M. Potter. 1990. *China's peasants: The anthropology of a revolution.* Cambridge: Cambridge University Press.

Propp, V. 1968. *Morphology of the folktale.* Trans. L. Scott, ed. L. A. Wagner. Austin: University of Texas Press.

Propp, V. 1984. *Theory and history of folklore.* Trans. A. Y. Martin, R. P. Martin, et al.; ed. A. Liberman. Minneapolis: University of Minnesota Press.

Rabinow, P. 1977. *Reflections on fieldwork in Morocco.* Berkeley: University of California Press.

Rabinow, P. 1984. Introduction. In *The Foucault reader,* ed. P. Rabinow, 3–29. New York: Random House.

Rabinow, P. 1986. Representations are social facts: Modernity and postmodernity in anthropology. In *Writing culture: The poetics and politics of ethnography,* ed. J. Clifford and G. E. Marcus, 234–61. Berkeley: University of California Press.

Radcliffe-Brown, A. R. 1952. *Structure and function in primitive society: Essays and addresses.* Foreword by E. E. Evans-Pritchard and Fred Eggan. Glencoe, Ill.: Free Press.

Radcliffe-Brown, A. R. 1957. *A natural science of society.* Glencoe, Ill.: Free Press.

Ricoeur, P. 1977. *The rule of metaphor: Multi-disciplinary studies of the creation of meaning in language.* Trans. R. Czerny with K. McLaughlin and J. Costello. Toronto: University of Toronto Press.

Ricoeur, P. 1984. *Time and narrative*. 3 vols. Trans. K. McLaughlin and D. Pellauer. Chicago: University of Chicago Press.

Ricoeur, P. 1991. *From text to action*. Trans. K. Blamey and J. B. Thompson. Evanston, Ill.: Northwestern University Press.

Rofel, L. 1999. *Other modernities: Gendered yearnings in China after socialism*. Berkeley: University of California Press.

Rosaldo, R. 1980. *Ilongot headhunting, 1883–1974: A study in society and history*. Stanford: Stanford University Press.

Sahlins, M. 1985. *Islands of history*. London: Tavistock.

Sangren, P. S. 1988. Rhetoric and the authority of ethnography: Postmodernism and the social reproduction of texts. *Current Anthropology* 29, no. 3: 415–24.

Sartre, J.-P. 1956. *Being and nothingness: An essay on phenomenological ontology*. Trans. and intro. H. E. Barnes. New York: Philosophical Library.

Sartre, J.-P. 1976. *Critique of dialectical reason*. Trans. A. Sheridan-Smith, ed. J. Ree. London: NLB; Atlantic Highlands, N.J.: Humanities Press.

Scholes, R., and R. Kellogg. 1966. *The nature of narrative*. New York: Oxford University Press.

Schram, S. R., ed. 1987. *Foundations and limits of state power in China*. London: School of Oriental and African Studies, University of London, on behalf of the European Science Foundation.

Schutz, A. 1967. *The phenomenology of the social world*. Trans. G. Walsh and F. Lehnert; intro. G. Walsh. Evanston, Ill.: Northwestern University Press.

Shue, V. 1980. *Peasant China in transition: The dynamics of development toward socialism, 1949–1956*. Berkeley: University of California Press.

Shue, V. 1988. *The reach of the state: Sketches of the Chinese body politic*. Stanford: Stanford University Press.

Smith, A. H. 1899. *Village life in China: A study in sociology*. New York: F. H. Revell.

Smith, A. M. 1998. *Laclau and Mouffe: The radical democratic imaginary*. London: Routledge.

Sokolowski, R. 2000. *Introduction to phenomenology*. Cambridge: Cambridge University Press.

Sperber, D. 1985. *On anthropological knowledge*. Cambridge: Cambridge University Press.

Spiegelberg, H. 1994. *The phenomenological movement: A historical introduction*. 3d rev. and enl. ed. With K. Schuhmann. Dordrecht: Kluwer.

Stocking, G. W., ed. 1984. *Functionalism historicized: Essays on British social anthropology*. Madison: University of Wisconsin Press.

Stocking, G. W., ed. 1986. *Malinowski, Rivers, Benedict, and others: Essays on culture and personality*. Madison: University of Wisconsin Press.

Stocking, G. W. 1992. *The ethnographer's magic and other essays in the history of anthropology*. Madison: University of Wisconsin Press.

Stocking, G. W. 1995. *After Tylor: British social anthropology, 1888–1951.* Madison: University of Wisconsin Press.

Taussig, M. T. 1987. *Shamanism, colonialism, and the wild man: A study in terror and healing.* Chicago: University of Chicago Press.

Taylor, C. 1985. *Human agency and language.* Cambridge: Cambridge University Press.

Taylor, C. 1989. *Sources of the self: The making of the modern identity.* Cambridge: Harvard University Press.

Taylor, C. 1993. To follow a rule . . . In *Bourdieu: Critical perspectives,* ed. C. Calhoun, E. LiPuma, and M. Postone, 45–60. Cambridge: Polity Press.

Thompson, E. P. [1967] 1993. Time, work-discipline, and industrial capitalism. In *Customs in common,* 352–403. New York: New Press.

Thompson, E. P. 1978. *The poverty of theory and other essays.* New York: Monthly Review.

Turner, V. W., and E. M. Bruner, eds. 1986. *The anthropology of experience.* Urbana: University of Illinois Press.

Volosinov, V. N. 1973. *Marxism and the philosophy of language.* New York: Seminar Press.

Wakeman, F., and W.-H. Yeh, eds. 1992. *Shanghai sojourners.* Berkeley: Institute of East Asian Studies.

Wallace, A. F. C. 1961. *Culture and personality.* New York: Random House.

Walsh, G. 1967. Introduction. In *The phenomenology of the social world,* by A. Schutz, trans. G. Walsh and F. Lehnert, xv–xxix. Evanston, Ill.: Northwestern University Press.

Wang, A. 1995. *Changhenge* (A song of everlasting sorrow). Beijing: Zuojia.

Wang, J. 1996. *High culture fever: politics, aesthetics, and ideology in Deng's China.* Berkeley: University of California Press.

Wang, Q.-H. 1997. *Yaoshi* (The key). Beijing: Zuojia.

Wank, D. L. 1999. *Commodifying communism: Business, trust, and politics in a Chinese city.* Cambridge: Cambridge University Press.

Watson, J. L. 1982. Chinese kinship reconsidered: Anthropological perspectives on historical research. *China Quarterly* 92:589–622.

Watson, J. L. 1986. An anthropological overview: The development of Chinese descent groups. In *Kinship organization in late imperial China: 1000–1940,* ed. P. B. Ebrey and J. L. Watson, 274–92. Berkeley: University of California Press.

Watson, R. S., ed. 1994. *Memory, history, and opposition under state socialism.* Sante Fe, N.M.: School of American Research Press; distributed by University of Washington Press.

Weber, M. 1958. *The Protestant ethic and the spirit of capitalism.* Trans. T. Parsons. New York: Scribner.

White, H. V. 1973. *Metahistory: The historical imagination in nineteenth-century Europe.* Baltimore: Johns Hopkins University Press.

White, H. V. 1978. *Tropics of discourse: Essays in cultural criticism*. Baltimore: Johns Hopkins University Press.

White, H. V. 1987. *The content of the form: Narrative discourse and historical representation*. Baltimore: John Hopkins University Press.

White, M. G. 1965. *Foundations of historical knowledge*. New York: Harper and Row.

Whyte, M. K., and W. L. Parish. 1984. *Urban life in contemporary China*. Chicago: University of Chicago Press.

Williams, R. 1977. *Marxism and literature*. Oxford: Oxford University Press.

Winch, P. [1958] 1990. *The idea of a social science and its relation to philosophy*. London: Routledge.

Wittgenstein, L. 1958a. *Philosophical investigations*. 2d ed. Trans. G. E. M. Anscombe. New York: Macmillan.

Wittgenstein, L. 1958b. *Preliminary studies for the "Philosophical investigations" generally known as the blue and brown books*. New York: Harper.

Wolf, E. 1982. *Europe and the people without history*. Berkeley: University of California Press.

Wolf, M. 1985. *Revolution postponed: Women in contemporary China*. Stanford: Stanford University Press.

Yan, Y.-X. 1996. *The flow of gifts: Reciprocity and social networks in a Chinese village*. Stanford: Stanford University Press.

Yang, M. C. 1945. *A Chinese village: Taitou, Shantung Province*. New York: Columbia University Press.

Yang, M. M.-H. 1994. *Gifts, favors, and banquets: The art of social relationships in China*. Ithaca, N.Y.: Cornell University Press.

Zhang X.-W., M.-G. Xie, and D. Li, eds. 1994. *Zhongguo siying jingji nianjian, 1978–1993* (The annals of private economy in China, 1978–1993). Hong Kong: Jingji Daobao.

Zhonghua renmin gongheguo dadian (The grand annals of the People's Republic of China). 1996. Beijing: Chinese Economy Press.

Index